The GETTYSBURG CAMPAIGN

in Numbers and Losses

Synopses, Orders of Battle, Strengths, Casualties, and Maps, June 9 – July 14, 1863

J. DAVID PETRUZZI AND STEVEN A. STANLEY

Authors of *The Complete Gettysburg Guide*
and *The New Gettysburg Campaign Handbook*

Library of Congress Cataloging-in-Publication Data

Petruzzi, J. David.

The Gettysburg Campaign in Numbers and Losses : Synopses, Orders of Battle, Strengths, Casualties, and Maps, June 9 – July 14, 1863 / J. David Petruzzi and Steven Stanley. – First edition. First printing.

pages cm

ISBN 978-1-61121-080-4

1. Gettysburg Campaign, 1863. I. Stanley, Steven. II. Title.
E475.51.P47 2013
973.7'349--dc23
2012038523

SB

Published by
Savas Beatie LLC
989 Governor Drive, Suite 102
El Dorado Hills, CA 95762

Mailing address:

Savas Beatie LLC
P.O. Box 4527
El Dorado Hills, CA 95762
Phone: 916-941-6896
(E-mail) editorial@savasbeatie.com

Savas Beatie titles are available at special discounts for bulk purchases worldwide by corporations, government agencies, institutions, and other organizations. For more details, please contact Special Sales, P.O. Box 4527, El Dorado Hills, CA 95762, or you may e-mail us at sales@savasbeatie.com, or visit our website at www.savasbeatie.com for additional information.

Cover Photo: "Sunset on the Field of Battle." ©2012 by Steven A. Stanley

J. David Petruzzi

*To the soldiers and volunteers who comprise the
seemingly faceless numbers herein – You are not forgotten.*

Steven A. Stanley

To those who have bravely fought to protect our way of life.

TABLE OF CONTENTS

FOREWORD

Considering that literally thousands of books have been written about the American Civil War, and that a large percentage of those have focused on the Gettysburg Campaign, it becomes increasingly difficult to find new ground to plow. I often look at a new offering with a jaundiced eye as a result, as it is so difficult to find something new. With so many books on the Gettysburg Campaign already in print, any time something new and unique is published, I get excited. My friends J. David Petruzzi and Steven Stanley have managed to publish two unique works to date. First is their epic *The Complete Gettysburg Guide: Walking and Driving Tours of the Battlefield, Town, Cemeteries, Field Hospital Sites, and other Topics of Historical Interest*, one of the most useful works on the Gettysburg Campaign to be published to date. Then came its first companion volume, published in 2011, *The New Gettysburg Campaign Handbook: Facts, Photos, and Artwork for Readers of All Ages, June 9 - July 14, 1863*. The *Handbook* provides lots of useful trivia and vignettes, including detailed discussions of the weather during the Campaign, the most comprehensive order of battle for the entire Gettysburg Campaign yet prepared, and lots of other fascinating tidbits that simply cannot be found elsewhere.

Just when I thought that Petruzzi and Stanley had run out of useful and unique ways to document the Gettysburg Campaign, they surprised me once again. This, their latest, *The Gettysburg Campaign in Numbers and Losses*, is yet another unique volume that provides new insights, even for someone who has devoted a lifetime to the study of this campaign. Herein, Petruzzi has meticulously researched the strengths and losses of each side during each and every notable engagement of the Gettysburg Campaign, beginning with the June 9, 1863, Battle of Brandy Station, and ending with the crossing of the Potomac River on July 14, 1863. Each engagement has a summary narrative written by Petruzzi, an order of battle with strengths and categorized losses, and at least one of master cartographer Stanley's superb maps. All maps are presented in full color, providing easy interpretation. This book is amply illustrated, and Stanley has designed an extremely handsome and user-friendly volume. Each engagement of the Campaign has its own complete order of battle — many of which are the subject of a formal order of battle for the first time in this volume — and ends with recommended reading for the discerning reader who is interested in learning more about a specific episode.

This book has something for everyone, from novice to Gettysburg Campaign fanatic. By providing an excellent overview of all of the actions in the entire campaign, including commentary that places each action within the larger context of the campaign, novices will gain interesting insights. Even the most fanatical Gettysburg devotees will undoubtedly find something new in

Petruzzi's meticulously researched orders of battle and in his detailed statistical analysis, and all will find surprising insight in the book's Epilogue. I have more than 40 years invested in the study of the Gettysburg Campaign, and I found Petruzzi's conclusions about the losses sustained by Maj. Gen. J.E.B. Stuart's cavalry division during the five weeks of the Gettysburg Campaign stunning. I came away from my review of this book with a more keen appreciation of the travails faced by Stuart's horse soldiers and of the ordeal faced by the blueclad horsemen who pursued them.

In short, I cannot recommend this volume more highly to anyone interested in learning more about the Gettysburg Campaign. Buy it, study it, then keep it handy on the shelf with the other two volumes by J. David Petruzzi and Steven Stanley, and you will have the nucleus of an essential collection of master reference works on the Civil War's most critical campaign.

Eric J. Wittenberg

Columbus, Ohio

INTRODUCTION

Orders of Battle are the roadmap of a conflict. They list all of the units involved, segmented (in the case of the Civil War) in descending order by Army, Corps, Division, Brigade, and finally the Regiment. Orders of Battle are nearly indispensible sources to have handy when one is studying a particular battle or skirmish. At a glance, one can find which particular units were involved in each confrontation.

However, Orders of Battle can be detailed in varying degrees. The simplest Orders list only the units that were present during the confrontation. These are typically the types of Orders that are found in the *Official Records of the Union and Confederate Armies* (the 70-volume compilation of reports, orders, and correspondence of the war published by the U.S. Government between 1880 – 1901). More detailed Orders go a step further by listing the commander of each unit. Some Orders include an additional useful detail by noting when such commanders were taken out of action during the conflict (by capture, wounding, death, or otherwise) and the name of the soldier who replaced him. In many cases, such as at the Battle of Gettysburg where an astonishing 68 percent of Robert E. Lee's officer corps became casualties, there were multiple replacements among regiments, brigades, and divisions.

In fewer instances still, Orders can be so detailed as to include the strengths of the units, as well as casualties suffered for each unit during the conflict, preferably broken down into categories such as: killed, wounded, mortally wounded, and captured (and perhaps even those wound and captured). For many of the more than 10,000 conflicts that occurred during the Civil War, calculating accurate casualty figures can be extremely challenging however. First and foremost, Confederate casualty reports are missing (or were never completed) for many of them. Second, in many cases the casualties suffered during minor conflicts during a larger campaign were simply grouped into reports for campaign totals over several days or even weeks. Attempts, therefore, to break down the casualty counts by each of those separate conflicts can range from difficult to impossible.

We faced such daunting tasks when putting together these Orders of Battle for dozens of conflicts, large and small, that occurred over the five weeks of the Gettysburg Campaign we could document, beginning with the cavalry battle at Brandy Station, Virginia (June 9) and ending when the Confederate Army of Northern Virginia escaped across the Potomac (July 14). Thankfully, Orders of Battle for Gettysburg itself (July 1-3) exist in many sources (some including casualty calculations). We have found, however, that even the most recent versions contain a number of errors (most common among them being the commanders of regiments and smaller units). But with the notable exceptions of the battles of Brandy Station, Second Winchester, and a few other conflicts, Orders of Battle of any detail for the more than forty other engagements during the campaign have simply never been constructed. In those cases, we had to start completely from scratch, and they appear in this book for the very first time anywhere.

Books written about these conflicts, and then secondary works about them, in addition to reports in the *Official Records*, were the first sources used to construct these Orders over the years. But for smaller conflicts about which no books or other readily available material existed, Orders of Battle, unit strengths, and casualties could only be extracted by meticulously combing through manuscripts, magazine and newspaper articles, and letters and diary entries written by participants. Present-For-Duty rosters (when they exist) for regiments during the campaign were pulled from the National Archives and tabulated. Virtually any scrap of primary source material that could provide information was mined. In the end, however, there are still gaps to fill and mysteries left to solve. In some cases, we simply are not sure who may have commanded a particular regiment at the conclusion of a skirmish or battle. This is especially true concerning a few Confederate regiments following the Battle of Gettysburg for which no reports were filed or they were subsequently lost.

Accurate casualty figures for many conflicts proved to be even more elusive. Again, either reports were never filed, were lost, or simply are not detailed enough. Although primary and secondary books, reminiscences, letters, diaries, and articles provided a number of casualty counts and clues, a number of gaps still necessarily remain.

We hope, however, that the reader will find the Orders of Battle contained in this work to be the most accurate, complete, and up to date. More than two decades of research and compilation has found its way into this work. A commander of a particular unit has only been listed when his command has been duly documented. Strengths of particular units have been documented in the primary sources as much as possible. In some instances, unit strengths had to be estimated based on calculations that took into account muster rolls at an earlier time, then factoring in known, subsequent casualties. In these cases, we are confident that our numbers are reasonably close. In situations where the actual numbers may vary more than ten percent from our estimations, we have noted that figure as "est." (estimated). There are many situations where unit strengths or casualties are, unfortunately, impossible to even estimate because no reliable documentation has yet to be unearthed.

This is especially true during the latter engagements of the campaign. Because so few records exist of strengths and casualties during the conflicts of July 6-14 (or because commanders often combined casualties of these events together into one total listing, if they were reported at all), many unit strengths had to be estimated. By taking into account known casualties, and comparing the resulting strength calculations with existing muster reports compiled later in July, we are confident that our numbers are reasonably and usefully accurate.

The numbers still remain a problem with the Confederate units, admittedly. The Confederate infantry regiments that composed the rear guard at the final battle at Falling Waters on July 14, for instance, offer up only a few hints at strengths by veterans in diaries, reminiscences, etc. For example, a Southern veteran may have written in his diary that at Falling Waters, there were "barely 50 of us left" in his regiment. But after subtracting losses suffered at the Battle of Gettysburg, approximately 150 of his comrades should remain. What do we make of the disappearance of the other 100 soldiers? In many cases, a number of Rebels crossed the Potomac River ahead of their mates. Quite a few were conscripted to assist with the thousands of wounded that needed to be cared for. Most Confederate infantry regiments seem to have lost nearly all cohesion during the final week of the campaign, and this helps to explain why there are such small numbers left in regiments together in one spot at any one time with their commander. In attempting, then, to list reasonable and likely strengths of Confederate units during those final days, we have taken into account every shred of as many primary sources as possible and made careful estimates based on those accounts, as well as interpolating those numbers for units where no accounting otherwise exists. We believe, in the end, that we have provided a reasonable and educated picture of the state of pertinent Confederate commands during the final days leading up to the Southern army's final crossing of the Potomac.

Even though we have detailed such a large number of conflicts of the campaign in this book, it must be remembered that even all of these are only a fraction of the contests that actually took place in the Eastern Theater during the Gettysburg Campaign. Peruse the three volumes (Series 1, Volume 27) of the *Official Records* dealing with the campaign, and the reader will quickly see that there were dozens — perhaps even hundreds (with many having gone unreported or unnoted — of large and small skirmishes, raids, expeditions, reconnaissance, ambushes, and meeting engagements that took place during the campaign, which many scholars properly document as actually encompassing the dates of June 3 – August 1, 1863. We hope that the contests documented herein are more representative of the breadth and scope of the fighting during the campaign than has ever been detailed in lists of Orders of Battle and statistics than ever before.

We would be remiss if we did not acknowledge those before us who have done wonderful work in compiling data that has been indispensable in constructing detailed Orders of Battle for the battle of Gettysburg itself. Foremost on any list are John W. Busey and David G. Martin, whose *Regimental Strengths and Losses at Gettysburg* (4th edition, 2005) is a massive, meticulously documented compendium of strengths and casualties for every unit present at Gettysburg. Their work has also been useful for extrapolating such figures for the other conflicts during the campaign. Most recently, John Busey teamed with his son Travis W. Busey to produce the 3-volume set titled *Union Casualties at Gettysburg: A Comprehensive Record* (2011). This massive study provides the most detail that has ever been made available on more than 23,000 Union casualties of the battle, categorized by unit, company, and service. These volumes were of inestimable value in constructing the casualty data for the battle contained herein. For Philip Laino's *Gettysburg Campaign Atlas* (2009), Dr. Steve Floyd combined Busey and Martin's data (as well as other sources) to construct the detailed Gettysburg Order of Battle contained therein. Dr. Floyd also graciously assisted the authors during discussions for the preparation of this book.

It is our sincere hope that students and scholars of the Gettysburg Campaign will find this book to be a valuable and additional tool when reading about, researching, and studying various aspects of the campaign. Perhaps readers will find skirmishes and minor conflicts inside that they were previously unaware of. In many cases, readers will find casualty tallies herein (whether large or small) that will be surprising and revealing, and that might motivate the reader to want to learn more about a particular skirmish or battle. At the end of the book is a section that lists recommended reading titles.

A few words of caution are in order as well. The strengths of units listed herein for any engagement (particularly the larger ones) don't always tell the full story of how many "effectives" were actually active on a field of battle. In the case of cavalry, bear in mind that during engagements when cavalrymen fought dismounted (on foot), one-fourth of the forces present performed the duty of "horse-holder." In other words, it was military protocol at the time for every fourth man to hold his own horse, and the horses of his three comrades, behind the lines. Consequently, if, for example, a cavalry regiment of 400 troopers fought dismounted, 100 of those men would be holding horses and only 300 troopers would actually be on the firing line.

Additionally, whenever artillery was present on the field, a portion of the forces were detailed to "support" or protect the artillery. In the case of larger engagements, entire regiments of either infantry or cavalry would be detailed to support the cannoneers. Their mission was to help fight off any close enemy attackers, and if overrun, to provide enough defense and time so the artillerists could limber up and retreat or re-deploy. That mission carried an obvious danger of its own; because opposing artillery often specifically targeted one another, supporting forces suffered under a great deal of destructive enemy artillery fire.

Finally, several other factors reduced the number of effectives actively fighting on the field. Usually a commander kept a portion of his force in "reserve." The reserve's mission was to cover a withdrawal or retreat of the fighting forces, protect the line of retreat, or join in the fighting if the weight of additional numbers had the opportunity to turn the tide late in a conflict. Often, too, commanders sent units off to the flanks to watch for enemy activity and minimize the danger of being flanked. When soldiers were wounded, often a comrade or comrades would cease actively fighting and attempt to take the wounded out of harm's way. The point of considering all of these factors is that the strength numbers herein give the reader a guide as to the maximum number of troops that may have been actively in combat, but in most cases the true number of "trigger-pullers" during any particular conflict was considerably less.

Having studied Orders of Battle for so many years, we are of the opinion that they (and the information contained in them) are dynamic rather than static; due to constant scholarship and research, they can constantly be changed, revised, and updated. We encourage any reader who has documentary evidence that will help us to correct or revise any of the information in this book to please contact us through our publisher, Savas Beatie LLC, at their website at www.savasbeatie. com. We wish for these pages to be as plausible and correct as possible so that we all may continue to learn from them, and we will include such good information in any future editions of this book.

ACKNOWLEDGEMENTS

This book was the idea of Savas Beatie's (our publisher) Managing Director, Theodore P. Savas. After compiling the Gettysburg Campaign Order of Battle for another work, *The New Gettysburg Campaign Handbook*, Ted approached us with the idea of further detailing the Orders with the casualty tabulations, and compiling such Orders for as many conflicts during the campaign as possible. Such a project had never been done before, and we willingly dove into it. Ted felt that such a unique and novel effort would prove useful to students of the campaign, and we express our thanks to him for allowing us to present it to you.

The Savas Beatie marketing team — Marketing Director Sarah Keeney, Veronica Kane, Lindy Gervin, Mona Cole, Yvette Lewis, and Helene Dodier — always stand ready and willing to assist us through each project. No writer could ask for a more talented group to work with. This is our fifth book with these wonderful folks, and even though each successive project has entailed deeper research and work than the previous one, each new book is an even more enjoyable experience.

We are thankful for the assistance of cavalry historian and good friend Eric J. Wittenberg, who penned the Foreword, and also assisted with preparing several Orders of Battle herein.

Scott L. Mingus, Sr., the expert on Confederate general Richard Ewell's advance through Pennsylvania prior to the Gettysburg battle, was of immeasurable assistance in compiling the data necessary to construct the Orders of Battle and casualty counts for Second Winchester and the June 28 skirmish and bridge-burning at Wrightsville, Pennsylvania. We are likewise indebted to John W. Busey and his son Travis, today's foremost scholars of Gettysburg battle casualties, for examining the finished manuscript and providing crucial corrections and suggestions. Our good friend and scholar of the Confederate brigade of Georgians commanded by George "Tige" Anderson, Rick Allen, gave us the benefit of his years of study in trying to determine the still-elusive command hierarchy of Anderson's Brigade at Gettysburg.

Examine the Acknowledgements of virtually any book, and one will see that most authors fail to thank the most important people of all — their readers. Our readers have been very supportive and gracious with our writing and design team over the years, from our first collaboration *The Complete Gettysburg Guide* (2009) to the book you hold in your hands. Thank you for your continued kind words and assistance, and we hope to see you out on the fields of the Gettysburg Campaign — the best "books" ever written on those momentous days of June and July 1863 — very soon.

J. David Petruzzi
Brockway, Pennsylvania

Steven A. Stanley
Gettysburg, Pennsylvania

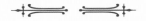

KEY TO THE

ORDERS OF BATTLE AND STRENGTHS/LOSSES

Each regiment, squadron, company, or detachment (or battery/section in the case of artillery) that was present and engaged on the field for each conflict listed during the campaign is listed under its highest army unit, or the unit to which it was formally or informally attached. For example, let's take the case of the June 23 Skirmish at the Cashtown Pass, west of Gettysburg. Only Company D of the 14th Virginia Cavalry was present on the Confederate side. This regiment was in Jenkins' Brigade in the Army of Northern Virginia Cavalry Division. Therefore, both the brigade and division are listed for identification purposes, but since neither Brig. Gen. Albert Gallatin Jenkins (commander of the brigade) nor Maj. Gen. J.E.B. Stuart (commander of the division) was present during this particular conflict, neither commander is listed. Commanders of units are only listed when they were present during a conflict, but the units are listed so that the reader will know the brigade, division, corps, etc. to which the particular engaged unit belonged.

Commanders of units that became casualties are identified by the following designations:

(k) – killed

(mw) – mortally wounded

(w) – wounded

(w-c) – wounded and captured

(c) – captured

(m) – missing

Unless otherwise noted, the last commander to appear on a list beneath a unit was the final commander on the field at the end of each engagement. In some cases (notably on the Confederate side for the main Gettysburg battle) however, the final commander is difficult or impossible to document. Much research is still ongoing by a number of scholars to determine both the hierarchy of command and the final command of a number of Southern regiments.

Beneath each unit, the strength and casualty tallies appear. The reported or calculated strength is in brackets [ ]. If a unit's strength has been difficult to determine, possibly varying more than ten percent from our calculations, it is denoted as estimated [est.] Next, in parentheses ( ), the casualty tallies are listed. In some cases, one side or the other provided a list of soldiers mortally wounded, and those are listed when known. In several cases, the casualty totals for a particular unit are simply unknown (they were likely never reported), and are denoted as such. The following designations are therefore used in the casualty tallies:

(k) – killed

(mw) – mortally wounded

(w) – wounded

(w-c) – wounded and captured

(c) – captured

(m) – missing

The total casualties are listed following the equal (=) sign, and then the percentage of casualties (%) is listed, carried to one decimal point, compared to the strength engaged of the particular unit. Whenever a commander of a unit filed a report of an action (or in other primary sources used to document an action), but listed no losses, it is shown as (No losses reported). Usually, this means that the unit actually suffered no reportable losses of any type. Sometimes, we have a report of the losses of a squadron, group of regiments, or a brigade (or higher unit), but not the specific categories of losses in a smaller member unit (such as a company or regiment). In those cases, they are listed with a question mark (?) meaning that a particular unit is known to have suffered killed, wounded, captured, missing, etc., but the exact number for that smaller unit is simply unknown.

It is important to point out that in the spring of 1863, prior to the Gettysburg Campaign, Confederate commander Robert E. Lee issued a directive that regiments were not to report the slightly wounded (including those wounded that were able to return to duty within a short time frame). Such a practice means that the numbers of wounded Southerners throughout the campaign (and subsequent conflicts) were grossly under-reported. If the "slightly wounded" numbers were known, the casualty tallies for the Confederates would be hundreds, and perhaps thousands, higher.

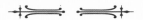

OVERVIEW

THE CAMPAIGN AND BATTLE OF GETTYSBURG, PA.

JUNE 9 – JULY 14, 1863

By the summer of 1863, the American Civil War had raged over the Nation's soil for two very bloody years. The Battle of Shiloh, Tennessee in April 1862, tallied a shocking butcher's bill with the death or wounding of nearly 20,000 men over two days. The Battle of Antietam, fought near the small Maryland hamlet of Sharpsburg on September 17, 1862, still stands as the bloodiest single day in American history when nearly 21,000 were killed , wounded or missing. Confederate **GEN. ROBERT E. LEE**'s impressive victories at the battles of Fredericksburg (December 11-15, 1862) and Chancellorsville (May 1-3, 1863) in Virginia motivated the Southern commander to put into motion his plan to march his Army of Northern Virginia onto Pennsylvania soil. The plan actually germinated in February 1863, when Confederate cartographer Jedediah Hotchkiss was tasked to prepare a secret map, one that included Virginia's Shenandoah Valley, Maryland, and southern Pennsylvania. The following month Confederate leaders gathered in Richmond to strategize, with Lee desirous of assuming the offensive no later than the first of May.

Following the death of Maj. Gen. Thomas "Stonewall" Jackson at Chancellorsville, Lee reorganized the Rebel army from two corps to three. Lee hoped that their march north would draw Maj. Gen. Joseph Hooker's Army of the Potomac out of its position north of the Rappahannock River. If the Yankees laid chase, and perceived a threat to Washington, Baltimore, Harrisburg, and other important Northern cities, Lee hoped to defeat portions of the Federal force while in Maryland and Pennsylvania.

On June 9, Brig. Gen. Alfred Pleasonton's Federal cavalry splashed across the Rappahannock in the early morning and surprised Maj. Gen. James Ewell Brown "J.E.B." Stuart's encamped Confederate horsemen, igniting an all-day brawl that delayed Lee's plans by one day. Following the battle, Lt. Gen. Richard S. Ewell's Second Corps advanced into the Shenandoah Valley, and a few

THE CAMPAIGN BEGINS JUNE 3

THE BATTLE OF GETTYSBURG JULY 1-3

LEE'S ARMY CROSSES THE POTOMAC RIVER JULY 14

days later laid siege to Maj. Gen. Robert Milroy's Federal stronghold at Winchester, Virginia. Ewell served up a Yankee embarrassment on a golden platter for Lee, when by June 15, Ewell inflicted some 4,500 casualties on Milroy's people (over 50% of the Federal strength) while suffering less than 300 of his own. Pennsylvania's Governor Andrew Curtain wasted no time in calling out for volunteers to defend the soil of the Keystone State against what was most assuredly a forthcoming Confederate invasion.

While the other two Confederate corps, commanded by Lt. Gens. James Longstreet and Ambrose P. Hill, advanced north along the Blue Ridge Mountains and the Shenandoah respectively, General Stuart took just over half his cavalry force on a detached ride across the river. The fight at Brandy Station had taken a bit of the polish off Stuart's golden legend, but the crimson-caped cavalier hoped to gallop through and around the Union army as he had done the year before. After setting the Federals back on their heels, Stuart was to link up with Ewell's command in Pennsylvania. As with any offensive military plan, it looked good on paper. Events as they soon transpired, however, began nudging the plans off their tracks toward an unanticipated derailment.

Stuart's foray was met with delays in the form of skirmishes and one, day-long pitched battle that kept him from making any progress in Pennsylvania until the evening of June 30 — six full days into his ride. Unable to locate Ewell's command, Stuart spent July 1 marching north to Carlisle while the first day of the Gettysburg battle raged to his southwest. That day, Lee's Southerners drove two Federal corps off the heights west of the town but onto ultimately better ground to the east and south. By the time the sun set over the Gettysburg landscape on the evening of July 3, blood painted the rocks of Devil's Den, the trampled stalks of farmer George Rose's wheatfield, the soil of Nicholas Codori's farm fronting the Federal defense at a stone wall, and a thousand other pockets and corners traversed by the troops.

With no alternative but to retreat from the field, Robert E. Lee gathered thousands of his wounded and began pulling his men from the field on the afternoon of July 4. Days of marching in biblical rainstorms brought the Confederates to a swollen Potomac River while the Federal forces tentatively pursued. Largely uncoordinated and led primarily by Federal cavalry, Northern attacks nonetheless led to more than two dozen additional battles and skirmishes (causing thousands more casualties) before the Confederates escaped across the water by the morning of July 14. Lee's army and officer corps had been decimated, leaving a lasting impact through to the end of the war, but the wounded lion had enough fight and determination left to battle for nearly two more years. Federal army commander **GEN. GEORGE G. MEADE** had repulsed the Confederates at Gettysburg but failed to crush them before they could safely escape Pennsylvania and Maryland.

THE CAMPAIGN BEGINS

THE BATTLE OF BRANDY STATION, VA.

JUNE 9, 1863

Maj. Gen. J.E.B. Stuart
Image courtesy of Library of Congress

Following the Confederate victory at Chancellorsville in Virginia in early May 1863, Gen. Robert E. Lee reorganized his army and agreed with President Jefferson Davis to undertake a second invasion north of the Potomac River. Lee intended to feed and equip his men while threatening major logistical centers and eventually win a decisive victory. This operation would spare Virginia for a time from the ravages of war, and hopefully convince the Union high command to withdraw forces away from Vicksburg, Mississippi. By June 5, two of his corps under James Longstreet and Richard S. Ewell were camped at Culpeper. Six miles northeast near a railroad stop named Brandy Station, **MAJ. GEN. JAMES EWELL BROWN "J.E.B." STUART** guarded the Rappahannock River crossings with his Confederate cavalry. Stuart held a "Grand Review" of his riders and horse artillery that same day, and another review three days later in the presence of Lee and other dignitaries. In preparation for the march north, Lee ordered Stuart to push across the river on June 9 and attack Federal picket positions.

Unknown to the Southerners, however, Federal cavalry and some infantry had moved just across the river with orders from Federal army commander Maj. Gen. Joseph Hooker to attack Stuart's cavalry and break it. Hooker was concerned that the concentration of Confederate cavalry around Brandy Station indicated that a large raid was in the offing. Cavalry Corps commander **BRIG. GEN. ALFRED PLEASONTON** led the expedition. Dividing the cavalry and infantry into two wings, Pleasonton planned for his right wing

Brig. Gen. Alfred Pleasonton
Image courtesy of Library of Congress

The Battle of Brandy Station – June 9, 1863

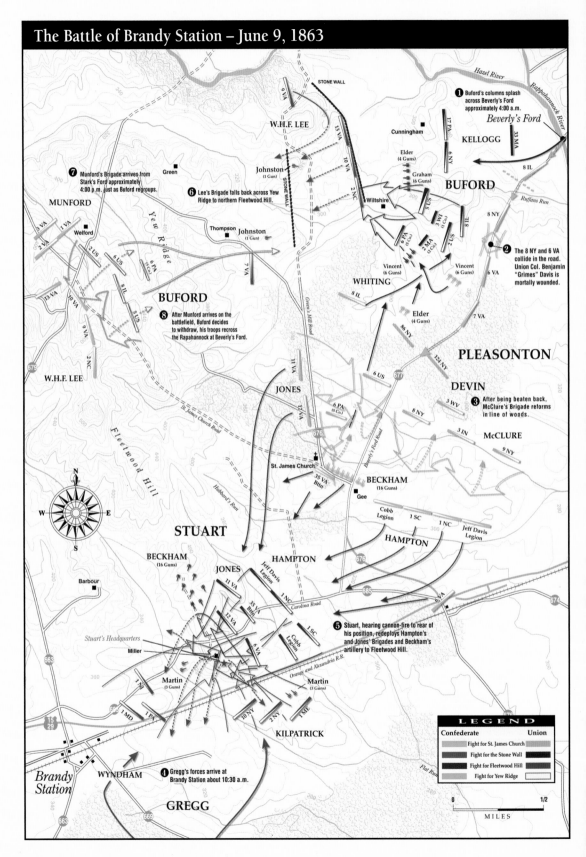

❶ Buford's columns splash across Beverly's Ford approximately 4:00 a.m.

❷ The 8 NY and 6 VA collide in the road. Union Col. Benjamin "Grimes" Davis is mortally wounded.

❸ After being beaten back, McClure's Brigade reforms in line of woods.

❹ Gregg's forces arrive at Brandy Station about 10:30 a.m.

❺ Stuart, hearing cannon-fire to rear of his position, redeploys Hampton's and Jones' Brigades and Beckham's artillery to Fleetwood Hill.

❻ Lee's Brigade falls back across Yew Ridge to northern Fleetwood Hill.

❼ Munford's Brigade arrives from Stark's Ford approximately 4:00 p.m. just as Buford regroups.

❽ After Munford arrives on the battlefield, Buford decides to withdraw, his troops recross the Rapahannock at Beverly's Ford.

LEGEND

Confederate	Union
Fight for St. James Church	
Fight for the Stone Wall	
Fight for Fleetwood Hill	
Fight for Yew Ridge	

0   1/2

MILES

under Brig. Gen. John Buford to attack across Beverly Ford, and the left wing under Brig. Gen. David M. Gregg to attack simultaneously across Kelly's Ford.

Buford's column began crossing at Beverly before dawn on June 9 and attacked Stuart's pickets there. Fighting broke out between a Federal cavalry brigade under Col. Benjamin F. "Grimes" Davis, who led Buford's thrust, and a Confederate cavalry brigade commanded by Brig. Gen. William E. "Grumble" Jones. The Confederates prevented Davis' troopers from reaching Southern horse artillery camped near St. James Church and Davis was killed in the effort. After two hours of heavy mounted and dismounted fighting and soaring casualties on both sides, there was still no sign of David Gregg's Federals who were to have crossed to the southeast at Kelly's Ford. The Confederates began pulling back south in the direction of Stuart's headquarters atop Fleetwood Hill when Gregg's late advance finally slipped across the Rappahannock.

After a series of mounted charges and countercharges on and around Fleetwood Hill throughout the afternoon, the Confederates repulsed the aggressive Federals. With his mission to scatter Stuart's forces in tatters after fourteen hours of fighting, Pleasonton withdrew his troopers across the river about sunset. Brandy Station — the largest, nearly-all cavalry battle ever witnessed in the western hemisphere — was finally over.

FEDERAL

ARMY OF THE POTOMAC
CAVALRY CORPS
[12,272 total forces] (82k, 394w, 383m = 859) 7.0%
Brig. Gen. Alfred Pleasonton, commanding

RIGHT WING
Brig. Gen. John Buford

FIRST CAVALRY DIVISION
[6,362] (50k, 284w, 164m = 498) 7.8%
Brig. Gen. John Buford (Right Wing Commander)
Col. Thomas Casimer Devin

FIRST BRIGADE
[1,700] (13k, 118w, 11m = 142) 8.4%
Col. Benjamin Franklin Davis (k)
Maj. William S. McClure

8th New York Cavalry
[560] (11k, 31w, 7m = 49) 8.8%
Maj. Edmund Mann Pope

8th Illinois Cavalry
[460] (1k, 46w, 3m = 50) 10.9%
Capt. Alpheus Clark (mw)
Capt. George Alexander Forsyth (w)
Capt. Elon John Farnsworth

3rd Indiana Cavalry (6 Companies)
[328] (1k, 23w = 24) 7.3%
Maj. William S. McClure
Maj. Charles Lemmon

9th New York Cavalry (5 Companies)
[290] (0k, 15w, 1m = 16) 5.5%
Maj. William B. Martin (w)

3rd (West) Virginia Cavalry (2 Companies)
[62] (0k, 3w = 3) 4.8%
Capt. Seymour Beach Conger

ATTACHED HORSE ARTILLERY
2nd United States Horse Artillery, Batteries B and L
(Six 3-inch Ordnance Rifles)
[106] (0k, 3w = 3) 2.8%
Lt. Albert Oliver Vincent

SECOND BRIGADE
[774] (0k, 7w = 7) 0.9%
Col. Thomas Casimer Devin
Col. Josiah Holcomb Kellogg

6th New York Cavalry
[254] (0k, 4w = 4) 1.6%
Maj. William Elliott Beardsley

17th Pennsylvania Cavalry (10 Companies)
[520] (0k, 3w = 3) 0.6%
Col. Josiah Holcomb Kellogg
Lt. Col. James Quigley Anderson

RESERVE BRIGADE
[1,935] (31k, 98w, 151m = 280) 14.5%
Maj. Charles Jarvis Whiting

1st United States Cavalry (10 Companies)
[350] (1k, 1w = 2) 0.6%
Capt. Richard Stanton C. Lord

2nd United States Cavalry
[435] (11k, 29w, 26m = 66) 15.2%
Capt. Wesley Merritt

5th United States Cavalry
[330] (6k, 17w, 15m = 38) 11.5%
Capt. James E. Harrison

6th United States Cavalry
[510] (8k, 26w, 32m = 66) 12.9%
Capt. George Clarence Cram

6th Pennsylvania Cavalry (10 Companies)
[310] (5k, 25w, 78m = 108) 34.8%
Maj. Robert Morris, Jr. (c)
Maj. Henry C. Whelan

ATTACHED HORSE ARTILLERY
4th United States Horse Artillery, Battery E
(Four 3-inch Ordnance Rifles)
[66] (No losses reported) 0.0%
Lt. Samuel Sherer Elder

ATTACHED INFANTRY BRIGADE
[1,658] (6k, 56w, 2m = 64) 3.9%
Brig. Gen. Adelbert Ames

33rd Massachusetts (11th Corps)
[496] (0k, 3w = 3) 0.6%
Col. Adin Ballou Underwood

2nd Massachusetts (12th Corps)
[322] (1k, 3w, 2m = 6) 1.9%
Lt. Col. Charles Redington Mudge

3rd Wisconsin (12th Corps)
[275] (1k, 14w = 15) 5.5%
Maj. Edwin L. Hubbard
(2nd MA and 3rd WI under command
of Lt. Col. Martin Flood)

86th New York (3rd Corps)
[313] (2k, 24w = 26) 8.3%
Maj. Jacob H. Lansing

124th New York (3rd Corps)
[252] (2k, 12w = 14) 5.6%
Lt. Col. Francis Markoe Cummins
(86th and 124th NY under command
of Col. A. Van Horne Ellis)

ATTACHED HORSE ARTILLERY
1st United States Horse Artillery, Battery K
(Six 3-inch Ordnance Rifles)
[123] (0k, 2w = 2) 1.6%
Capt. William Montrose Graham, Jr.

LEFT WING
[5,910 total forces] (32k, 110w, 219m = 361) 6.1%
Brig. Gen. David McMurtrie Gregg

SECOND CAVALRY DIVISION
[1,640] (5k, 11w, 13m = 29) 1.8%
Col. Alfred Napoléon Alexander Duffié

FIRST BRIGADE
[915] (5k, 10w, 9m = 24) 2.6%
Col. Luigi Palma di Cesnola

1st Massachusetts Cavalry (8 Companies)
[260] (2k, 9w, 5m = 16) 6.2%
Lt. Col. Greely Stevenson Curtis

6th Ohio Cavalry (8 Companies)
[370] (1k, 1w, 1m = 3) 0.8%
Maj. William Steadman

1st Rhode Island Cavalry
[285] (2k, 3m = 5) 1.8%
Lt. Col. John L. Thompson

SECOND BRIGADE
[595] (0k, 1w, 4m = 5) 0.8%
Col. John Irvin Gregg

3rd Pennsylvania Cavalry
[335] (No losses reported) 0.0%
Lt. Col. Edward S. Jones

4th Pennsylvania Cavalry
[260] (0k, 1w, 4m = 5) 1.9%
Lt. Col. William Emile Doster

16th Pennsylvania Cavalry
(guarding division wagons)
Maj. William H. Fry

ATTACHED HORSE ARTILLERY

2nd United States Horse Artillery, Battery M
(Six 3-inch Ordnance Rifles)
[130] (No losses reported) 0.0%
Lt. Alexander Cummings McWhorter Pennington, Jr.

THIRD CAVALRY DIVISION
[4,270] (27k, 99w, 206m = 332) 7.8%
Brig. Gen. David McMurtrie Gregg

FIRST BRIGADE
[1,240] (8k, 34w, 110m = 152) 12.3%
Col. Hugh Judson Kilpatrick

1st Maine Cavalry (11 Companies)
[340] (1k, 2w, 28m = 31) 9.1%
Col. Calvin Sanger Douty

2nd New York Cavalry
[440] (4k, 14w, 21m = 39) 8.9%
Lt. Col. Henry Eugene Davies

10th New York Cavalry
[400] (3k, 18w, 61m = 82) 20.5%
Lt. Col. William Irvine (c)
Maj. Matthew Henry Avery

Orton's Independent Company, District
of Columbia Volunteer Cavalry (attached)
[60] (No losses reported) 0.0%
Capt. William H. Orton

SECOND BRIGADE
[930] (18k, 52w, 80m = 150) 16.1%
Col. Percy Wyndham (w)
Col. John P. Taylor

1st Maryland Cavalry
[340] (6k, 13w, 44m = 63) 18.5%
Lt. Col. James Monroe Deems

1st New Jersey Cavalry (11 Companies)
[240] (7k, 21w, 24m = 52) 21.7%
Lt. Col. Virgil Broderick (k)
Maj. John H. Shelmire (k)
Maj. Myron Holley Beaumont

1st Pennsylvania Cavalry (11 Companies)
[350] (5k, 18w, 12m = 35) 10.0%
Col. John P. Taylor
Lt. Col. David Gardner

12th Illinois Cavalry
(not present on the field)
Col. Arno Voss

ATTACHED HORSE ARTILLERY
6th New York Light Independent Artillery
(Six 3-inch Ordnance Rifles)
[111] (0k, 8w, 13m = 21) 18.9%
Capt. Joseph W. Martin

ATTACHED INFANTRY BRIGADE
[1,847] (1k, 5w, 3m = 9) 0.5%
Brig. Gen. David Allen Russell

7th Wisconsin (1st Corps)
[364] (No losses reported) 0.0%

2nd Wisconsin (Companies A and I) (1st Corps)
[50] (No losses reported) 0.0%
Col. William Robinson

56th Pennsylvania (1st Corps)
[261] (1k, 5w, 3m = 9) 3.4%
Col. J. William Hoffman
(7th and 2nd WI and 56th PA
under command of Col. William Robinson)

5th New Hampshire (2nd Corps)
[179] (No losses reported) 0.0%
Col. Edward Cross

81st Pennsylvania (2nd Corps)
[175] (No losses reported) 0.0%
(5th NH and 81st PA
under command of Col. Edward Cross)

6th Maine (6th Corps)
[395] (No losses reported) 0.0%
Col. Hiram Burnham

119th Pennsylvania (6th Corps)
[423] (No losses reported) 0.0%
Maj. Henry P. Truefitt, Jr.
(6th ME and 119th PA
under command of Col. Hiram Burnham)

ATTACHED ARTILLERY
3rd United States Horse Artillery, Battery C
(Six 3-inch Ordnance Rifles)
[142] (No losses reported) 0.0%
Lt. William Duncan Fuller

CASUALTY TOTALS BY BRANCH

CAVALRY [8,089] (75k, 320w, 365m = 760) 9.4%
INFANTRY [3,505] (7k, 61w, 5m = 73) 2.1%
ARTILLERY [678] (0k, 13w, 13m = 26) 3.8%

CONFEDERATE

ARMY OF NORTHERN VIRGINIA
CAVALRY DIVISION
[10,258 total forces] (71k, 16mw, 267w, 224m = 578) 5.6%
Maj. Gen. James Ewell Brown Stuart

JONES' BRIGADE
[2,020] (27k, 9mw, 112w, 122m = 270) 13.4%
Brig. Gen. William Edmondson Jones

6th Virginia Cavalry
[600] (6k, 6mw, 11w, 29m = 52) 8.7%
Maj. Cabell Edward Flournoy

7th Virginia Cavalry
[400] (2k, 2mw, 18w, 2m = 24) 6.0%
Lt. Col. Thomas A. Marshall Jr.

11th Virginia Cavalry
[400] (5k, 13w, 4m = 22) 5.5%
Col. Lunsford Lindsay Lomax

12th Virginia Cavalry
[290] (6k, 1mw, 31w, 21m = 59) 20.3%
Col. Asher Waterman Harman (w)
Lt. Col. Thomas Benjamin Massie

35th Battalion Virginia Cavalry
[330] (8k, 39w, 66m = 113) 34.2%
Lt. Col. Elijah Viers White (w)

WILLIAM HENRY FITZHUGH LEE'S BRIGADE
[1,910] (23k, 4mw, 76w, 26m = 129) 6.8%
Brig. Gen. William Henry Fitzhugh Lee (w)
Col. James Lucius Davis (w)
Col. John Randolph Chambliss, Jr.

2nd North Carolina Cavalry
[264] (4k, 2mw, 14w, 10m = 30) 11.4%
Col. Solomon Williams (k)
Lt. Col. William Henry Fitzhugh Payne

9th Virginia Cavalry
[716] (15k, 21w = 36) 5.0%
Col. Richard Lee Turberville Beale

10th Virginia Cavalry
[359] (4k, 2mw, 37w, 16m = 59) 16.4%
Col. James Lucius Davis (w)
Maj. Joseph Rosser

13th Virginia Cavalry
[571] (0k, 4w = 4) 0.7%
Col. John Randolph Chambliss, Jr.
Maj. Joseph Ezra Gillette

15th Virginia Cavalry
(on Rappahannock picket duty)
Maj. Charles Reed Collins

HAMPTON'S BRIGADE
[2,576] (14k, 2mw, 47w, 49m = 112) 4.3%
Brig. Gen. Wade Hampton

Cobb's Legion (Georgia)
[524] (6k, 22w, 16m = 44) 8.4%
Col. Pierce Manning Butler Young (w)

Jeff Davis Legion (Mississippi)
[361] (0k, 4w = 4) 1.1%
Lt. Col. Joseph Frederick Waring

1st South Carolina Cavalry
[558] (3k, 1mw, 8w, 4m = 17) 3.1%
Col. John Logan Black

2nd South Carolina Cavalry
[443] (0k, 1mw, 1w, 15m = 17) 3.8%
Col. Matthew Calbraith Butler (w)
Maj. Thomas Jefferson Lipscomb

1st North Carolina Cavalry
[690] (5k, 12w, 14m = 31) 4.5%
Col. Laurence Simmons Baker

Phillips' Legion (Georgia)
(on Rappahannock picket duty)
Lt. Col. William Wofford Rich

FITZHUGH LEE'S BRIGADE
[2,244] (6k, 1mw, 22w, 26m = 55) 2.5%
Col. Thomas Taylor Munford

1st Virginia Cavalry
[517] (0k, 1w = 1) 0.2%
Col. James Henry Drake

2nd Virginia Cavalry
[668] (5k, 12w = 17) 2.5%
Lt. Col. James Winston Watts

3rd Virginia Cavalry
[489] (1k, 8w = 9) 1.8%
Col. Thomas Howerton Owen

4th Virginia Cavalry
[570] (0k, 1mw, 1w, 26m = 28) 4.9%
Col. Williams Carter Wickham

5th Virginia Cavalry
(on Rappahannock picket duty)
Col. Thomas Lafayette Rosser

ROBERTSON'S BRIGADE

[985] (No losses reported) 0.0%
Brig. Gen. Beverly Holcombe Robertson

4th North Carolina Cavalry (8 Companies)
[515] (No losses reported) 0.0%
Col. Dennis Dozier Ferebee

5th North Carolina Cavalry
[470] (No losses reported) 0.0%
Col. Peter Gustavus Evans

STUART HORSE ARTILLERY

[523] (1k, 10w, 1m = 12) 2.3%
Maj. Robert Franklin Beckham

**Hart's Battery, Washington (South Carolina)
Horse Artillery (Four Blakely Rifles)**
[107] (0k, 1w = 1) 0.9%
Capt. James Franklin Hart

**Breathed's Battery, 1st Stuart (Virginia)
Horse Artillery (Four 3-inch Ordnance Rifles)**
[108] (0k, 3w = 3) 2.8%
Capt. James Williams Breathed

**Chew's Battery, Ashby (Virginia) Horse Artillery
(One 3-inch Ordnance Rifle,
One 12-pounder Howitzer)**
[95] (0k, 3w = 3) 3.2%
Capt. Roger Preston Chew

**Lynchburg "Beauregard" Rifles, Moorman's
(Virginia) Battery (One Napoleon, Three unknown)**
[107] (1k, 3w, 1m = 5) 4.7%
Capt. Marcellus Newton Moorman

**2nd Stuart Horse Artillery, McGregor's (Virginia)
Battery (One Blakely, Three unknown)**
[106] (No losses reported) 0.0%
Capt. William Morrell McGregor

CASUALTY TOTALS BY BRANCH

CAVALRY [9,735] (70k, 16mw, 257w, 241m = 584) 6.0%
ARTILLERY [523] (1k, 10w, 1m = 12) 2.3%

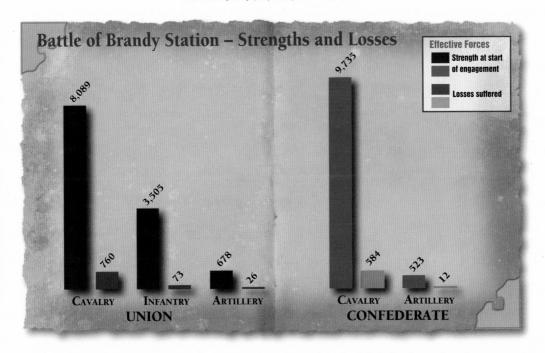

Both sides claimed victory after the battle. Although he had failed in his ordered mission to disperse and destroy the Confederate cavalry, Pleasonton later argued that he had only meant to conduct a reconnaissance of Stuart's position and forces, and that he had succeeded in doing so. Although caught off guard by the large-scale attack, Stuart claimed the laurels because he held the field at the end of the day. Southern papers and some of his own men, however, excoriated Stuart for conducting the review and not paying attention to the enemy, all of which combined to create a large embarrassment. The criticism stung Stuart, and some have speculated that this may have influenced his decisions during the ensuing campaign into Pennsylvania.

Regardless of who "won" Brandy Station, the fighting indisputably delayed Lee's northward advance one full day. Just as important, the ability of the Federal cavalry to fight their counterparts hard all day long, as a cohesive corps, earned them a grudging new respect. After he took command of the Federal army, Joseph Hooker brought together the scattered regiments and companies of his cavalry to create a tight Cavalry Corps. The blue troopers had previously been characterized as little more than errand boys for the Federal infantry commanders. As Maj. Henry B. McClellan, J.E.B. Stuart's adjutant, later admitted, "[The Battle of Brandy Station] made the Federal cavalry. Up to that time confessedly inferior to the Southern horsemen, they gained on this day that confidence in themselves and in their commanders which enabled them to contest so fiercely the subsequent battlefields."

Lee waited through much of the following day, June 10, to ascertain Hooker's intentions. When no further attacks came and no movement of any consequence was detected, Lee ordered corps commander Ewell to march his men northeast from Culpeper late that afternoon toward the Shenandoah Valley. The move toward Pennsylvania was about to get underway.

THE SKIRMISH AT SENECA MILLS, MD.

JUNE 10, 1863

On the evening of June 9, Confederate partisan **MAJ. JOHN S. MOSBY** set off for the Potomac River with two newly organized companies of his 43rd Battalion of Virginia Cavalry (better known as "Mosby's Rangers"). Mosby intended to cross the river that night to attack Federal troopers of the 6th Michigan Cavalry picketing the river at Seneca Mills, Maryland. Mosby's guide got lost and led the Rangers along the wrong road, so it was after daylight on June 10 before the Virginians arrived at Rowser's Ford about one mile downstream from the Federals. Three of Mosby's troopers crossed the river and captured a Wolverine picket post at the Seneca Locks of the Chesapeake and Ohio (C&O) Canal.

Maj. John S. Mosby
Image courtesy of Library of Congress

The bulk of Mosby's raiders then crossed the canal and rode toward the Federal cavalry camp, which was located about midway

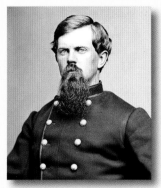

Capt. Charles W. Deane
Image courtesy of Library of Congress

between the canal and Seneca Mills. **CAPT. CHARLES W. DEANE**, commanding Company I of the 6th Michigan Cavalry, exhorted his men to stand and fight, but they fled when Mosby's men charged. Deane reorganized his Northern troopers behind a defensive position along a narrow bridge spanning Seneca Creek near the grist mill, but a second mounted assault broke their line. Deane tried to rally his men, but they were chased all the way to Poolesville, Maryland, before Mosby gave up the pursuit.

The Rangers returned to the Wolverines' camp, gathered up everything of value, burned the rest, and then crossed back over the Potomac River with their prisoners in tow.

FEDERAL

DEPARTMENT OF WASHINGTON
XXII ARMY CORPS CAVALRY DIVISION

FIRST BRIGADE
6th Michigan Cavalry (Company I)
[90] (4k, 1w, 16m = 21) 23.3%
Capt. Charles Werden Deane

CONFEDERATE

ARMY OF NORTHERN VIRGINIA

43rd Battalion Virginia Cavalry (2 Companies)
[90] (2k, 1w = 3) 3.3%
Maj. John Singleton Mosby

The raid upon Seneca Mills, one of the first with organized companies of the 43rd Battalion, began cementing Mosby's reputation among the Federals as a dangerous and effective partisan raider in Northern Virginia. As he would time and again, Mosby inflicted many more casualties than he suffered, regardless of the odds he faced. After the attack, several Federal cavalry regiments set out to intercept Mosby, but most of his men escaped. As a result of Mosby's Seneca Mills success, Confederate cavalry commander J.E.B. Stuart recommended a promotion for Mosby, one of his most valuable scouts. Mosby continued using his raiding and reconnaissance talents to inflict casualties and embarrass the Federal high command, and to assist Stuart as the Pennsylvania campaign unfolded.

On the same afternoon that Mosby raided Seneca Mills, Lt. Gen. Richard S. Ewell's Second Corps marched twenty miles northeast toward Winchester; Lt. Gen. James Longstreet's First Corps practiced drill at Culpeper; and Lt. Gen. Ambrose P. Hill's Third Corps remained below the Rappahannock River in its Fredericksburg defenses. Most of Alfred Pleasonton's Federal cavalrymen moved to Warrenton Junction, where they guarded the creek fords. President Abraham Lincoln's General-in-Chief Henry W. Halleck's grave concern about the safety of the Federal troops garrisoning Winchester, Virginia, would soon be validated.

CONFEDERATES CLEAR THE VALLEY

THE SECOND BATTLE OF WINCHESTER, VA.

JUNE 13-15, 1863

After the swirling all-day cavalry battle at Brandy Station, General Lee ordered **LT. GEN. RICHARD S. EWELL** and his Second Corps to clear the lower (northern) Shenandoah Valley of Federal forces. The operation was undertaken to facilitate the Army of Northern Virginia's use of the valley for its march northward to Pennsylvania, as well as enable the Confederates to use the Blue Ridge Mountains as a screen against probing Federal eyes. It was cavalry commander J.E.B. Stuart's role to defend the gaps and passes and keep the enemy away from the main body of the army. Ewell's Corps passed through Chester's Gap southeast of Front Royal on June 12 and was joined by a cavalry brigade under Brig. Gen. Albert G. Jenkins. Ewell's goal was the Federal garrison at Winchester, Virginia, a well-fortified, important crossroads center with long-range, heavy artillery guarded by **MAJ.**

Lt. Gen. Richard S. Ewell
Image courtesy of Library of Congress

GEN. ROBERT H. MILROY's XIII Corps division, composed of more than 8,000 infantry, cavalry, and artillery.

Ewell sent two of his three divisions (about 13,000 men under Maj. Gens. Jubal A. Early and Edward Johnson) down the Valley Pike and Front Royal Road to converge on Milroy simultaneously from the east and west. (Maj. Gen. Robert E. Rodes' Division was not engaged in the main battle.) Milroy was under orders to evacuate Winchester and retreat to Harpers Ferry if he was attacked by a superior force. A series of ridges west of Winchester were strongly fortified and linked to reinforced bastions, including Fort Milroy, Star Fort, and West Fort. Milroy was confident his position was sound and his defenses more than adequate to repel the enemy.

Maj. Gen. Robert H. Milroy
Image courtesy of Library of Congress

1863

| THE CAMPAIGN BEGINS JUNE 3 | THE SECOND BATTLE OF WINCHESTER JUNE 13-15 | THE BATTLE OF GETTYSBURG JULY 1-3 | LEE'S ARMY CROSSES THE POTOMAC RIVER JULY 14 |

The Second Battle of Winchester – June 13, 1863

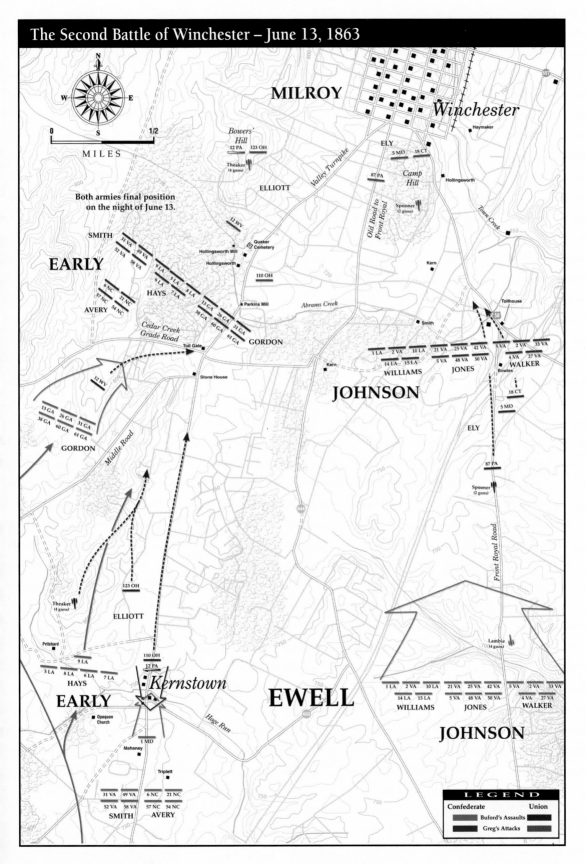

MILROY

Winchester

Haymaker

Bowers'
Hill
12 PA 123 OH

ELY
5 MD 18 CT

Theaker
(4 guns)

87 PA

Camp
Hill

Hollingsworth

ELLIOTT

12 WV

Spooner
(2 guns)

Town Creek

Both armies final position
on the night of June 13.

SMITH
31 VA 49 VA
52 VA 58 VA

Quaker
Cemetery

Hollingsworth Mill

Hollingsworth

Kern

EARLY
9 LA 5 LA
6 LA 5 LA
6 NC 21 NC
HAYS 7 LA
57 NC 54 NC
AVERY

110 OH

Parkins Mill

Abrams Creek

Smith

Tollhouse

38 GA 26 GA
60 GA 31 GA
61 GA

GORDON

1 LA 2 VA 10 LA   21 VA 25 VA 42 VA   5 VA 2 VA 33 VA
14 LA 15 LA   5 VA 48 VA 50 VA   4 VA 27 VA
WILLIAMS   JONES   WALKER
Bowles

Cedar Creek
Grade Road

Toll Gate

Kern

18 CT

JOHNSON

5 MD

Stone House

12 WV

13 GA 26 GA 31 GA
38 GA 60 GA 61 GA

GORDON

ELY

87 PA

Spooner
(2 guns)

Front Royal Road

Middle Road

123 OH

ELLIOTT

Theaker
(4 guns)

Pritchard

9 LA

Lambie
(4 guns)

5 LA 8 LA 6 LA 7 LA
HAYS

110 OH
12 PA

Kernstown

EWELL

1 LA 2 VA 10 LA   21 VA 25 VA 42 VA   5 VA 2 VA 33 VA
14 LA 15 LA   5 VA 48 VA 50 VA   4 VA 27 VA
WILLIAMS   JONES   WALKER

EARLY

Opequon
Church

1 MD
Mahaney

Hoge Run

JOHNSON

Triplett

31 VA 49 VA 6 NC 21 NC
52 VA 58 VA 57 NC 54 NC
SMITH   AVERY

LEGEND

Confederate	Union
Buford's Assaults	
Greg's Attacks	

The Second Battle of Winchester – June 14, 1863

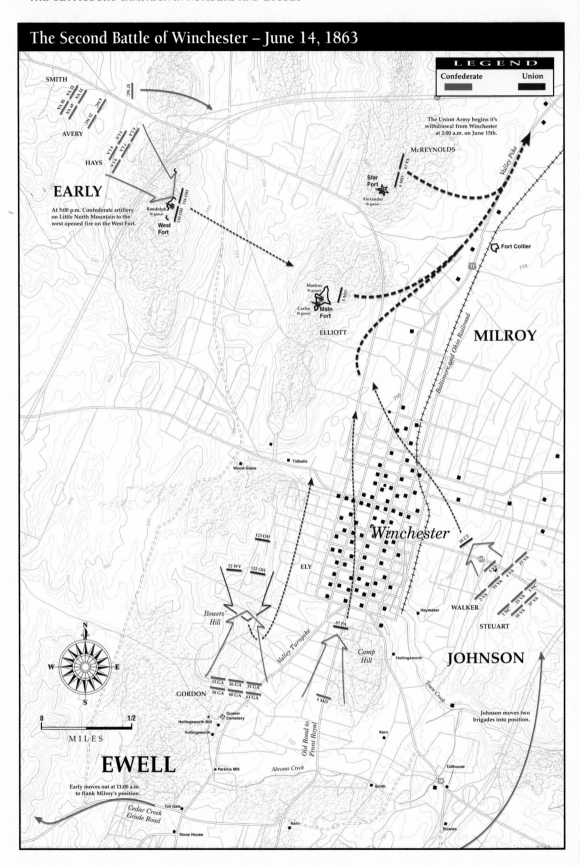

LEGEND
Confederate   Union

SMITH

55 NC

9 LA 6 VA 8 VA 31 VA 21 NC

AVERY

57 VA 21 VA 58 VA 72 VA

HAYS

6 OH 110 OH

EARLY

At 5:00 p.m. Confederate artillery on Little North Mountain to the west opened fire on the West Fort.

Randolph (6 guns)

West Fort

The Union Army begins it's withdrawal from Winchester at 2:00 a.m. on June 15th.

McREYNOLDS

Star Fort

6 MD 67 PA

Alexander (6 guns)

Valley Pike

Fort Collier

710

Martins (6 guns)

5 MD

Carlin (6 guns) Main Fort

ELLIOTT

MILROY

Baltimore and Ohio Railroad

750

730

Tidballs

Wood-Glass

123 OH

Winchester

18 CT

5 MD

33 VA 4 VA 27 VA

12 WV 122 OH

ELY

2 VA

1 NC 23 VA 3 NC

10 VA 37 VA

WALKER

Bowers' Hill

87 PA

Haymaker

STEUART

Camp Hill

Hollingsworth

JOHNSON

N
W   E
S

13 GA 26 GA 31 GA

38 GA 60 GA 61 GA

GORDON

Valley Turnpike

Town Creek

Johnson moves two brigades into position.

0   1/2
MILES

Quaker Cemetery

Hollingsworth Mill

Hollingsworth

1 MD

Kern

Toolhouse

EWELL

★ Parkins Mill

Abrams Creek

Smith

Early moves out at 11:00 a.m. to flank Milroy's position.

Old Road to Front Royal

Toll Gate

Cedar Creek Grade Road

Stone House

Kern

Bowles

Moving northwest on the Front Royal Pike, Johnson's men found Federal pickets holding the crossing of the Opequon River. The Yankees were easily driven back toward Fort Milroy. Federal artillery from the fort opened on Johnson's column and prevented an immediate assault. Johnson held his ground, however, and waited for Early's division to arrive. Milroy seems not to have realized he was about to face the bulk of Ewell's Corps. As a result, the Federals remained inside their defenses.

On the following day (June 14) skirmishing broke out in the streets of Winchester and the Confederates captured the eminence known as Bower's Hill. Ewell positioned his men to surround the forts and choke off any escape route, especially the Charles Town Road. Ewell bombarded the forts with artillery from Bower's Hill and other positions until after dark as he readied his men for the forthcoming assault.

Milroy called a council of war that night and decided to retreat to Harpers Ferry under the cover of darkness. The Federals began quietly slipping away from their defenses sometime after midnight along the Charles Town Road—the route Ewell expected them to utilize. About dawn, Confederate skirmishers from Johnson's division discovered Milroy's retreating column near Stephenson's Depot and attacked. Milroy formed his men into battle lines and attempted to cut his way out, but within a short time Johnson's infantry had nearly surrounded the Federals. Milroy's

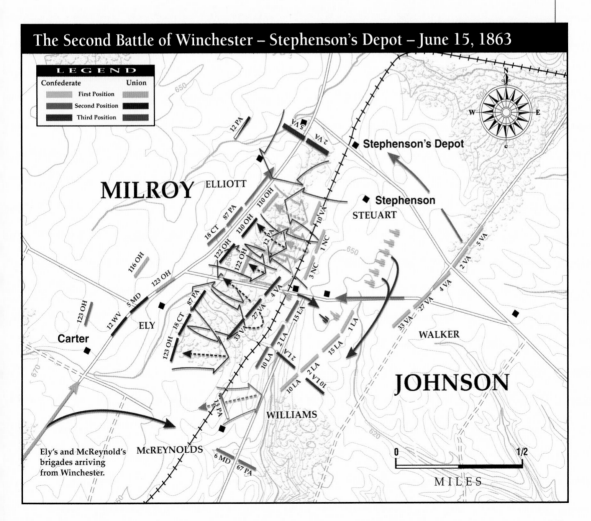

The Second Battle of Winchester – Stephenson's Depot – June 15, 1863

men attempted to scatter and run, but before the morning was over Ewell bagged 4,000 Federal prisoners, twenty-three pieces of artillery, hundreds of wagons, tons of material, and more than 300 horses.

The Second Battle of Winchester was one of the most lopsided engagements in terms of troops engaged and casualties suffered during the entire Civil War. Milroy's 8,300 men (about 6,900 effectives) suffered about 4,500 casualties in killed, wounded, missing, and captured—more than 50% of his total forces and 65% of his effective strength. Ewell's casualty rate over the three days was barely two percent. Some 1,200 Federals managed to escape to Harpers Ferry, and another 2,600 trickled into Bloody Run (today Everett), Pennsylvania, over the following days.

FEDERAL

MIDDLE DEPARTMENT
VIII ARMY CORPS

SECOND DIVISION
[8,324] (96k, 3mw, 349w, 3,999m = 4,447) 53.4%
Maj. Gen. Robert Huston Milroy, commanding

FIRST BRIGADE
[2,989] (24k, 121w, 1,214m = 1,359) 45.5%
Brig. Gen. Washington Lafayette Elliott

110th Ohio
[569] (4k, 51w, 210m = 265) 46.6%
Col. Joseph Warren Keifer

116th Ohio
[240] (8k, 29w, 141m = 178) 74.2%
Col. James Washburn

122nd Ohio
[810] (8k, 25w, 380m = 413) 51.0%
Col. William H. Ball

12th Pennsylvania Cavalry
[620] (4k, 12w, 156m = 172) 27.7%
Col. Lewis B. Pierce

13th Pennsylvania Cavalry
[655] (0k, 1w, 247m = 248) 37.9%
Col. James A. Gallagher

1st (West) Virginia Light Artillery, Battery D
(Six 3-inch Ordnance Rifles)
[95] (0k, 3w, 80m = 83) 87.4%
Capt. John Carlin

SECOND BRIGADE
[3,305] (52k, 173w, 1,752m = 1,977) 59.8%
Col. William G. Ely (c)

18th Connecticut
[820] (18k, 46w, 534m = 598) 72.9%
Lt. Col. Monroe Nichols (c)
Maj. Henry Peale

5th Maryland
[645 est.] (0k, 5w, 315m = 320) 49.6% est.
Maj. Salome Marsh

123rd Ohio
[720 est.] (21k, 62w, 466m = 549) 76.3% est.
Col. William T. Nelson (c)

87th Pennsylvania
[400] (4k, 21w, 87m = 112) 28.0%
Col. John W. Schall

12th (West) Virginia
[440] (6k, 36w, 191m = 233) 53.0%
Col. John B. Klunk

1st (West) Virginia Cavalry, Company K
[65] (0k, 1w, 11m = 12) 18.5%
Capt. Weston Rowand

3rd (West) Virginia Cavalry, Companies D and E
[125] (0k, 1w, 71m = 72) 57.6%
Capt. James R. Utt

5th United States Artillery, Battery L
(Six 3-inch Ordnance Rifles)
[90] (3k, 1w, 77m = 81) 90.0%
Lt. Wallace F. Randolph (c)
Lt. Edmund D. Spooner

THIRD BRIGADE
[1,925] (20k, 3mw, 52w, 993m = 1,068) 55.5%
Col. Andrew T. McReynolds

6th Maryland
[580] (1k, 6w, 167m = 174) 26.5%
Col. John W. Horn

67th Pennsylvania
[830] (17k, 38w, 736m = 791) 5.3%
Lt. Col. Horace B. Burnham

1st New York (Lincoln) Cavalry
[420] (2k, 3mw, 3w, 56m = 64) 15.2%
Maj. Alonzo W. Adams (final command of regiment)
(Adams was placed under arrest on
June 13 then restored to command later that day)
Maj. Timothy Quinn

Baltimore Battery, Maryland Light Artillery
(Six 3-inch Ordnance Rifles)
[95] (0k, 5w, 34m = 39) 41.0%
Capt. Frederick W. Alexander

HEAVY ARTILLERY
1st Massachusetts Heavy Artillery (Four 20-pounder
Parrotts, Two 24-pounder Howitzers)
[105] (0k, 3w, 40m = 43) 41.0%
Capt. William F. Martins (c)
Lt. Jonathan B. Hanson

CONFEDERATE

ARMY OF NORTHERN VIRGINIA
EWELL'S CORPS
[14,008] (49k, 1mw, 238w, 12m = 300) 2.1%
Lt. Gen. Richard Stoddert Ewell, commanding

EARLY'S DIVISION
[6,350] (26k, 1mw, 136w = 163) 2.6%
Maj. Gen. Jubal Anderson Early, commanding

HAYS' BRIGADE
[1,272] (13k, 75w = 88) 6.9%
Brig. Gen. Harry Thompson Hays

5th Louisiana
[206] (1k, 5w = 6) 2.9%
Maj. Alexander Hart

6th Louisiana
[255] (7k, 36w = 43) 16.9%
Col. William Monaghan
(Monaghan became ill at Winchester –
regiment led to Gettysburg, and commanded
there by Lt. Col. Joseph Hanlon)

7th Louisiana
[255] (1k, 22w = 23) 9.0%
Col. Davidson Bradfute Penn

8th Louisiana
[296] (1k, 3w =4) 1.4%
Col. Trevanion Dudley Lewis

9th Louisiana
[260] (3k, 9w = 12) 4.6%
Col. Leroy Augustus Stafford

HOKE'S BRIGADE
[1,750] (1k, 1w = 2) 0.1%
Col. Isaac Erwin Avery

1st North Carolina Battalion
[77] (No losses reported) 0.0%
Maj. Rufus H. Wharton

6th North Carolina
[515] (No losses reported) 0.0%
Maj. Samuel McDowell Tate

21st North Carolina
[445] (No losses reported) 0.0%
Col. William Whedbee Kirkland

54th North Carolina
[408] (No losses reported) 0.0%
Col. J. C. T. McDonald

57th North Carolina
[305] (1k, 1w = 2) 0.7%
Col. Archibald Campbell Godwin

SMITH'S BRIGADE
[1,180] (0k, 3w = 3) 0.3%
Brig. Gen. William Smith

13th Virginia
[102] (No losses reported) 0.0%
Col. James B. Terrill

31st Virginia
[270] (0k, 1w = 1) 0.4%
Col. John Stringer Hoffman

49th Virginia
[281] (0k, 1w = 1) 0.4%
Lt. Col. Jonathan Catlett Gibson

52nd Virginia
[255] (0k, 1w = 1) 0.4%
Lt. Col. James Henry Skinner

58th Virginia
[272] (No losses reported) 0.0%
Col. Francis H. Board

GORDON'S BRIGADE
[1,850] (11k, 55w = 66) 3.6%
Brig. Gen. John Brown Gordon

13th Georgia
[322] (3k, 10w = 13) 4.0%
Col. James Milton Smith

26th Georgia
[320] (0k, 8w = 8) 2.5%
Col. Edmund Nathan Atkinson

31st Georgia
[260] (1k, 7w = 8) 3.1%
Col. Clement Anselm Evans

38th Georgia
[350] (2k, 14w = 16) 4.6%
Capt. William L. McLeod

60th Georgia
[305] (5k, 16w = 21) 6.9%
Capt. Walter Burrus Jones

61st Georgia
[293] (No losses reported) 0.0%
Col. John Hill Lamar

ARTILLERY BATTALION
[298] (1k, 2w, 1mw = 4) 1.3%
Lt. Col. Hilary Pollard Jones

Carrington's Battery, Charlottesville (Virginia) Artillery (Four Napoleons)
[75] (1k, 1w = 2) 2.7%
Capt. James McD. Carrington

Tanner's Battery, Richmond (Virginia) "Courtney" Artillery (Four 3-inch Ordnance Rifles)
[95] (No losses reported) 0.0%
Capt. William A. Tanner

Garber's Battery, Staunton (Virginia) Artillery (Four Napoleons)
[64] (0k, 1w = 1) 1.6%
Capt. Asher W. Garber

Thompson's Battery, Louisiana Guard Artillery (Two 3-inch Ordnance Rifles, Two 10-pounder Parrotts)
[64] (0k, 1mw = 1) 1.6%
Capt. Charles Thompson (mw)
Lt. Charles A. Green

JOHNSON'S DIVISION
[6,473] (22k, 101w, 10m = 133) 2.1%
Maj. Gen. Edward Johnson

STEUART'S BRIGADE
[2,178] (14k, 54w = 68) 3.1%
Brig. Gen. George Hume Steuart

1st Maryland Battalion
[400] (No losses reported) 0.0%
Lt. Col. James Rawlings Herbert

1st North Carolina
[396] (5k, 14w = 19) 4.8%
Lt. Col. Hamilton Allen Brown

3rd North Carolina
[585] (9k, 34w = 43) 7.4%
Maj. William Murdock Parsley

10th Virginia
[282] (0k, 6w = 6) 2.1%
Col. Edward Tiffin Harrison Warren

23rd Virginia
[251] (not engaged)
Lt. Col. Simeon Taylor Walton

37th Virginia
[264] (not engaged)
Maj. Henry Clinton Wood

NICHOLL'S BRIGADE
[1,038] (2k, 13w = 15) 1.4%
Col. Jesse Milton Williams

1st Louisiana
[172] (0k, 1w =1) 0.6%
Capt. Edward D. Willett

2nd Louisiana
[236] (2k, 9w =11) 4.7%
Lt. Col. Ross Edwin Burke

10th Louisiana
[226] (0k, 3w = 3) 1.3%
Maj. Thomas N. Powell

14th Louisiana
[218] (No losses reported) 0.0%
Lt. Col. David Zable

15th Louisiana
[186] (not engaged)
Maj. Andrew Brady

THE STONEWALL BRIGADE
[1,346] (3k, 19w, 10m = 32) 2.4%
Brig. Gen. James Alexander Walker

2nd Virginia
[335] (0k, 2w = 2) 0.6%
Col. John Quincy Adams Nadenbousch

4th Virginia
[257] (No losses reported) 0.0%
Maj. William Terry

5th Virginia
[370] (3k, 16w, 10m = 29) 7.8%
Lt. Col. Hazael Joseph Williams (w)
Maj. James William Newton

27th Virginia
[148] (No losses reported) 0.0%
Lt. Col. Daniel McElheran Shriver

33rd Virginia
[236] (0k, 1w = 1) 0.4%
Capt. Jacob Burner Golladay

JONES' BRIGADE
[1,446] (0k, 1w =1) 0.07%
Brig. Gen. John Marshall Jones

21st Virginia
[183] (No losses reported) 0.0%
Capt. William Perkins Moseley

25th Virginia
[280] (No losses reported) 0.0%
Col. John Carlton Higginbotham

42nd Virginia
[252] (No losses reported) 0.0%
Lt. Col. Robert Woodson Withers

44th Virginia
[227] (No losses reported) 0.0%
Maj. Norvell Cobb

48th Virginia
[252] (0k, 1w = 1) 0.4%
Lt. Col. Robert Henry Dungan

50th Virginia
[252] (No losses reported) 0.0%
Lt. Col. Logan Henry Neil Salyer

ARTILLERY BATTALION
[380] (3k, 14w = 17) 4.5%
Lt. Col. Richard Snowden Andrews (w)
Maj. Joseph White Latimer

**Dement's Battery, 1st Maryland Battery
(Four Napoleons)**
[105] (2k, 13w = 15) 14.3%
Capt. William F. Dement

**Brown's Battery, 4th Maryland "Chesapeake"
Artillery (Four 10-pounder Parrotts)**
[81] (not engaged)
Capt. William D. Brown

**Carpenter's Battery, Alleghany (Virginia)
Rough Artillery (Two Napoleons,
Two 3-inch Ordnance Rifles)**
[99] (1k, 1w = 2) 2.0%
Lt. William T. Lambie

**Raine's Battery, Lynchburg (Virginia) "Lee"
Battery (One 3-inch Ordnance Rifle,
One 10-pounder Parrott, Two 20-pounder Parrotts)**
[95] (No losses reported) 0.0%
Capt. Charles I. Raine

ARTILLERY RESERVE
[85] (No losses reported) 0.0%

1ST VIRGINIA BATTALION
**1st Rockbridge (Virginia) Artillery
(Two Blakely, Two 20-pounder Parrotts)**
[85] (No losses reported) 0.0%
Capt. Archibald Graham
*(Captured two 20-pounder Parrotts and
disposed of the Blakely guns)*

CAVALRY DIVISION

JENKIN'S BRIGADE
[1,072] (1k, 1w, 2m = 4+) 0.4%+
Brig. Gen. Albert Gallatin Jenkins

14th Virginia Cavalry (7 Companies)
[268] (1k, 2m = 3) 1.1%
Col. James Addison Cochran

16th Virginia Cavalry
[265] (Unknown losses)
Maj. James Henry Nounnan

17th Virginia Cavalry
[242] (0k, 1w = 1) 0.4%
Col. William Henderson French

34th Battalion Virginia Cavalry
[172] (Unknown losses)
Lt. Col. Vincent Addison Witcher

36th Battalion Virginia Cavalry
[125] (Unknown losses)
Capt. Cornelius Timothy Smith

ARTILLERY
**Jackson's Battery, Charlottesville (Virginia)
Horse Artillery (Two 12-pounder Howitzers,
Two 3-inch Ordnance Rifles)**
[113] (Unknown losses)
Capt. Thomas Edwin Jackson

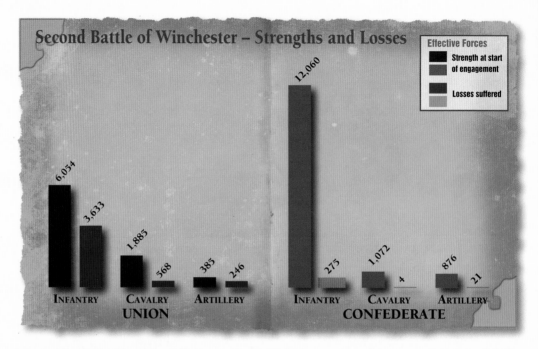

Ewell's decisive defeat of Milroy at Second Winchester cleared the lower Shenandoah Valley of most Federal forces and paved the way for Lee's army to march north into Maryland and then into Pennsylvania. The defeat shocked the Northern population in general and President Abraham Lincoln in particular. A court of inquiry was called to determine why the defenses were not immediately evacuated as ordered. Although Milroy was exonerated ten months later, he was transferred to the Western Theater and held minor administrative positions until the end of the war.

Following the Winchester debacle, Pennsylvania Governor Andrew G. Curtin placed an immediate call for 50,000 volunteer troops to defend the state against what seemed a likely enemy invasion—even before a single Confederate soldier stepped foot on Keystone State soil. Lincoln followed with a plea of his own for 100,000 additional volunteer troops.

Ewell's brilliant performance at Winchester may have had an influence on the manner in which the three-day battle of Gettysburg (July 1-3) was carried out. Lee had reorganized the army following Stonewall Jackson's death after Chancellorsville and elevated Ewell to lead Jackson's former corps. As many in the army now believed, Ewell's aggressive marching and attacking at Winchester made it seem as though Jackson was back with the army. Lee's confidence in Ewell soared. Late on the first day at Gettysburg, Lee gave Ewell discretionary orders regarding an attack against the Federals gathering atop Cemetery Hill. Ewell temporized and in the end decided not to attack. His decision (whether correct or incorrect can never be known) permitted the Federals to reorganize and entrench on the high ground east and south of Gettysburg with Cemetery Hill serving as the line's linchpin. Lee would spend the next two days trying unsuccessfully to carry that line.

After Second Winchester, all three of Lee's infantry corps were on the move for the first time since the campaign began. A. P. Hill's Third Corps left the area around Fredericksburg and was marching to Culpeper Court House, and Longstreet's First Corps continued the march it had begun east of the Blue Ridge Mountains. Most of the Federal army, in contrast, was resting. The I Corps and XI Corps camped around Centreville, Virginia; the III Corps camped near Bull Run; the V Corps was near Warrenton Station; and the XII Corps was near Fairfax. Only two Federal corps were on the move: the II Corps (with its new commander Maj. Gen. Winfield S. Hancock) marched from Acquia Creek to Wolf Run Shoals, and the VI Corps tramped from Dumfries to Fairfax Station.

Federal commander Joseph Hooker betrayed some uncertainty, likely intensified by his lack of knowledge of Confederate movements and intentions, by asking President Lincoln for instructions on how to proceed. General-in-Chief Halleck wired Hooker to send a force to Leesburg, Virginia, to find the enemy, and thereafter to move as conditions dictated. Hooker asked repeatedly for more troops, but was informed that none would be forthcoming.

STUART SHIELDS THE ARMY'S ADVANCE

THE BATTLE OF ALDIE, VA.

JUNE 17, 1863

Sheltered by the Blue Ridge Mountains, Lee's Army of Northern Virginia continued tramping north down the Shenandoah Valley while **MAJ. GEN. J.E.B. STUART**'s cavalry screened the march by guarding mountain passes and keeping the Federals at a distance. Federal cavalry commander **BRIG. GEN. ALFRED PLEASONTON**'s inability to crack Stuart's screen and bring him reliable information on Southern movements frustrated Joe Hooker. Determined to break through, Pleasonton ordered Brig. Gen. David M. Gregg and his Second Cavalry Division westward from Manassas Junction to Aldie, Virginia, a crucially important hub near the Little River Turnpike, the thoroughfare that connected both of the roads to Ashby's Gap and Snicker's Gap in the Blue Ridge.

Maj. Gen. J.E.B. Stuart
Image courtesy of Library of Congress

1863

THE CAMPAIGN BEGINS JUNE 3 | THE BATTLES OF ALDIE, MIDDLEBURG, AND UPPERVILLE JUNE 17-21 | THE BATTLE OF GETTYSBURG JULY 1-3 | LEE'S ARMY CROSSES THE POTOMAC RIVER JULY 14

Brig. Gen. Alfred Pleasonton
Image courtesy of Library of Congress

Two Virginia cavalry regiments under Col. Thomas T. Munford were conducting a foraging mission around Aldie while picketing the road to Snicker's Gap. Gregg's leading brigade under the impetuous Brig. Gen. Judson Kilpatrick arrived at Aldie late that afternoon. Munford's pickets west of town were driven out by the troopers of the 1st Massachusetts Cavalry, but the Federals were driven back through Aldie when the rest of Munford's brigade arrived. The Massachusetts men and the 4th New York charged the Virginians, but a Southern countercharge swept the Federals back and the road to Ashby's Gap was secure.

Kilpatrick tried to capture the road leading to Snicker's Gap as an artillery duel broke out. Mounted and dismounted fighting erupted along the road. Trapped along a curve in the road, the Massachusetts troopers suffered more than 50% casualties. Still, Kilpatrick gained the upper hand when he was reinforced by the 1st Maine Cavalry, but its commander, Col. Calvin S. Douty, was killed during the subsequent fighting. After four hours of combat, Munford withdrew his troopers about 8:00 p.m. west toward Middleburg.

FEDERAL

ARMY OF THE POTOMAC
CAVALRY CORPS
Brig. Gen. Alfred Pleasonton

SECOND CAVALRY DIVISION
[1,580] (50k, 1mw, 130w, 124m = 305) 19.3%

SECOND BRIGADE
[1,311] (44k, 1mw, 111w, 120m = 276) 21.1%
Brig. Gen. Hugh Judson Kilpatrick

1st Massachusetts Cavalry (8 Companies)
[294] (20k, 57w, 90m = 167) 56.8%
Lt. Col. Greeley Stevenson Curtis

2nd New York Cavalry
[310] (16k, 19w, 15m = 50) 16.1%
Col. Henry Eugene Davies

4th New York Cavalry
[340] (5k, 22w, 15m = 42) 12.4%
Col. Luigi Palma di Cesnola (w-c)
Lt. Col. Augustus Pruyn

6th Ohio Cavalry (8 Companies)
[367] (3k, 1mw, 13w = 17) 4.6%
Col. William Stedman

ARTILLERY
**1st United States Horse Artillery,
Batteries E and G (Four 12-pounder Napoleons)**
[91] (No losses reported) 0.0%
Capt. Alanson Merwin Randol

THIRD BRIGADE
1st Maine Cavalry (6 Companies engaged)
[178] (6k, 19w, 4m = 29) 16.3%
Col. Calvin Sanger Douty (k)
Lt. Col. Charles Henry Smith

CONFEDERATE

ARMY OF NORTHERN VIRGINIA

CAVALRY DIVISION

[2,144] (9k, 47w, 63m = 119) 5.6%

Maj. Gen. James Ewell Brown Stuart

FITZHUGH LEE'S BRIGADE

[2,028] (7k, 44w, 63m = 114) 5.6%

Col. Thomas Taylor Munford

1st Virginia Cavalry

[376] (1k, 4w, 1m = 6) 1.6%

Col. James Henry Drake

2nd Virginia Cavalry

[487] (2k, 11w = 13) 2.7%

Col. Thomas Taylor Munford
Lt. Col. James Winston Watts (w)
Maj. Cary Breckenridge

3rd Virginia Cavalry

[274] (0k, 5w, 15m = 20) 7.3%

Col. Thomas Howerton Owen

4th Virginia Cavalry

[654] (1k, 7w, 9m = 17) 2.6%

Col. Williams Carter Wickham
Capt. William Brockenbrough Newton

5th Virginia Cavalry

[237] (3k, 17w, 38m = 58) 24.5%

Col. Thomas Lafayette Rosser

ARTILLERY

Breathed's Battery, 1st Stuart (Virginia) Horse
Artillery (Four 3-inch Ordnance Rifles)

[116] (2k, 3w = 5) 4.3%

Capt. James Williams Breathed

The Battle of Aldie – June 17, 1863

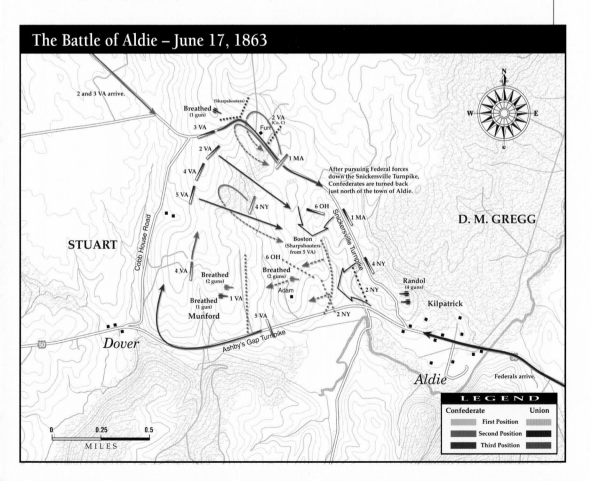

The skirmish at Aldie was the first in a series of several small but bloody cavalry fights near the mountain gaps. Once again, Stuart's troopers foiled Pleasonton's attempt to thrust his way into the Loudoun Valley, depriving Hooker of reliable information on Confederate positions, movements, and intentions.

Meanwhile, Robert E. Lee's army was stretched across more than 100 miles of Virginia. The head of Ewell's Second Corps had reached the Potomac River, Longstreet's divisions were behind Ewell in the Shenandoah Valley, and A. P. Hill's Third Corps was marching for the valley from Culpeper. A few days earlier, Brig. Gen. Albert G. Jenkins' Confederate cavalry had ridden ahead of Ewell and entered Pennsylvania, a move that panicked the officials of the state's new Department of the Susquehanna. Most of the Federal army in Virginia remained largely inactive for the next several days while, as Hooker explained, "the enemy develops his intention or force."

THE SKIRMISHES AT MIDDLEBURG, VA.

JUNE 17-18, 1863

Early on the morning of June 17, Federal cavalry commander Brig. Gen. Alfred Pleasonton ordered French-born **COL. ALFRED DUFFIÉ** on a reconnaissance mission with his 1st Rhode Island Cavalry, part of Brig. Gen. Judson Kilpatrick's brigade. The regiment was to leave from the army's camp near Centreville, Virginia, on the way to Middleburg. The Rhode Islanders had orders to ride the next day as far west as Snickersville and report on any enemy activity they discovered. The mission would be conducted deep into enemy territory, but Duffié and his men were dispatched alone without any other units in supporting distance.

Col. Alfred N. A. Duffié
Image courtesy of Library of Congress

The Rhode Islanders passed through Thoroughfare Gap and brushed aside Rebel pickets belonging to Col. Richard L. T. Beale's 9th Virginia Cavalry. (Beale was under orders not to engage the enemy.) The Federals arrived in Middleburg about 4:00 p.m., about the same time Kilpatrick and the rest of the brigade arrived at Aldie five miles to the east. The Rhode Islanders had no idea that Confederate cavalry commander

Maj. Gen. J.E.B. Stuart
Image courtesy of Library of Congress

MAJ. GEN. J.E.B. STUART had established his headquarters at Middleburg. As Duffié's men drove in Southern cavalry pickets near the town, Stuart, his staff, and members of the 4th Virginia Cavalry abandoned their lunch and sought safer ground in the direction of Rector's Crossroads, where the demi-brigade of North Carolina cavalrymen under Brig. Gen. Beverly Robertson was located. Stuart ordered Robertson to ride to Middleburg to punish the intruders.

Duffié intended to hold Middleburg as his orders directed, so he barricaded the streets and dismounted one-half of his men in strategic positions behind stone walls. Dusk was falling when Robertson's North Carolinians charged into the town and captured dozens of Duffié's men. Duffié fell back with his remaining troopers and made camp. When they tried to escape back east, they were ambushed by Beale's 9th Virginia Cavalry and most of the Federals were captured.

FEDERAL

ARMY OF THE POTOMAC

CAVALRY CORPS
Brig. Gen. Alfred Pleasonton

SECOND BRIGADE
1st Rhode Island Cavalry
[280] (6k, 9w, 210m = 225) 80.4%
Col. Alfred Napoléon Alexander Duffié

CONFEDERATE

ARMY OF NORTHERN VIRGINIA

CAVALRY DIVISION
[2,207] (25+ total est.) 1.1%+ est.
Maj. Gen. James Ewell Brown Stuart

WILLIAM HENRY FITZHUGH LEE'S BRIGADE
9th Virginia Cavalry
[680] (Unknown losses)
Col. Richard Lee Turberville Beale

FITZHUGH LEE'S BRIGADE
4th Virginia Cavalry
[542] (Unknown losses)
Col. Williams Carter Wickham

ROBERTSON'S BRIGADE
[985] (6k est. = 25 est.) 2.5% est.
Brig. Gen. Beverly Holcombe Robertson

4th North Carolina Cavalry
[515] (15 est.) 2.9% est.
Col. Dennis Dozier Ferebee

5th North Carolina Cavalry
[470] (10 est.) 2.1% est.
Col. Peter Gustavus Evans

Duffié and only a few dozen of his men escaped capture and returned that night to Centreville. Because Pleasonton distrusted foreigners and systematically purged his cavalry corps of foreign-born officers throughout the month of June, many historians postulate that Pleasonton sent Duffié on the suicidal 'fool's errand' to Middleburg, alone and unsupported deep behind enemy lines, in an effort to get rid of him. Duffié had also fallen into disfavor because of his poor performance at the June 9 battle at Brandy Station. Whatever the motivation, the price for his foray was the death, wounding, and capture of most of his regiment. Duffié never again commanded troops in the Army of the Potomac.

THE SKIRMISHES AT CATOCTIN CREEK, MD.

JUNE 17, 1863

Just before sunset on June 17, Confederate partisan **LT. COL. ELIJAH V. WHITE** crossed the Potomac River at Grubb's Ford just below Brunswick with 165 of his men of the 35th Battalion Virginia Cavalry on his way to attack an enemy encampment at Point of Rocks, Maryland. The enemy there was a unit of pro-Union Virginia cavalry partisans called the Independent Loudoun Virginia Rangers under the command of **CAPT. SAMUEL A. MEANS**. White divided his force when he reached the north shore, sending Company B under Lt. Joshua Randolph Crown north along the Frederick Road to attack from the north while White led the balance of his men along the canal towpath to attack from the south. (See the narrative on the Skirmish at Point of Rocks for more information.)

Lt. Col. Elijah V. White
Image courtesy of Library of Congress

Some of Crown's men were dressed in Federal uniforms to deceive the loyalist Virginians. After an advance of about two miles, Crown's men captured a Federal. According to the prisoner, he was making his way to the camp at Point of Rocks. Crown's men wounded another Federal soon thereafter and killed a third. The shooting was heard by troopers of the 1st Potomac Home Brigade Cavalry, a Maryland unit numbering some 200 men locally known as "Cole's Cavalry."

The first company of Cole's Cavalry, Company A, was raised in Maryland during the fall of 1861 by Capt. Henry A. Cole. Four companies of Maryland and southern Pennsylvania men

Capt. Samuel A. Means
Image courtesy of J. D. Petruzzi

were consolidated under Cole, who was promoted to major. Cole's horsemen often operated as partisans, patrolling and conducting raids and attacks on Confederate units in Maryland and northern Virginia.

When Cole's Federals heard the shots fired by Crown's Confederates, they crossed Catoctin Creek and formed a battle line along a slight ridge. Although Crown was outnumbered, he ordered his men to set their spurs and charge. Cole's troopers unleashed a volley of bullets, but Crown's men closed the distance, crashed into the Federals, and scattered them. A running fight ensued that lasted for four miles. By the time it was over, Crown captured several dozen members of Cole's Cavalry and their horses. With his prisoners in tow, Crown proceeded to Point of Rocks to ride to Lt. Col. White's aid in the second attack taking place there.

FEDERAL

MIDDLE DEPARTMENT
VIII ARMY CORPS

FIRST DIVISION

THIRD BRIGADE

Cole's Battalion, 1st Potomac Home Brigade Cavalry (4 Companies)
[200] (1k, 2w, 37m = 40) 20.0%
Maj. Henry A. Cole

CONFEDERATE

ARMY OF NORTHERN VIRGINIA
CAVALRY DIVISION

JONES' BRIGADE

35th Battalion Virginia Cavalry (Company B)
[63] (No losses reported) 0.0%
Lt. Joshua Randolph Crown

Even though outnumbered more than two to one, Crown was able to scatter the Federal force and capture half his own number in prisoners, while losing none of his men. The Virginia horsemen were additionally able to stop Cole's men from reaching Samuel Means' encampment at Point of Rocks, where the Federals would have been able to assist their comrades in the surprise attack that was about to be launched there by Elijah White.

THE SKIRMISHES AT PHILOMONT, VA.

JUNE 18, 1863

While John Gregg was skirmishing with Stuart near Middleburg, **COL. WILLIAM GAMBLE**'s cavalry brigade, part of Brig. Gen. John Buford's First Cavalry Division, was riding toward Philomont, Virginia. About mid-morning, Gamble, accompanied by six guns of horse artillery, cautiously proceeded along the Snickersville Pike and across Goose Creek at Carter's Bridge. Two of his guns remained at the bridge to protect the crossing. Troopers under **COL. THOMAS MUNFORD** stood in Gamble's path on the way to Philomont and triggered a series of running skirmishes in an effort to slow down his advance.

Col. Thomas Munford
Image courtesy of Library of Congress

Munford was in command of Fitz Lee's cavalry brigade. He prepared for Gamble's full arrival by forming a line of battle near Snickersville early that afternoon. After passing through Philomont, Munford's pickets increased the pressure on Gamble. Ten miles ahead of any supports and not knowing what or who was waiting ahead, Gamble decided to turn his column back toward Aldie, where he arrived about 9:00 p.m. Neither side reported any casualties.

Col. William Gamble
Image courtesy of Library of Congress

FEDERAL

ARMY OF THE POTOMAC
CAVALRY CORPS

FIRST CAVALRY DIVISION
[1,550] (No losses reported) 0.0%

FIRST BRIGADE
[1,475] (No losses reported) 0.0%
Col. William Gamble

8th Illinois Cavalry
[415] (No losses reported) 0.0%
Maj. John Lourie Beveridge

12th Illinois Cavalry (4 Companies)
[237] (No losses reported) 0.0%

3rd Indiana Cavalry (6 Companies)
[308] (No losses reported) 0.0%
Col. George Henry Chapman
(Capt. George Washington Shears had
subordinate command of the 12th Illinois Cavalry)

8th New York Cavalry
[515] (No losses reported) 0.0%
Lt. Col. William L. Markell

ATTACHED ARTILLERY
2ND UNITED STATES HORSE
ARTILLERY BRIGADE

2nd United States Horse Artillery, Battery A
(Six 3-inch Ordnance Rifles)
[75] (No losses reported) 0.0%
Lt. John Haskell Calef

CONFEDERATE

ARMY OF NORTHERN VIRGINIA
CAVALRY DIVISION

FITZ LEE'S BRIGADE
[1,922] (No losses reported) 0.0%
Col. Thomas Taylor Munford

1st Virginia Cavalry
[370] (No losses reported) 0.0%
Col. James Henry Drake

2nd Virginia Cavalry
[476] (No losses reported) 0.0%
Col. Thomas Taylor Munford
Maj. Cary Breckenridge

3rd Virginia Cavalry
[255] (No losses reported) 0.0%
Col. Thomas Howerton Owen

4th Virginia Cavalry
[636] (No losses reported) 0.0%
Col. Williams Carter Wickham

5th Virginia Cavalry
[185] (No losses reported) 0.0%
Col. Thomas Lafayette Rosser

Colonel Gamble had little to show for his long ride. Still, he had managed to thrust as far as two miles from Snicker's Gap and the Blue Ridge, and he had kept Munford and his Virginians on the defensive. Buford's other two brigades, one comprised of volunteers and the other Regular Army cavalry, were scattered from Aldie to Thoroughfare Gap. The fighting thus far, coupled with the Federals' urgent need to discover the location and intention of Lee's Army of Northern Virginia, suggested that a major fight was about to get underway. The only question was where the combat would take place.

THE SKIRMISHES AT WARRENTON, VA.

JUNE 18, 1863

The final Federal cavalry force dispatched to conduct a scouting mission included two regiments from Maj. Gen. Julius Stahel's division. Vermonters and cavalry from western Virginia (West Virginia was formally admitted to the Union as a separate state on June 20, 1863) under **COL. OTHNEIL DEFOREST** camped at Centreville, Virginia on the night of June 17. It left the next morning to scout toward Warrenton and Sulphur Springs.

Brig. Gen. Wade Hampton
Image courtesy of Library of Congress

DeForest spotted a Confederate battle line about two miles outside of Warrenton, midway between his men and the town. DeForest ordered his men to advance against the Southerners, composed of a brigade of cavalry under **BRIG. GEN. WADE HAMPTON**. A heavy thunder and lightning storm broke out as the Federal line of battle advanced. The Federal skirmishers pushed back Hampton's skirmish line a short distance, but the rain, coupled with the onset of darkness and a lack of artillery support convinced DeForest to pull his men back. No losses were reported by either side.

Col. Othneil DeForest
Image courtesy of J. D. Petruzzi

FEDERAL

DEPARTMENT OF WASHINGTON
CAVALRY DIVISION

SECOND BRIGADE
[995] (No losses reported) 0.0%
Col. Othneil DeForest

1st Vermont Cavalry
[600] (No losses reported) 0.0%
Lt. Col. Addison Webster Preston

1st (West) Virginia Cavalry
[395] (No losses reported) 0.0%
Col. Nathaniel Pendleton Richmond

CONFEDERATE

ARMY OF NORTHERN VIRGINIA
CAVALRY DIVISION

HAMPTON'S BRIGADE
[2,572] (No losses reported) 0.0%
Brig. Gen. Wade Hampton

Cobb's Legion (Georgia)
[575] (No losses reported) 0.0%
Col. Pierce Manning Butler Young

Jeff Davis Legion (Mississippi)
[357] (No losses reported) 0.0%
Lt. Col. Joseph Frederick Waring

1st South Carolina Cavalry
[545] (No losses reported) 0.0%
Col. John Logan Black

2nd South Carolina Cavalry
[430] (No losses reported) 0.0%
Maj. Thomas Jefferson Lipscomb

1st North Carolina Cavalry
[665] (No losses reported) 0.0%
Col. Laurence Simmons Baker

DeForest was outnumbered nearly three to one, so it was fortuitous that he broke off the engagement with Hampton's troopers when he did. By the end of the day on June 18, Federal cavalry commander Alfred Pleasonton's troopers had been stopped on three separate fronts, and army commander Maj. Gen. Joseph Hooker had not gained any significant information about the Army of Northern Virginia. Pleasonton believed any threat Lee's army posed was nothing but a "grand dodge." It is doubtful he would have thought this way had he known that one of Lee's corps under Lt. Gen. Richard S. Ewell would cross into Pennsylvania within a few short days; most of Lt. Gen. James Longstreet's Corps was in the western part of the Shenandoah Valley; and the third corps under Lt. Gen. Ambrose P. Hill was marching just behind Longstreet.

It was now more imperative than ever that Hooker gain intelligence as to Lee's designs. As a result, Federal cavalry probes would begin again in earnest near Middleburg the next day (June 19).

THE BATTLE OF MIDDLEBURG, VA.

JUNE 19, 1863

Confederate Cavalry leader **MAJ. GEN. J.E.B. STUART** continued holding his high ground west of Middleburg on the morning of June 19. **BRIG. GEN. DAVID M. GREGG** determined to move against him once again, and sent forward one of his cavalry brigades under his cousin Col. John I. Gregg. In the meantime, two more brigades from Brig. Gen. John Buford's cavalry division rode north toward Pot House (also called Leithtown then and New Lisbon today) to try and turn Stuart's left flank. This time Colonel Gregg's troopers cleared Confederate pickets away from Middleburg after a sharp fight, and Buford's men pushed back the North Carolina cavalry of Brig. Gen. Beverly Robertson near Pot House.

Maj. Gen. J.E.B. Stuart
Image courtesy of Library of Congress

By midday the temperature was approaching an enervating 100 degrees. Colonel Gregg occupied Middleburg while assessing Stuart's position on Mount Defiance. Gregg needed reinforcements to attack the hill and was reinforced by the 2nd New York and 6th Ohio troopers from Judson Kilpatrick's brigade. When a wave of mounted charges pushed the Confederate artillery from the hill, Stuart and his cavalry retreated westward. Buford's presence to the north forced Stuart to abandon the Middleburg area as far as Kirk's Branch. Federal cavalry commander Alfred Pleasonton, however, was cautious about driving too far west too quickly and refused to allow further pursuit.

Unfortunately, detailed loss reports for this engagement are missing for both sides. Federal losses were at least 109 from all causes (killed, wounded, captured, and missing) with most of them suffered by Gregg's division; Buford's losses were probably very light. Confederate casualty tallies are even more elusive. Primary sources have only turned up an estimate of some forty losses from all causes for J.E.B. Stuart's men.

Brig. Gen. David M. Gregg
Image courtesy of Library of Congress

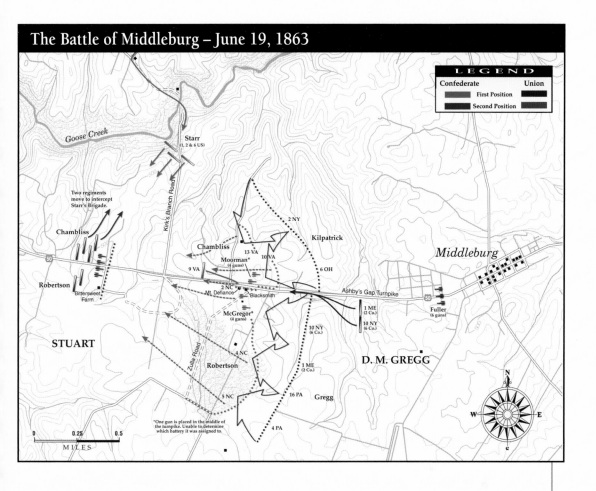

The Battle of Middleburg – June 19, 1863

FEDERAL

ARMY OF THE POTOMAC
CAVALRY CORPS
[5,643] (16k, 1mw, 55w, 23m = 95+) 1.7%+

FIRST CAVALRY DIVISION
[3,436] (Unknown losses)
Brig. Gen. John Buford

FIRST BRIGADE
[1,475] (Unknown losses)
Col. William Gamble

8th Illinois Cavalry
[415] (Unknown losses)
Maj. John Lourie Beveridge

12th Illinois Cavalry (4 Companies)
[237] (Unknown losses)

3rd Indiana Cavalry (6 Companies)
[308] (Unknown losses)
Col. George Henry Chapman
*(Capt. George Washington Shears had
subordinate command of the 12th Illinois)*

8th New York Cavalry
[515] (Unknown losses)
Lt. Col. William L. Markell

RESERVE BRIGADE
[1,735] (Unknown losses)
Maj. Samuel Henry Starr

1st United States Cavalry (10 Companies)
[348] (Unknown losses)
Capt. Richard Stanton C. Lord

2nd United States Cavalry
[375] (Unknown losses)
Capt. Wesley Merritt

5th United States Cavalry
[305] (Unknown losses)
Capt. James E. Harrison

6th United States Cavalry
[465] (Unknown losses)
Capt. George Clarence Cram

6th Pennsylvania Cavalry (10 Companies)
[242] (Unknown losses)
Maj. Henry C. Whelan

ATTACHED ARTILLERY
**1st United States Artillery, Battery K
(Six 3-inch Ordnance Rifles)**
[121] (No losses reported) 0.0%
Capt. William Montrose Graham, Jr.

ATTACHED HORSE ARTILLERY
**2nd United States Horse Artillery, Batteries B and L
(Six 3-inch Ordnance Rifles)**
[105] (No losses reported) 0.0%
Lt. Albert Oliver Vincent

SECOND CAVALRY DIVISION
[2,207] (16k, 1mw, 55w, 23m = 95) 4.3%
Brig. Gen. David McMurtrie Gregg

SECOND BRIGADE
[627] (0k, 1mw, 1w = 2) 0.3%

2nd New York Cavalry
[275] (No losses reported) 0.0%
Col. Henry Eugene Davies

6th Ohio Cavalry
[352] (0k, 1mw, 1w = 2) 0.6%
Col. William Stedman

THIRD BRIGADE
[1,475] (16k, 54w, 23m = 93) 6.3%
Col. John Irvin Gregg

1st Maine Cavalry
[355] (10k, 27w = 37) 10.4%
Lt. Col. Charles H. Smith

10th New York Cavalry
[435] (3k, 8w, 18m = 29) 6.7%
Maj. Matthew H. Avery

4th Pennsylvania Cavalry
[270] (2k, 9w, 5m = 16) 5.9%
Col. William Emile Doster (c – escaped)

16th Pennsylvania Cavalry
[415] (1k, 10w = 11) 2.7%
Col. John K. Robinson

ATTACHED ARTILLERY
**3rd United States Horse Artillery, Battery C
(Six 3-inch Ordnance Rifles)**
[105] (No losses reported) 0.0%
Lt. William Duncan Fuller

CONFEDERATE

ARMY OF NORTHERN VIRGINIA

CAVALRY DIVISION
[5,028] (11k+, 24w+, 1w-c+, ?m = 36+) 0.7%+
Maj. Gen. James Ewell Brown Stuart

FITZHUGH LEE'S BRIGADE
[1,823] (Unknown losses)
Col. Thomas Taylor Munford

1st Virginia Cavalry
[370] (Unknown losses)
Col. James Henry Drake

2nd Virginia Cavalry
[476] (Not engaged – kept in reserve)
Col. Thomas Taylor Munford
Maj. Cary Breckenridge

3rd Virginia Cavalry
[255] (Not on field – patrolling near Snickersville)
Col. Thomas Howerton Owen

4th Virginia Cavalry
[537] (Not on field – patrolling near Snickersville)
Col. Williams Carter Wickham

5th Virginia Cavalry
[185] (Unknown losses)
Col. Thomas Lafayette Rosser

WILLIAM HENRY FITZHUGH LEE'S BRIGADE
[1,636] (11k+, 22w+, 1w-c = 34+) 2.1%+
Col. John Randolph Chambliss, Jr.

2nd North Carolina Cavalry
[80] (3k, 1w-c = 4) 5.0%
Lt. Col. William Henry Fitzhugh Payne

9th Virginia Cavalry
[678] (4k+, 4w+ = 8+) 1.2%+
Col. Richard Lee Turberville Beale (w)
Lt. Col. Meriwether Lewis

10th Virginia Cavalry
[310] (Unknown losses)
Col. James Lucius Davis

13th Virginia Cavalry
[568] (4k, 18w = 22) 3.9%
Maj. Joseph Ezra Gillette

ROBERTSON'S BRIGADE
[960] (Unknown losses)
Brig. Gen. Beverly Holcombe Robertson

4th North Carolina Cavalry
[500] (Unknown losses)
Col. Dennis Dozier Ferebee

5th North Carolina Cavalry
[460] (Unknown losses)
Col. Peter Gustavus Evans

JONES' BRIGADE

7th Virginia Cavalry
[401] (0k, 1w = 1) 0.2%
Lt. Col. Thomas A. Marshall, Jr.

ATTACHED ARTILLERY
[208] (0k, 1w = 1) 0.5%

**2nd Stuart Horse Artillery, McGregor's (Virginia)
Battery (One Blakely, One unknown)**
[106] (0k, 1w = 1) 0.9%
Capt. William Morrell McGregor

**Lynchburg "Beauregard" Rifles, Moorman's
(Virginia) Battery (One Napoleon, Three unknown)**
[102] (No losses reported) 0.0%
Capt. Marcellus Newton Moorman

Although Stuart was knocked off his perch at Mount Defiance, he had again managed to keep Pleasonton's cavalry out of the Valley, albeit assisted by Pleasonton's own unwillingness to aggressively advance when he had the opportunity to do so. The mounting casualties suffered by both sides (as well as the exhausted horses) continued to take their toll on the mounted forces.

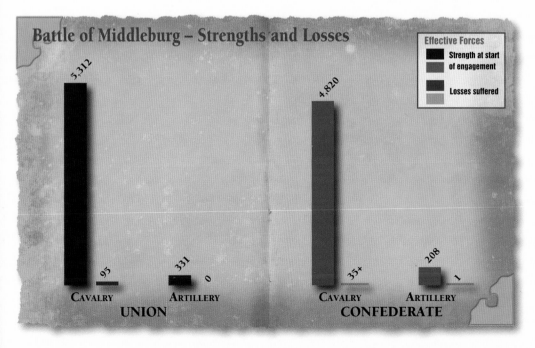

Battle of Middleburg – Strengths and Losses

Effective Forces
■ Strength at start of engagement
■ Losses suffered

5,312
95
331
0
4,820
35+
208
1

CAVALRY   ARTILLERY
UNION

CAVALRY   ARTILLERY
CONFEDERATE

During the afternoon of June 19, when a Federal staff officer heard the sound of guns at Pot House, he mistakenly thought Buford's men and the Union flank were endangered. The officer ordered the bridge over Goose Creek burned. The result was that after the fighting Gamble's men had to ford the stream, which was swollen by the previous night's torrential downpour. Gamble's troopers sent up "hearty curses" against the misguided officer as they guided their mounts through the fast-running and nearly saddle-deep creek.

By the next day (June 20), J.E.B. Stuart had all five of his cavalry brigades in Loudoun Valley. The Federals still threatened the gaps near Upperville and Ashby's Gap because they were concentrated around Aldie. To counter this threat, Stuart put John R. Chambliss' and William E. Jones' brigades near Union, positioned Beverly Robertson's and Wade Hampton's brigades around Middleburg, and used Thomas Munford's men to anchor Snickersville.

Middleburg was the heart of Virginia's horse country, and it had witnessed some of the sharpest cavalry fighting of the week along its streets and the hills and fields surrounding the town. These swirling combats for control of access to the mountain passes and by extension the Shenandoah Valley, was far from over. Stuart preferred to avoid fighting on Sunday (June 21) but that morning he was given no choice.

THE BATTLE OF UPPERVILLE, VA.

JUNE 21, 1863

Two days after the cavalry fighting at Aldie, the Federal horsemen determined to deliver one more heavy thrust in their attempt to enter the Shenandoah Valley and gain intelligence on the Confederate army's whereabouts and intentions. The previous day (June 20), Federal cavalry commander **BRIG. GEN. ALFRED PLEASONTON** pleaded for infantry support and was given Col. Strong Vincent's brigade of nearly 1,400 men from Maj. Gen. George G. Meade's V Corps. The Confederates also received reinforcements with the arrival of Brig. Gen. Wade Hampton's veteran cavalry brigade. The combatants were about evenly matched with roughly 8,000 men on each side.

Brig. Gen. Alfred Pleasonton
Image courtesy of Library of Congress

Maj. Gen. J.E.B. Stuart
Image courtesy of Library of Congress

Although June 21 was a Sunday, neither side would enjoy a day of rest. Just after daybreak Federal horse artillery moved into position and lobbed shells against **MAJ. GEN. J.E.B. STUART**'s position at the Bittersweet Farm two miles west of Middleburg, followed by an attack by Brig. Gen. Judson Kilpatrick's Federal cavalry brigade. Stuart's men held their own for a while until Vincent's infantry advanced. The Confederates retreated westward while conducting a classic delaying action by using natural terrain features such as ridges, waterways, and low stone walls to slow the Federal advance. Stuart attempted a determined stand along a stone bridge spanning Goose Creek west of the little hamlet of Rector's Crossroads. He kept the Federals at bay for several hours by using his artillery to his advantage. Eventually, however, the weight of the Federal attacks wore down the defense and Stuart's gunners limbered their pieces and withdrew. The artillerists were moving off when one of Capt. James F. Hart's prized English Blakely rifled guns flipped over and had to be abandoned. This was the first piece of Stuart's artillery captured during the war.

Stuart's troopers withdrew west toward Upperville with his left flank resting near the town. Brigadier General John Buford's Federal division arrived after its detour to the north and attacked the flank while Col. John Gregg's and Kilpatrick's cavalry brigades advanced on Stuart's front along Vineyard Hill. Both sides launched mounted attacks and counterattacks across the fields and ridges

The Battle of Upperville – June 21, 1863

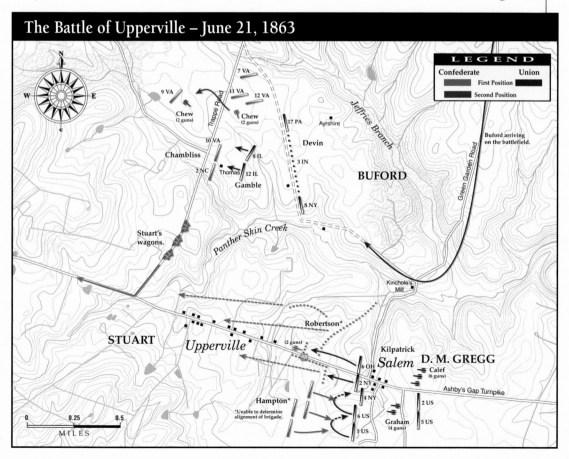

for about two hours. During one such attack Confederate artillery fired a blast of canister at close range against an assault led by Federal brigade commander Col. William Gamble. Somehow the officer escaped with but a slight wound although his horse was torn to pieces. In the end Stuart withdrew in what was his first sound defeat on a field of battle. The Confederates retreated that evening to a defensive position in Ashby's Gap. Several Confederate casualty reports are missing, but a solid estimate for Stuart's losses is about 210 killed, wounded, captured, and missing. Federal losses were nearly the same at 209.

Of the fighting at Upperville, Stuart wrote in a letter to his wife Flora, "The First Dragoons [1st U.S. Cavalry, a regiment in which Stuart had served prior to the war] tried very hard to kill me."

FEDERAL

ARMY OF THE POTOMAC
CAVALRY CORPS
[8,227 total forces] (12k, 134w, 7w-c, 60m = 213) 2.6%
Brig. Gen. Alfred Pleasonton

FIRST DIVISION
[4,321] (6k, 62w, 47m = 115) 2.7%
Brig. Gen. John Buford

FIRST BRIGADE
[1,462] (4k, 35w, 5m = 44) 3.0%
Col. William Gamble (w) (final command of brigade)
Maj. William H. Medill

8th Illinois Cavalry
[412] (2k, 17w = 19) 4.6%
Maj. John Lourie Beveridge

12th Illinois Cavalry (4 Companies)
[235] (2k, 14w, 4m = 20) 8.5%

3rd Indiana Cavalry (6 Companies)
[305] (0k, 4w, 1m = 5) 1.6%
Col. George Henry Chapman
(Capt. George Washington Shears had subordinate command of the 12th Illinois)

8th New York Cavalry
[510] (No losses reported – supported artillery) 0.0%
Lt. Col. William L. Markell

ATTACHED ARTILLERY

1st United States Horse Artillery, Battery K
(One Section of Two 3-inch Ordnance Rifles)
[36] (No losses reported) 0.0%
Lt. Theophilus B. von Michalowski

SECOND BRIGADE
[1,102] (0k, 8w = 8) 0.7%
Col. Thomas Casimer Devin

6th New York Cavalry (6 Companies)
[250] (No losses reported) 0.0%
Maj. William Elliott Beardsley

9th New York Cavalry
[275] (No losses reported) 0.0%
Col. William Sackett

17th Pennsylvania Cavalry (9 Companies)
[517] (0k, 8w = 8) 1.5%
Col. Josiah Holcomb Kellogg

3rd West Virginia Cavalry (Companies A and C)
[60] (No losses reported) 0.0%
Capt. Seymour Beach Conger

RESERVE BRIGADE
[1,721] (2k, 19w, 42m = 63) 3.7%
Maj. Samuel Henry Starr

1st United States Cavalry
[345] (1k, 13w, 39m = 53) 15.4%
Capt. Richard Stanton C. Lord

2nd United States Cavalry
[372] (No losses reported) 0.0%
Capt. Wesley Merritt

5th United States Cavalry
[301] (1k = 1) 0.3%
Capt. Julius Wilmot Mason

6th United States Cavalry
[463] (0k, 6w, 3m = 9) 1.9%
Capt. George Clarence Cram

6th Pennsylvania Cavalry (10 Companies)
[240] (No losses reported) 0.0%
Maj. Henry C. Whelan

SECOND DIVISION
[2,540] (4k, 53w, 7w-c, 13m = 77) 3.0%
Brig. Gen. David McMurtrie Gregg

SECOND BRIGADE
[1,063] (2k, 39w, 7w-c, 9m = 57) 5.4%
Brig. Gen. Hugh Judson Kilpatrick

1st Massachusetts Cavalry
[132] (No losses reported) 0.0%
Lt. Col. Greeley S. Curtis

2nd New York Cavalry
[275] (1k, 5w = 6) 2.2%
Col. Henry Eugene Davies

4th New York Cavalry
[305] (0k, 18w, 9m = 27) 8.9%
Lt. Col. Augustus Pruyn

6th Ohio Cavalry
[351] (1k, 16w, 7w-c = 24) 6.8%
Col. William Stedman

THIRD BRIGADE
[1,248] (1k, 11w, 4m = 16) 1.3%
Col. John Irvin Gregg

1st Maine Cavalry
[153] (0k, 7w, 2m = 9) 5.9%
Lt. Col. Charles H. Smith

10th New York Cavalry
[431] (No losses reported) 0.0%
Maj. Matthew Henry Avery

4th Pennsylvania Cavalry
[252] (1k, 4w, 2m = 7) 2.8%
Col. William Emile Doster

16th Pennsylvania Cavalry
[412] (No losses reported) 0.0%
Col. John K. Robinson

ATTACHED ARTILLERY
[229] (1k, 3w = 4) 1.7%

**1st United States Horse Artillery, Battery K
(Two Sections) (Four 3-inch Ordnance Rifles)**
[79] (No losses reported) 0.0%
Capt. William Montrose Graham, Jr.
(One section attached to Gamble's cavalry brigade)

**2nd United States Horse Artillery, Battery A
(Six 3-inch Ordnance Rifles)**
[75] (No losses reported) 0.0%
Lt. John Haskell Calef

**3rd United States Horse Artillery, Battery C
(Six 3-inch Ordnance Rifles)**
[75] (1k, 3w = 4) 5.3%
Lt. William Duncan Fuller

V ARMY CORPS
FIRST DIVISION

THIRD BRIGADE
[1,366] (2k, 19w = 21) 1.5%
Col. Strong Vincent

20th Maine
[404] (1k, 7w = 8) 2.0%
(Strength includes 116 men of the 2nd Maine,
who joined the regiment on May 20)
Col. Joshua Lawrence Chamberlain

16th Michigan
[272] (0k, 9w = 9) 3.3%
Lt. Col. Norval E. Welch

44th New York
[394] (1k, 2w = 3) 0.8%
Col. James C. Rice

83rd Pennsylvania
[296] (0k, 1w = 1) 0.3%
Capt. Orpheus S. Woodward

CONFEDERATE

ARMY OF NORTHERN VIRGINIA
CAVALRY DIVISION
[7,065] (41k+, 4mw+, 95w+, 5w-c+, 55c+, 39m = 239+) 3.4%+
Maj. Gen. James Ewell Brown Stuart

HAMPTON'S BRIGADE
[2,490] (6k+, 18w+, 21c+ = 45+) 1.8+%
Brig. Gen. Wade Hampton

Cobb's Legion (Georgia)
[490] (0k, 3w, 10c = 13) 2.7%
Col. Pierce Manning Butler Young

Jeff Davis Legion (Mississippi)
[358] (6k, 15w, 11c = 32) 8.9%
Lt. Col. Joseph Frederick Waring

1st South Carolina Cavalry
[544] (Unknown losses)
Col. John Logan Black (w)
Lt. Col. John David Twiggs

2nd South Carolina Cavalry
[430] (Unknown losses)
Maj. Thomas Jefferson Lipscomb

1st North Carolina Cavalry
[668] (Unknown losses)
Col. Laurence Simmons Baker

WILLIAM HENRY FITZHUGH LEE'S BRIGADE
[1,625] (16k, 19w, 4w-c, 7c, 33m = 79) 4.9%
Col. John Randolph Chambliss, Jr.

2nd North Carolina Cavalry
[75] (7k, 11w, 3w-c, 1c = 22) 29.3%
Lt. Col. William Henry Fitzhugh Payne

9th Virginia Cavalry
[675] (3k, 1w, 1w-c, 27m = 32) 4.7%
Col. Richard Lee Turberville Beale

10th Virginia Cavalry
[309] (4k, 4w, 6m = 14) 4.5%
Col. James Lucius Davis

13th Virginia Cavalry
[566] (2k, 3w, 6c = 11) 1.9%
Maj. Joseph Ezra Gillette

JONES' BRIGADE
[1,590] (14k, 3mw, 47w, 1w-c, 6m = 71) 4.5%
Brig. Gen. William Edmundson Jones

6th Virginia Cavalry
[560] (2k, 10w, 1m = 13) 2.3%
Maj. Cabell Edward Flournoy

7th Virginia Cavalry
[400] (5k, 3mw, 13w, 1m = 22) 5.5%
Lt. Col. Thomas A. Marshall Jr.

11th Virginia Cavalry
[385] (5k, 13w, 1w-c, 4m = 23) 6.0%
Col. Lunsford Lindsay Lomax
(final command of regiment)
Lt. Col. Oliver Ridgeway Funsten

12th Virginia Cavalry (7 Companies)
[245] (2k, 11w = 13) 5.3%
Col. Thomas Benjamin Massie

ROBERTSON'S BRIGADE
[953] (3k+, 10w+, 26c+ = 39+) 4.1%+
Brig. Gen. Beverly Holcombe Robertson

4th North Carolina Cavalry
[498] (3k, 10w, 26c = 39) 7.8%
Col. Dennis Dozier Ferebee

5th North Carolina Cavalry
[455] (Unknown losses)
Col. Peter Gustavus Evans (mw-c)
Lt. Col. Stephen B. Evans

ATTACHED ARTILLERY
[407] (2k, 1mw, 1w, 1c = 5) 1.2%

Ashby Horse Artillery, Chew's (Virginia) Battery
(One 3-inch Ordnance Rifle,
One 12-pounder Howitzer)
[93] (1k, 1w = 2) 2.2%
Capt. Roger Preston Chew

2nd Stuart Horse Artillery, McGregor's (Virginia)
Battery (One Blakely, One unknown)
[106] (No losses reported) 0.0%
Capt. William Morrell McGregor

Washington (South Carolina) Horse Artillery,
Hart's Battery (Four Blakely)
[106] (No losses reported) 0.0%
Capt. James Franklin Hart

Lynchburg (Virginia) "Beauregard" Rifles,
Moorman's Battery (One Napoleon, Three unknown)
[102] (1k, 1mw, 1c = 3) 2.9%
Capt. Marcellus Newton Moorman

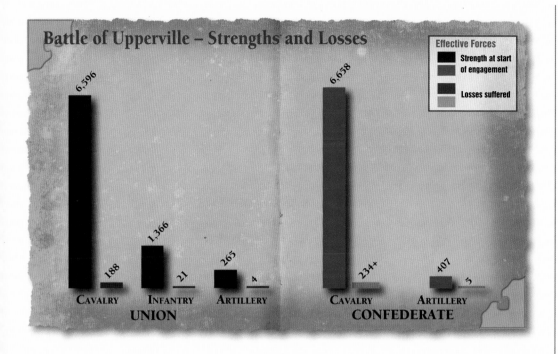

Battle of Upperville – Strengths and Losses

Effective Forces

■ Strength at start of engagement

■ Losses suffered

UNION — CAVALRY 6,596 / 188 — INFANTRY 1,366 / 21 — ARTILLERY 265 / 4

CONFEDERATE — CAVALRY 6,658 / 234+ — ARTILLERY 407 / 5

After Stuart fell back to Ashby's Gap, Gregg's Federal troopers went into camp east of Upperville and Vincent's infantry returned to Aldie. Although Upperville was a tactical defeat for Stuart, it was a significant strategic success. His magnificent fluid defensive effort had once again prevented the Federals from piercing his shield and driving into the Shenandoah Valley. The running combats were taking a toll on the Southern mounted arm, however. Stuart had already suffered several hundred casualties defending the gaps and passes. As of the night of June 21, Pleasonton had still not located the main body of the Army of Northern Virginia. Without this intelligence the Union war effort in the Eastern Theater was temporarily blind and unable to determine a proper course of action.

Early the next morning, June 22, Stuart submitted a plan to General Lee proposing that his cavalry ride around Joe Hooker's Army of the Potomac while the main Confederate army continued its march north to Pennsylvania. The operation was reminiscent of his ride around Maj. Gen. George B. McClellan's men the year before. Stuart offered to insert his three best brigades between Hooker and the Northern capital in Washington, and then ride through Maryland and into Pennsylvania to join with Lee's army on Yankee soil. Lee approved the plan later that afternoon, setting into motion a chain of events that would have a significant impact on the Pennsylvania campaign. Within a few short days Lee and Stuart would lose communication with one another, an important lapse that would not be re-established until the armies were already fighting at Gettysburg.

The aggressive Federal cavalry (and it infantry support) did cause some alarm within the circles of the Confederate high command. Although much of the Southern army remained in its camps in northern Virginia and southern Maryland, Lee ordered James Longstreet to send one of his divisions to help secure Ashby's Gap. When no further Yankee attacks materialized on June 22, Lee ordered the rest of his army to cross the Potomac River. James Longstreet's Corps continued its march toward Winchester, Ambrose P. Hill's Corps gathered around Charlestown, and Richard S. Ewell's Corps were already across the Maryland border and moving north.

On the Federal side, meanwhile, frustration reigned at both army headquarters and in the War Department in Washington as a result of Pleasonton's inability to gather reliable information. Pleasonton reported (erroneously) to General Hooker that Lee's army was concentrated in the area around Winchester at the northern end of the Shenandoah Valley, oblivious of the fact that Brig. Gen. Albert G. Jenkins' cavalry brigade, screening Ewell's march, was already in Pennsylvania. In fact, Jenkins' men would that same day spill the first enemy blood of the campaign north of the Mason-Dixon line.

EARLY ADVANCES INTO PENNSYLVANIA

THE SKIRMISH AT GREENCASTLE, PA.

JUNE 22, 1863

After the Federal shellacking at Second Winchester, companies of the 1st New York Cavalry (the "Lincoln Cavalry") helped cover the Federal retreat. **CAPT. WILLIAM BOYD**'s Company C of the Lincoln Cavalry harassed Confederate units as they crossed into Pennsylvania, particularly **BRIG. GEN. ALBERT G. JENKINS**' cavalry. On June 15, Brig. Gen. Albert G. Jenkins' Confederate cavalry brigade crossed north over the Potomac River. Jenkins and his brigade of Virginians were tasked with scouting south-central Pennsylvania to prepare the way for the advance of Lt. Gen. Richard S. Ewell's Corps. After breakfasting

Brig. Gen. Albert G. Jenkins
Image courtesy of Library of Congress

1863

| THE CAMPAIGN BEGINS JUNE 3 | | MARSH CREEK & WITMER FARM — JUNE 26 | THE BATTLE OF GETTYSBURG JULY 1-3 | LEE'S ARMY CROSSES THE POTOMAC RIVER JULY 14 |

GREENCASTLE & MONTEREY PASS — JUNE 22

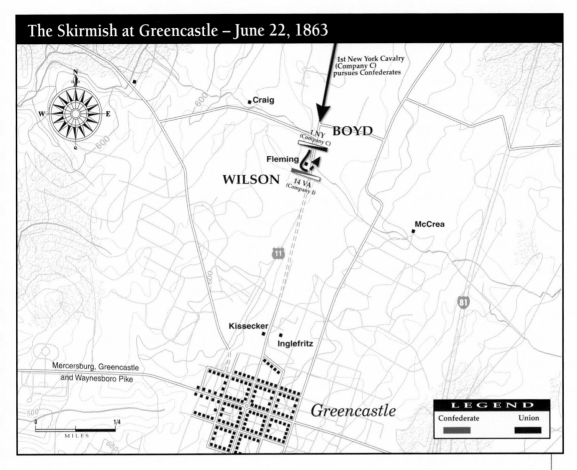

The Skirmish at Greencastle – June 22, 1863

at friendly Williamsport, Maryland, Jenkins and his men rode to Hagerstown and stopped to eat lunch. The Virginians destroyed the railroad depot at Greencastle that afternoon before heading for Chambersburg, Pennsylvania, where they skirmished briefly with Federal cavalry. After driving off the enemy troopers, Jenkins camped at Chambersburg and spent the next day destroying the railroad and collecting supplies. On June 17 Jenkins fell back to Hagerstown, Maryland, where word of a large advancing Federal force reached him. The next day Jenkins sent out several companies back into the Keystone State to forage, gather supplies, and capture any Federals they could find.

Just north of Greencastle, Pennsylvania, on June 22, Boyd and his few dozen troopers gave chase to mounted Rebels. Concerned that he was being drawn into an ambush, Boyd reined in his men at the Archibald Fleming farmhouse and sent Cpl. William Rihl and Sgt. Milton Cafferty around the house to reconnoiter. The Rebels, a company of Jenkins' 14th Virginia Cavalry, were waiting for them and opened fire, killing Rihl with a shot to the head and wounding Cafferty in the leg. Boyd turned the rest of his men and galloped to Chambersburg, Pennsylvania, to report that a large column of Confederates were on the move north.

Rihl, a 21-year-old Philadelphia native, was buried where he fell in Fleming's yard but was later reinterred in a local cemetery. In 1886, Greencastle's Grand Army of the Republic post reburied Rihl where he fell in Fleming's yard and installed a small marker. The following year the state of Pennsylvania placed an impressive monument over his grave to honor the "humble but brave defender of the Union." Rihl holds the unenviable distinction of being the first Federal killed in Pennsylvania during the campaign and the first man killed north of the Mason-Dixon line during the Civil War.

FEDERAL

DEPARTMENT OF THE SUSQUEHANNA

1st New York (Lincoln) Cavalry (Company C)
[35] (1k, 1w, 2m = 4) 11.4%
Capt. William Boyd

CONFEDERATE

ARMY OF NORTHERN VIRGINIA
CAVALRY DIVISION

Jenkins' Brigade
14th Virginia Cavalry (Company I)
[45] (No losses reported) 0.0%
Capt. Joseph Alfred Wilson

The skirmish at Greencastle, like the several skirmishes yet to occur, did not impact the movement of the respective armies. Boyd's report of the clash, however, validated the wildly circulating reports of Southern troops crossing into Pennsylvania and the suspicion that Lee was undertaking a large-scale invasion. This and additional clashes to come spread excitement and panic among the emergency troops raised by Pennsylvania Governor Andrew Curtin, and increased the consternation and political heartburn President Abraham Lincoln was feeling. Lincoln and his cabinet could not understand why Joe Hooker was unable to fully discover or interrupt Lee's movement.

THE SKIRMISH AT MONTEREY PASS, PA.

JUNE 22, 1863

Another of Jenkins' foraging detachments, Company D of the 14th Virginia Cavalry under **CAPT. ROBERT B. MOORMAN**, foraged in the area of Waynesborough, Pennsylvania, and captured a number of horses and supplies. On the night of June 21, most of Jenkins' brigade rode again toward Chambersburg and the next day Moorman's company moved toward South Mountain to appropriate horses from local farmers. Major James Bryan, a quartermaster in Ewell's Corps, rode along for logistical support. As Lt. Hermann Schuricht of the company later wrote, the next couple of days proved that the region was "a very dangerous section for cavalry movements."

About midday the Virginians rode within a mile east of Fairfield just below the mountain. Unknown to the Virginians, a detail of Federal militia was on the way from Gettysburg to reconnoiter the mountain passes. The First Troop, Philadelphia City Cavalry (originally formed in 1774 and still the oldest active military unit in the nation today) volunteered its services in mid-June and arrived in Gettysburg on June 21. That day a detail of ten of the Philadelphians skirmished with members of the 14th Virginia Cavalry at Chambersburg. On the afternoon of June 22, the First Troop (under Capt. Samuel Randall, a future Speaker of the House of Representatives) was sent to Fairfield with about forty members of **CAPT. ROBERT BELL**'s militia cavalry formed of volunteers from the Gettysburg area, leading the way. Also along were a couple dozen members of Gettysburg's Home Guard. When the Virginians were spotted, the Federals opened fire, galloped through Fairfield and drove the Rebels into the Fairfield Pass and the Monterey Pass beyond.

Capt. Robert Bell
Image courtesy of J. D. Petruzzi

FEDERAL

DEPARTMENT OF THE SUSQUEHANNA

Capt. Robert Bell's Independent Adams County Cavalry
[40] (No losses reported) 0.0%
Capt. Robert Bell

First Troop, Philadelphia City Cavalry
[40] (No losses reported) 0.0%
Capt. Samuel Jackson Randall

Gettysburg Home Guard
[25] (No losses reported) 0.0%
Capt. Elias Spangler

CONFEDERATE

ARMY OF NORTHERN VIRGINIA
CAVALRY DIVISION

JENKINS' BRIGADE

14th Virginia Cavalry (Company D)
[45] (No losses reported) 0.0%
Capt. Robert Bruce Moorman
(Tactical command – Maj. James Bryan, quartermaster of O'Neill's Brigade of Rodes' Division, Ewell's Corps)

No casualties were reportedly suffered by either side, but the running skirmish was only one of several that took place in the Gettysburg area during the week preceding the main July 1-3 battle. The mountains and valleys around Gettysburg proved to be a very dangerous place for local militia units and armed citizen Home Guards, as well as for the Confederates moving through the area during the coming days. Another contest confronted Moorman's Federal company the following day (June 23), but this one would have deadly consequences.

On June 22, General Lee ordered General Ewell and his Second Corps near Hagerstown, Maryland, to continue north into Pennsylvania. "If you are ready to move, you can do so," Lee wrote. "I think your best course will be toward the Susquehanna . . . if Harrisburg comes within your means, capture it." Longstreet's Corps was making for Winchester, Virginia, while A. P. Hill's Corps was at Charlestown farther north. Ewell's men continued as ordered and one of his divisions under Maj. Gen. Robert E. Rodes crossed into Pennsylvania by midday. Confederate infantry was now in Northern territory.

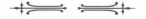

THE SKIRMISH AT CASHTOWN GAP, PA. AND THE AMBUSH AT GALLAGHER'S KNOB

JUNE 23, 1863

Along with other parts of Brig. Gen. Albert Jenkins' cavalry brigade, Company D of the 14th Virginia Cavalry continued scouting and foraging in the Chambersburg-Gettysburg areas of Franklin and Adams counties. At dawn on June 23, **CAPT. ROBERT B. MOORMAN**'s troopers rode along the Cashtown Pike to the Caledonia Iron Works fourteen miles west of Gettysburg. These works were owned by U.S. Congressman Thaddeus Stevens. Three days later Maj. Gen. Jubal A. Early's infantry division would destroy the works on their way to Gettysburg and the Susquehanna River. On this day, however, Moorman and his Virginians were only concerned with capturing much-needed horses and supplies. After seizing several dozen horses and mules, Moorman continued east toward Cashtown, a small village at the base of the South Mountain pass.

When the Virginia cavalrymen reached the pass, they found it blocked with felled trees, and some unidentified men manned the obstruction. Confederate Maj. James Bryan consulted with Moorman, and the Virginias decided to attack. About half the company dismounted and approached the obstruction with carbines raised. Manning the blockade was **CAPT. ROBERT BELL**'s militia cavalry, who had fought with Moorman's men the previous day near Fairfield, together with a couple dozen Home Guard troops from Gettysburg under Capt. Elias Spangler. One of the Home Guard members may have been Gettysburg's John Burns, the 69-year-old former town constable who helped the Home Guard patrol area mountain passes. Burns was later wounded on July 1 while fighting with Federal infantry west of town during the Battle of Gettysburg. The "Hero of Gettysburg" is the only private citizen known to have fought with the Federals at the battle.

Capt. Robert Bell
Image courtesy of J. D. Petruzzi

As the Virginians approached the blockaded pass, Bell's cavalry and much of the Home Guard fled, but most of the Home

Guard's pickets were captured. After clearing the obstruction and interviewing their captives, the Virginians continued their ride toward Cashtown.

A short distance beyond the pass, the road ran just north of a hill known as "Gallagher's Knob." When a shotgun blast erupted from the bushes south of the road, 42-year-old Pvt. Eli Amick, riding at the head of the cavalry column, clutched his belly and cried out, "I'm shot!" His horse bolted in surprise and Amick fell hard to the ground. The trigger-puller was local citizen Henry Hahn, who was hiding in the bushes with three comrades to ambush Confederates. According to local lore, Hahn had scratched a line in the road and vowed to shoot the first Rebel who crossed it. Ironically, Amick was known in Federal circles as a "notorious Guerilla and bushwacker" and had been captured and imprisoned earlier in the war for ambushing and killing Federal soldiers in rural Virginia.

Hahn and his party escaped into the woods, but Pvt. Amick's war was over. Moorman decided it was too dangerous to continue, so they recovered the wounded private and returned the way they had come. The Confederates were fired upon several times before they reached Greenwood, where Amick died later that night.

FEDERAL

DEPARTMENT OF THE SUSQUEHANNA

Capt. Robert Bell's Independent Adams County Cavalry
[40 est.] (No losses reported) 0.0%
Capt. Robert Bell

Gettysburg Home Guard
[25] (Pickets temporarily detained, but no losses reported) 0.0%
Capt. Elias Spangler

Local citizen ambush party
[4] (No losses reported) 0.0%
Henry Hahn, leader

CONFEDERATE

ARMY OF NORTHERN VIRGINIA

CAVALRY DIVISION

Jenkins' Brigade

14th Virginia Cavalry (Company D)
[45] (0k, 1mw = 1) 2.2%
Capt. Robert Bruce Moorman
(Tactical command – Maj. James Bryan, quartermaster of O'Neill's Brigade of Rodes' Division, Ewell's Corps)

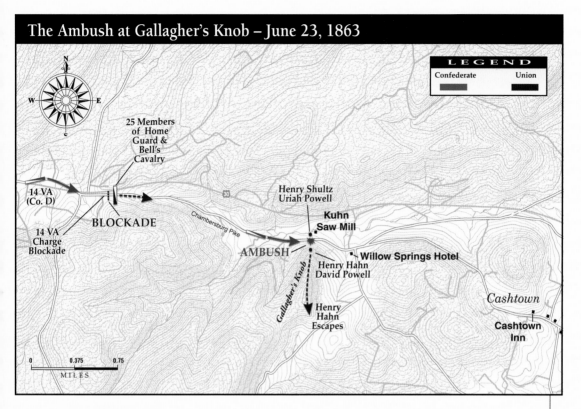

The Ambush at Gallagher's Knob – June 23, 1863

Amick earned the unfortunate distinction of being the first Confederate killed near Gettysburg. It was this episode that convinced Lt. Hermann Schuricht of Moorman's company to lament in his diary that "this section of Pennsylvania seems to be full of 'bushwackers.'" Within only a few days, tens of thousands of Amick's comrades would also pass through the Cashtown Gap, and like him, many would also give up their life near Gettysburg.

By June 23, Gen. Richard S. Ewell's Second Corps was on the march toward Harrisburg and Gen. James Longstreet's First Corps was west of the Shenandoah River following Gen. A. P. Hill's Third Corps marching for the Potomac River. The Army of the Potomac was still in Virginia. Hill's Corps crossed the Potomac into Maryland the following day, and Longstreet's infantry crossed on June 26. On June 23, however, Gen. Joseph Hooker finally received news of Lee's movements when his Signal Corps reported long columns of Confederate infantry approaching Charlestown from the south. Brigadier General Henry W. Benham, leading the Engineer Brigade, was ordered to build a pontoon bridge across the mouth of the Monocacy Creek in Maryland for elements of the Army of the Potomac to use for their march north.

THE SKIRMISH AT MARSH CREEK, PA.

JUNE 26, 1863

On June 24, Confederate corps commander Lt. Gen. Richard S. Ewell sent one of his divisions under Maj. Gen. Jubal A. Early through Chambersburg, Pennsylvania. The 17th Virginia Cavalry, together with Early's pet cadre of horsemen and **LT. COL. ELIJAH V. WHITE**'s 35th Battalion Virginia Cavalry, escorted the division. Early reached Chambersburg the next day. Ewell ordered Early to continue on to Gettysburg and then York. Once these tasks were completed, Early would link up with Ewell across the Susquehanna for an assault on the state capital at Harrisburg.

Lt. Col. Elijah V. White
Image courtesy of Library of Congress

Early roused his men on June 26 and had them marching under a cool rain for Gettysburg just after dawn. At Caledonia, Early burned Thaddeus Stevens' iron works and continued toward Cashtown. Shortly thereafter Early's advance guard warned that armed militia was ahead near Gettysburg. Once through the Cashtown Gap Early divided his division. Brigadier General John B. Gordon's brigade, screened by Elijah V. White's cavalry, would move directly toward Gettysburg while the balance of Early's command marched along the Hilltown Road to flank the militia from the north.

The 743 men of the 26th Pennsylvania Volunteer Militia comprised part of the thousands of emergency troops raised in Pennsylvania to help repel the Confederate invasion. They arrived in Gettysburg from Harrisburg by train on the morning of June 26 to join forces with Capt. Robert Bell's militia cavalry and the First Troop, Philadelphia City Cavalry. Just one hour after the 26th Pennsylvania military arrived the volunteers (minus one company left in town with the Philadelphia cavalry) and Bell's troopers marched west along the Cashtown Pike to watch for any Confederates approaching from that direction. They had no idea Early's veteran division was bearing down on them. A few miles outside town, militia commander **COL. WILLIAM W. JENNINGS** halted the men at the Samuel Lohr farm near Marsh Creek and went into camp. Jennings sent some of Bell's men ahead as a picket detail to scout the road.

It wasn't long before one of Bell's men came galloping back to report that a large force of Confederates—White's cavalry and Gordon's Brigade—were approaching. Knowing they were no match for what was heading their way, the nervous militia gathered their equipment to retreat. White's cavalry, however, spotted the bluecoats and one of his companies, led by Lt. Harrison Strickler, charged the panicked volunteers. Forty pickets were captured and White's battalion chased the rest into and through Gettysburg. Later that afternoon Pvt. George Washington Sandoe of nearby Mt. Joy, a member of Bell's militia cavalry, was shot and killed along the Baltimore Pike southeast of town when he tried to escape. Sandoe was the first Federal to die within sight of Gettysburg. His counterpart, Pvt. Eli Amick of the 14th Virginia Cavalry, had been the first Confederate to fall just a few miles away three days earlier.

FEDERAL

DEPARTMENT OF THE SUSQUEHANNA

26th Pennsylvania Volunteer Militia
[675] (0k, 40m = 40) 5.9%
Col. William Wesley Jennings

Capt. Robert Bell's Independent Adams County Cavalry
[76] (1k, 9w, 2m = 12) 15.8%
Capt. Robert Bell

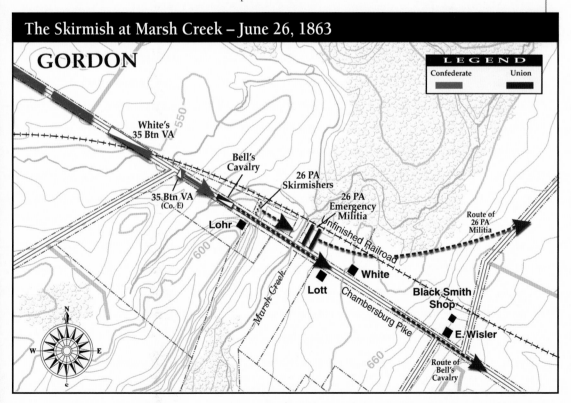

The Skirmish at Marsh Creek – June 26, 1863

CONFEDERATE

ARMY OF NORTHERN VIRGINIA
CAVALRY DIVISION

35th Battalion Virginia Cavalry
[242] (No losses reported) 0.0%
Lt. Col. Elijah Viers White
(Attached to Early's infantry division, Gordon's Brigade)

After scattering the militia, Gordon continued marching his brigade to Gettysburg. The balance of Early's Division and Col. William French's 17th Virginia Cavalry arrived from the north after the running action with the volunteers had ended. Gettysburg was now in Confederate hands. Colonel William Jennings' Federals were fleeing northeast, and Early intended to bag as many of them as possible.

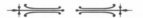

THE SKIRMISH AT WITMER'S FARM, PA.

JUNE 26, 1863

Most of the twelve companies of **COLONEL JENNINGS**' militia that escaped the initial skirmish west of Gettysburg regrouped at Henry and Catherine Witmer's farm a few miles northeast of town. The exhausted men drank from the well and reorganized. Jennings placed a rearguard of about eighty men a couple hundred yards behind them along the road.

The Skirmish at Witmer's Farm – June 26, 1863

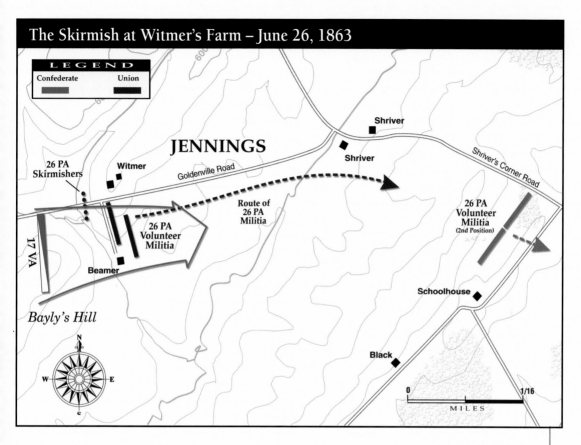

While most of Jubal Early's men secured Gettysburg and engaged in some looting, **COL. WILLIAM H. FRENCH**'s 17th Virginia Cavalry followed Jennings' fleeing militia. Once the Yankees were located, the Virginians formed a mounted battle line atop Bayly's Hill west of Jennings' position and trotted toward them. The militia managed a volley, but if any round killed or wounded any Virginian it went unrecorded. One Federal was killed and about a dozen wounded. About 150 more Federals were taken prisoner, including most of Jennings' rearguard.

FEDERAL

DEPARTMENT OF THE SUSQUEHANNA

26th Pennsylvania Volunteer Militia
[625 est.] (1k, 12w est., 176m = 189) 30.2% est.
Col. William Wesley Jennings

CONFEDERATE

ARMY OF NORTHERN VIRGINIA
CAVALRY DIVISION

Jenkins' Brigade
17th Virginia Cavalry
[274] (Unknown losses)
Col. William Henderson French

Jennings escaped with the balance of his men. Two days later he arrived in Harrisburg to report to Pennsylvania Governor Andrew Curtin that Gettysburg and its important road network was in Confederate hands.

STUART'S RIDE TO PENNSYLVANIA BEGINS

THE SKIRMISH AT
FAIRFAX COURT HOUSE, VA.

JUNE 27, 1863

It was about 1:00 a.m. on June 25 when Confederate cavalry commander **MAJ. GEN. J.E.B. STUART** set out on what would become his most controversial action of the war: his ride to Pennsylvania. He left his camp at Rector's Crossroads with three of his brigades, or just more than one-half his command. Shortly after dawn Stuart's column discovered the wagon train and tail of Maj. Gen. Winfield S. Hancock's Federal 2nd Corps near Haymarket, Virginia. Stuart's men unlimbered some artillery and fired at the Federals, killing and wounding a few before capturing several prisoners during the resulting skirmish. More important was the fact that Hancock's corps blocked Stuart's intended route north, so the Confederates disengaged and withdrew to Buckland.

The following day Stuart advanced to Wolf Run Shoals on the Occoquan Creek and on June 27 turned his column toward Fairfax Court House. Once there, the Confederates rested and turned out their horses to graze. In accordance with his orders to report any enemy movement north to General Lee (and contrary to conventional accounts of the campaign), Stuart sent a dispatch advising the Confederate commander that, according to his scouting reports, the Army of the Potomac was heading toward Leesburg. In a twist of fate that would later prove disastrous to Confederate campaign plans, the courier failed to deliver the dispatch to Lee.

Stuart's respite was broken when a squadron of Federal horsemen galloped into the perimeter of their camp. This squadron of the 11th New York Cavalry (known as "Scott's 900") was assigned to the defenses of Washington and was on a reconnaissance to Centreville when it ran into Stuart's position. The Federals believed the Rebels only consisted of a small detached force, and so **MAJ. S. PIERRE REMINGTON** ordered his men to charge. Within minutes the New Yorkers were fighting the 1st North Carolina Cavalry, which Stuart had dispatched to deal with the intruders.

| THE CAMPAIGN BEGINS JUNE 3 | | SKIRMISH AT FAIRFAX COURT HOUSE JUNE 27 | | THE BATTLE OF GETTYSBURG JULY 1-3 | LEE'S ARMY CROSSES THE POTOMAC RIVER JULY 14 |

The New Yorkers were outnumbered nearly five-to-one. They lost several killed and wounded and most of the rest were surrounded and captured. Only about eighteen made their escape. Stuart suffered one casualty: the mortal wounding of Maj. John H. Whitaker, who had led the North Carolinians in the initial counterassault.

FEDERAL

DEPARTMENT OF WASHINGTON CAVALRY DIVISION

11th New York Cavalry (2 Companies)
[100] (4k, 21w-c, 57c = 82) 82.0%
Maj. Seth Pierre Remington

CONFEDERATE

ARMY OF NORTHERN VIRGINIA
CAVALRY DIVISION

HAMPTON'S BRIGADE
Brig. Gen. Wade Hampton

1st North Carolina Cavalry
[468] (0k, 1mw = 1) 0.2%
Maj. John H. Whitaker (mw)
Col. Laurence Simmons Baker

The run-in with Hancock's corps at Haymarket delayed Stuart's progress north by a full day, and he lost another half day at Fairfax Court House. After three full days Stuart was still struggling to get out of Virginia, and the Federal army was marching north. Unbeknownst to Stuart, General Lee had no news of either because his courier would never reach army headquarters.

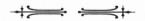

EARLY MARCHES TO THE SUSQUEHANNA

THE RAID ON HANOVER JUNCTION, PA.

JUNE 27, 1863

After having his way with the town of Gettysburg on June 26, Maj. Gen. Jubal A. Early marched his division toward historic York, Pennsylvania. He planned to destroy the tracks of the Northern Central Railway there (which connected Harrisburg to Baltimore and Washington) while unleashing **LT. COL. ELIJAH WHITE**'s and William French's Virginia cavalry to wreak havoc against bridges, telegraphs, and anything of military value to the Federals.

Lt. Col. Elijah V. White
Image courtesy of Library of Congress

Confederate cavalry raided several towns and dozens of farms east of Gettysburg, from Hanover to Spring Forge and then Jefferson. The mounted men generally followed the trace of the Hanover Branch Railroad during their raid to destroy bridges and railroad and telegraph equipment. Farther east at Hanover Junction, the Northern Central Railway met the Hanover Branch Railroad. Although militarily important, Hanover Junction was only lightly guarded by a portion of the 20th Pennsylvania Volunteer Militia, about 225 men under **LT. COL. WILLIAM H. SICKLES**. The militia occupied a defensive line along a hill near the junction.

White's troopers arrived at Hanover Junction early that afternoon with pistols blazing. Sickles and his men repeated the performance Col. William Jennings had turned in outside Gettysburg the previous day by scattering at the first sign of danger. Most of them sought refuge on a hill behind their lines. From this vantage point they watched White's men destroy rail cars and equipment. When the Rebels finished and moved on, Sickles led his green troops northward to Wrightsville, where he expected to find militia support.

| THE CAMPAIGN BEGINS JUNE 3 | | HANOVER JUNCTION & WRIGHTSVILLE JUNE 27-28 | THE BATTLE OF GETTYSBURG JULY 1-3 | LEE'S ARMY CROSSES THE POTOMAC RIVER JULY 14 |

FEDERAL

DEPARTMENT OF THE SUSQUEHANNA

20th Pennsylvania Volunteer Militia (Companies B, F, and H)
[225 est.] (No losses reported) 0.0%
Lt. Col. William H. Sickles

CONFEDERATE

35th Battalion Virginia Cavalry (Detachment)
[150 est.] (No losses reported) 0.0%
Lt. Col. Elijah Viers White

The only loss suffered during the skirmish at Hanover Junction was the damage inflicted upon the railroad and telegraph equipment. Despite White's best efforts, the Military Railroad Department had the junction back up and running within a few days. The skirmish, however, was another indication that green Federal militia were incapable of standing up to Confederate troops.

For Lt. Col. Sickles, however, the ignominious loss of Hanover Junction was the beginning of the worst few days of his military career. When he arrived at Wrightsville early on the morning of June 28, the stage was already set for an even more humiliating encounter with Confederates from Richard Ewell's Second Corps.

Except for part of A. P. Hill's Third Corps, by June 27, all of Lee's infantry was in Pennsylvania. James Longstreet's First Corps was stretched from Greencastle to Chambersburg. Rodes' Division of Ewell's Second Corps marched toward Carlisle, with most of Johnson's Division following. Early's Division paroled its prisoners from the June 26 skirmishing near Gettysburg and continued onward to East Berlin. Anderson's Division of Hill's Third Corps marched through Chambersburg, while Heth's and Pender's divisions passed through Hagerstown, Maryland and reached Pennsylvania by midday. The Army of the Potomac was also on the move, with the 1st, 3rd, and 11th corps approaching the passes of the South Mountain range and the balance of the army making for Frederick, Maryland. General Hooker, who was ordered to cover both Harpers Ferry and Washington, once again asked for reinforcements because he believed he was outnumbered and his assignments were impossible with the troops under his command. "I am unable to comply with this condition with the means at my disposal," he wired General Henry Halleck, "and earnestly request that I may at once be relieved from the position I occupy." Halleck and President Lincoln moved quickly to comply with Hooker's request. Early the next morning on June 28, 5th

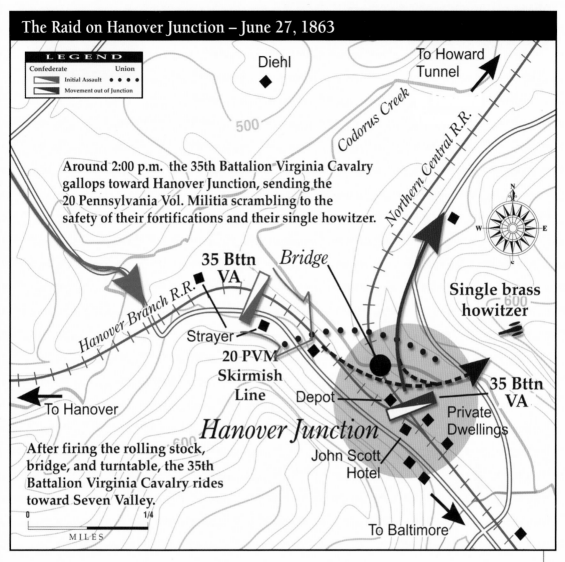

The Raid on Hanover Junction – June 27, 1863

LEGEND

Confederate Union

Initial Assault ● ● ●

Movement out of Junction

Diehl

To Howard Tunnel

500

Codorus Creek

Northern Central R.R.

Around 2:00 p.m. the 35th Battalion Virginia Cavalry gallops toward Hanover Junction, sending the 20 Pennsylvania Vol. Militia scrambling to the safety of their fortifications and their single howitzer.

35 Bttn VA

Bridge

Single brass howitzer

600

Hanover Branch R.R.

Strayer

20 PVM Skirmish Line

Depot

35 Bttn VA

Private Dwellings

To Hanover

Hanover Junction

John Scott Hotel

After firing the rolling stock, bridge, and turntable, the 35th Battalion Virginia Cavalry rides toward Seven Valley.

0 1/4

MILES

To Baltimore

Corps commander Maj. Gen. George G. Meade was roused from his slumber by Col. James Hardie of Halleck's staff. At first Meade thought he was being arrested. In fact, he had just been given command of the Army of the Potomac.

THE SKIRMISH AT
WRIGHTSVILLE, PA.

JUNE 28, 1863

Throughout the weekend of June 27 and 28, green Federal militia tirelessly worked to strengthen the defenses at Wrightsville, Pennsylvania, and especially the enormous covered bridge spanning the Susquehanna River — a bridge that Confederates could use to advance upon Harrisburg. When he learned that a large contingent of Rebels (a brigade of Lt. Gen. Richard S. Ewell's Second Corps under **BRIG. GEN. JOHN B. GORDON**) had passed through York, Federal **COL. JACOB G. FRICK**, commanding the newly formed 27th Pennsylvania Volunteer Militia, determined to deny the enemy possession or use of the important bridge. Existing rifle pits were expanded and nearly 3,000 militia and local volunteers stood ready to resist the advance. On the evening of June 27, Capt. Samuel Randall and his First Troop, Philadelphia City Cavalry arrived from Gettysburg and confirmed reports that York had surrendered to the Confederates.

Brig. Gen. John B. Gordon
Image courtesy of Library of Congress

With Company C of the 17th Virginia Cavalry leading the way, General Gordon and his brigade approached Wrightsville about 5:00 p.m. on June 28. Gordon inspected Wrightsville from a high hill just out of sight of the Federal militia. There was no enemy artillery within sight and scouting reports indicated that only militia occupied the defenses. Gordon deployed his command to attack. Captain William Tanner's "Courtney" artillery unlimbered on a ridge overlooking the town, and Gordon's Georgia infantry formed a line of battle.

Skirmishing began when Lt. Col. Elijah White's Virginia cavalry approached Yankees guarding the railroad. By the time Gordon's Georgians began pressuring the Federal defenses, however, Col. Frick concluded that a resistance would end in slaughter. Major Granville Haller, who had retreated from west of Gettysburg on June 26 with his 26th Pennsylvania volunteers, suggested that the bridge be destroyed to deny its use to the Southerners so they could not reach Columbia and beyond. Tanner's Southern guns began raking the defenses and

Col. Jacob G. Frick
Image courtesy of Historical Society of Schuylkill County

sporadic musket fire broke out along the front. Frick held on for a little more than an hour before ordering his militia to retreat to the bridge.

Following an often disorderly retreat, most of the militia crossed the bridge into Columbia. By this time it was after 7:00 p.m. and Gordon's victorious infantry took possession of Wrightsville.

FEDERAL

DEPARTMENT OF THE SUSQUEHANNA
[1,461] (1k, 9w, 1w-c, 18m = 29) 2.0%

COLUMBIA-WRIGHTSVILLE DEFENSES
[783] (1k, 9w = 10) 1.3%
Col. Jacob Gilbert Frick

27th Pennsylvania Volunteer Militia
[650] (0k, 9w = 9) 1.4%
Col. Jacob Gilbert Frick

Columbia Company of "Negro Volunteers"
[53] (1k = 1) 1.9%

ARTILLERY
Lt. Delaplaine J. Ridgway

Columbia Artillery (Two 12-Pounder Napoleons, One 3-inch Ordnance Rifle)
[est. 80 of 27th Pennsylvania Militia]
(No losses reported) 0.0%
Capt. E. K. Smith

ADAMS-YORK COUNTY DEFENSES
[678 est.] (0k, 1w-c, 18m = 19) 2.8% est.
Maj. Granville Owen Haller

[RIGHT FLANK]

20th Pennsylvania Volunteer Militia (Companies B, F, and H)
[200] (0k, 18m = 18) 9.0%
Lt. Col. William H. Sickles (c)

[COLUMBIA BRIDGE GUARDS]

26th Pennsylvania Volunteer Militia (Commissary Guard)
[50] (No losses reported) 0.0%
Capt. Christopher Wilson Walker

[LEFT FLANK]
[298] (No losses reported) 0.0%
Lt. Col. David B. Green

Patapsco (Maryland) Guards, York Battalion
[60] (No losses reported) 0.0%
Capt. Thomas McGowan

87th Pennsylvania Infantry (remnant)
York Military Hospital Invalids ("Invalid Battalion")
Small group of local citizens
[238] (No losses reported) 0.0%

CAVALRY
[130] (0k, 1w-c = 1) 0.8%
Maj. Charles McLean Knox, Jr.

First Troop, Philadelphia City Cavalry
[45] (No losses reported) 0.0%
Capt. Samuel Jackson Randall

Capt. Robert Bell's Adams County Independent Cavalry
[60] (0k, 1w-c = 1) 1.7%
Capt. Robert Bell

Lancaster County Scouts
[25 est.] (No losses reported) 0.0%
Capt. Matthew M. Strickler

CONFEDERATE

ARMY OF NORTHERN VIRGINIA
EWELL'S CORPS

[2,113 est.] (0k, 1w, 1m = 2) 0.09% est.

GORDON'S BRIGADE
[1,808] (0k, 1w, 1m = 2) 0.01%
Brig. Gen. John Brown Gordon

13th Georgia
[312] (No losses reported) 0.0%
Col. James Milton Smith

26th Georgia
[315] (No losses reported) 0.0%
Col. Edmund Nathan Atkinson

31st Georgia
[252] (0k, 1m = 1) 0.4%
Col. Clement Anselm Evans

38th Georgia
[341] (No losses reported) 0.0%
Capt. William L. McLeod

60th Georgia
[300] (0k, 1w = 1) 0.3%
Capt. Walter Burrus Jones

61st Georgia
[288] (No losses reported) 0.0%
Col. John Hill Lamar

CAVALRY

17th Virginia Cavalry, Company C
[40 est.] (No losses reported) 0.0%
Capt. Thaddeus P. Waldo

35th Battalion Virginia Cavalry
[175 est.] (No losses reported) 0.0%
Lt. Col. Elijah Viers White

ARTILLERY

**Tanner's Battery, Richmond (Virginia) "Courtney"
Artillery (Four 3-inch Ordnance Rifles)**
[90] (No losses reported) 0.0%
Capt. William A. Tanner

To their credit, Cols. Frick and Haller had anticipated the militia's ultimate retreat from Wrightsville and made preparations to explode a section of the western end of the Wrightsville-Columbia Bridge. When the explosives detonated about 7:30 p.m. but proved inadequate to destroy the section, Frick ordered the bridge burned. Despite a light rain, the western end of the long structure was soon engulfed in flames. When Gordon's efforts to extinguish the fire failed, he watched the bridge collapse into the river.

Gordon's division commander, Maj. Gen. Jubal Early, arrived while the bridge was burning to find his hope of attacking Harrisburg from the rear through Lancaster County dashed. After collecting usable supplies in Wrightsville, Gordon and his men retraced their steps west toward York the next morning. Early still hoped to attack Harrisburg in a frontal assault with the rest of Ewell's Corps, but those plans were also about to change.

While the bridge was burning at Wrightsville, one of Lt. Gen. James Longstreet's scouts named Henry Thomas Harrison rode into the Confederate camp at Messersmith's Woods east of Chambersburg, Pennsylvania. After consulting with Longstreet, Harrison was given an audience with the Confederate commander to share his news: the Federal Army of the Potomac — under its new commander General Meade — was on the move and had already crossed the Potomac River north into Maryland. The news surprised Lee, who had expected J.E.B. Stuart to keep him informed of

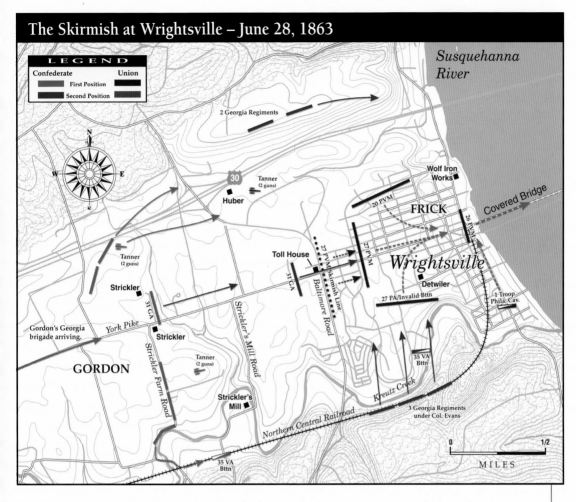

The Skirmish at Wrightsville – June 28, 1863

LEGEND

Confederate	Union
First Position	
Second Position	

Susquehanna River

2 Georgia Regiments

Wolf Iron Works

30

Tanner (2 guns)

Huber

20 PVM

FRICK

Covered Bridge

26 PVM

Tanner (2 guns)

Toll House

27 PVM

27 PVM Skirmish Line

Wrightsville

31 GA

Baltimore Road

Strickler

Detwiler

1 Troop Phila. Cav.

31 GA

Strickler

York Pike

Strickler's Mill Road

Strickler Farm Road

Tanner (2 guns)

27 PA/Invalid Bttn

35 VA Bttn

Gordon's Georgia brigade arriving.

GORDON

Strickler's Mill

Kreutz Creek

3 Georgia Regiments under Col. Evans

Northern Central Railroad

35 VA Bttn

0   1/2

MILES

just such an event. (As noted earlier, Stuart had dispatched a courier to Lee with this information, but the rider failed to arrive.) In order to protect his lines of communications and meet this threat, Lee ordered his army to concentrate east of South Mountain in the area of Cashtown, Pennsylvania. The new orders meant there would be no attack on Harrisburg.

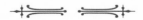

RAIDING SOUTHERN PENNSYLVANIA

THE SKIRMISH AT McCONNELLSBURG, PA.

JUNE 29, 1863

Upon the news that the Federal army was on the pursuit, Lee ordered Ewell and his corps to march in the direction of Gettysburg and rejoin the rest of the Army of Northern Virginia. Ewell was disappointed but reluctantly complied. Lee had still heard nothing from his cavalry commander, J.E.B. Stuart, and did not know his location.

With his cavalry guarding his flanks and rear, new Federal commander Maj. Gen. George G. Meade ordered his various corps to the Maryland towns of Emmitsburg, Taneytown, Frizzleburg, and New Windsor. Meade held out hope that some part of his army would meet and give battle to units of Lee's dispersed troops.

Meanwhile, elements of the Confederate cavalry not with Stuart on his mission continued to raid the southern Pennsylvania countryside. About 8:30 a.m. on June 29, **CAPT. ABRAM JONES** led his Company A of the 1st New York (Lincoln) Cavalry into the town of McConnellsburg, west of Chambersburg in Fulton County, to the cheers of its citizens. Jones sent a few men to picket toward Chambersburg while he rested his men and horses. A short time later, a company of unarmed militia cavalry from Huntington County arrived and its captain, H. M. Morrow, began conferring with Jones. Suddenly, Jones' pickets galloped in with news that Confederate cavalry were coming down the mountain toward town.

Jones told Morrow to ride his men to the town square, then retreat further westward when the Confederates spotted them. Jones then mounted his New Yorkers and waited.

At the top of a small hill appeared just less than 100 troopers of Company G of the 18th Virginia Cavalry of **BRIG. GEN. JOHN D. IMBODEN**'s Northwestern Brigade, a mix of cavalry and mounted infantry. Imboden had brought his men north across the Potomac River to guard the rear of Lee's advance through Pennsylvania. Company G's commander, Capt. William D. Ervin, saw Jones' men and immediately ordered his troopers to "Charge the damn Yankees!" When

1863

Morrow's men rode from the square to see what was happening, the Virginians feared they were being flanked. Their hesitation gave Jones the opportunity he needed to launch a countercharge. With their sabers held high, the New Yorkers drove the Rebels out of town. Jones' men, even though outnumbered, soon overtook their prey and killed two, wounded a few more, and captured nearly two dozen including Captain Ervin. Now commanded by Lt. John Byrd, the rest of the Virginians galloped onward away from McConnellsburg.

FEDERAL

DEPARTMENT OF SUSQUEHANNA

1st New York (Lincoln) Cavalry, Company A
[32 est.] (0k, 4w est. = 4 est.) 12.5% est.
Capt. Abram Jones

Huntington County Militia Cavalry Company (unarmed)
[25 est.] (No losses reported) 0.0%
Capt. H. M. Morrow

CONFEDERATE

ARMY OF NORTHERN VIRGINIA
CAVALRY DIVISION

IMBODEN'S NORTHWESTERN BRIGADE

18th Virginia Cavalry, Company G
[90 est.] (2k, 5w est., 22c = 29 est.) 32.2% est.
Capt. William Dickinson Ervin (c)
Lt. John Thomas Byrd

A victorious Jones and his New York cavalrymen marched their prisoners onward to Bloody Run (Everett today). Following the skirmish, the citizens of McConnellsburg performed a kindness for the two dead Confederates; after coffins were secured, they were buried along the Mercersburg Pike near where they fell during the fight. The funeral procession for Sgt. William Brice Moore and Pvt. Thomas A. Shelton (of North Carolina) was taking place as General Imboden arrived in town with the rest of his brigade. Satisfied there were no Federal soldiers left in McConnellsburg, Imboden returned to the Cumberland Valley.

In 1929, the Daughters of the Confederacy installed a granite monument over the graves of Moore and Shelton, who still repose at their little battlefield along modern Route 16, just outside town to the southeast.

J.E.B. STUART'S MARCH DELAYED

THE BATTLE OF
WESTMINSTER, MD.

JUNE 29, 1863

Following the brief engagement with the 11th New York Cavalry at Fairfax Court House on June 27, J.E.B. Stuart collected supplies in the town and rested his men and horses. His troopers crossed the Potomac River that night at Rowser's Ford below Leesburg, Virginia. Once across, they damaged the Chesapeake & Ohio Canal and continued north toward Rockville, Maryland. Stuart realized he was behind schedule and making slow progress to Pennsylvania. That fact that he had not yet found any sign of Lee's army compounded his problems.

Troopers riding in advance of Brig. Gen. Wade Hampton's Brigade spotted a long Federal supply wagon train heading for Rockville from Washington. A running fight ensued and Col. John R. Chambliss'

Brig. Gen. Fitzhugh Lee
Image courtesy of Library of Congress

Brigade captured most of the wagons. The train was carrying grain and forage for the animals of the Federal army that Stuart's horses desperately needed. Instead of burning the booty, Stuart took along about 125 wagons and his column continued riding and rolling to Brookeville, where it turned north in the direction of Westminster, Maryland.

The railhead at Westminster was a vitally important supply and transportation route for the Federals. For much of June a small detachment of the 150th New York led by Lt. Pulaski Bowman guarded the town. On the morning of June 28, about 100 troopers of the 1st Delaware Cavalry arrived in Westminster to augment the New Yorkers. The Delaware horsemen offered much-needed assistance picketing roads leading into town.

Capt. Charles Corbit
Image courtesy of J. D. Petruzzi

About 5:00 p.m. on June 29, **BRIG. GEN. FITZHUGH LEE**'s Brigade, leading Stuart's column, approached Westminster. Lee's advance guard snatched up five Delawareans picketing east of town, prompting a citizen to gallop into Westminster to warn of the approaching Rebels. Major Napoleon B. Knight, the commander of the 1st Delaware Cavalry, was imbibing in a local establishment so the regiment's senior captain, 25-year-old **CHARLES CORBIT**, mounted his men and formed a line of battle across Westminster's main street. When Fitz Lee's men appeared, Corbit ordered his troopers to set their spurs and charge. Lee counterattacked into the heavily outnumbered Federals. Hand-to-hand fighting in the fence-lined streets left two troopers on each side dead. Lee's superior force wounded or captured most of Corbit's men and drove the balance out of town.

FEDERAL

MIDDLE DEPARTMENT

Combined Cavalry and Infantry: [123] (2k, 2mw, 5w, 9w-c, 10c, 52m = 80) 65.0%

CAVALRY

1st Delaware Cavalry (Companies C and D)
[108] (2k, 2mw, 5w, 9w-c, 49m = 67) 62.0%
Maj. Napoleon Bonaparte Knight (final command of squadron)
Capt. Charles Corbit (c) (Tactical command)
Lt. Caleb Churchman (c)

INFANTRY

150th New York (detachment)
[15] (0k, 10c, 3m = 13) 86.7%
Lt. Pulaski Bowman (c)

CONFEDERATE

ARMY OF NORTHERN VIRGINIA

CAVALRY DIVISION

[1,653] (2k, 6w, 3w-c, 8c = 19) 1.1%

FITZ LEE'S BRIGADE

[1,410] (2k, 6w, 3w-c, 6c = 17) 1.2%
Brig. Gen. Fitzhugh Lee

1st Virginia Cavalry
[320] (0k, 1w-c, 3c = 4) 1.3%
Col. James Henry Drake

2nd Virginia Cavalry
[452] (0k, 4w, 2c = 6) 1.3%
Col. Thomas Taylor Munford

4th Virginia Cavalry
[638] (2k, 2w, 2w-c, 1c = 7) 1.1%
Col. Williams Carter Wickham

WILLIAM HENRY FITZHUGH LEE'S BRIGADE

10th Virginia Cavalry
[243] (0k, 2c = 2) 0.8%
Col. James Lucius Davis

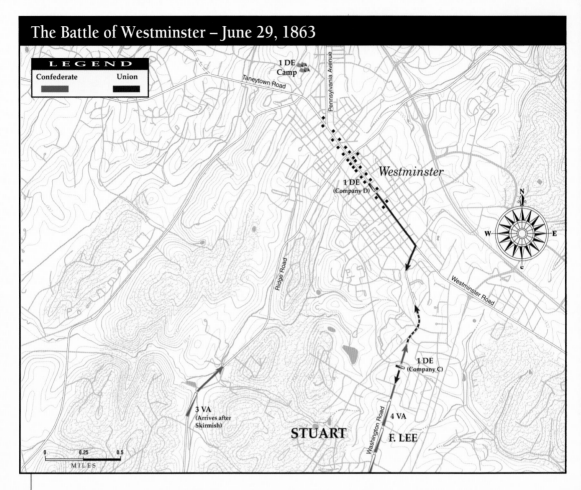

The Battle of Westminster – June 29, 1863

When the short but desperate skirmish ended, Maj. Knight had barely forty men left unscathed. Corbit's audacious charge, however, demonstrated "an almost suicidal bravery" according to one witness and once again brought Stuart's progress to a standstill. The necessity of processing prisoners and restoring order wasted another half a day.

The two dead Confederates, Lts. John W. Murray and William St. Pierre Gibson, were buried in the graveyard of the Ascension Episcopal Church. In 1867, Gibson's body was claimed by his Virginia family and returned home, but Murray still rests in the cemetery.

Stuart intended to pass through Hanover, Pennsylvania the following day to continue toward the Susquehanna River in an effort to find Lt. Gen. Richard Ewell's Second Corps in the region surrounding York. Stuart, however, still did not have any real idea where Lee's army was, and he was several days behind schedule. Stretched out along the road between Westminster and the tiny hamlet of Union Mills, Stuart's troopers were in for yet another rude surprise when they crossed the Mason-Dixon Line into Pennsylvania. Each infantry corps of the Federal Army of the Potomac was marching hard toward Pennsylvania on June 29. But like Stuart, Brig. Gen. Judson Kilpatrick's cavalry division, fronting the center of the Union advance, was also making for Hanover.

THE BATTLE OF HANOVER, PA.

JUNE 30, 1863

BRIG. GEN. JUDSON KILPATRICK, recently installed as commander of the Army of the Potomac's new Third Cavalry Division, was tasked with finding Lt. Gen. Richard Ewell's Confederate corps. The Federals believed Ewell was operating somewhere east of Chambersburg. Kilpatrick's two brigades were led by two young, recently promoted officers. The First Brigade was commanded by Brig. Gen. Elon J. Farnsworth, and the Second Brigade by a dapper, golden-locked 23-year-old brigadier named George Armstrong Custer.

Long before daylight on June 30, Custer led two of his four regiments of the Michigan cavalry brigade north from Emmitsburg, Maryland, through Hanover, Pennsylvania, to scout in the direction of Abbottstown in search of Ewell. Riding a few hours behind Custer, Kilpatrick led Farnsworth and his brigade north from its camps at Littlestown, Pennsylvania, toward Hanover, which they reached about 8:00 a.m. The jittery Hanoverians greeted the blue troopers with food, refreshments, and song, but the patriotic respite ended soon thereafter south of town when Kilpatrick's rearguard, the green 18th Pennsylvania Cavalry, began fighting with Confederate cavalry.

Maj. Gen. J.E.B. Stuart
Image courtesy of Library of Congress

Confederate cavalry commander **MAJ. GEN. J.E.B. STUART** had broken camp prior to daylight along the road from Westminster to Union Mills in Maryland and led his column on two parallel paths across the Pennsylvania border to Hanover. Stuart intended to pass through Hanover and then ride north through the Pigeon Hills in search of Ewell. Three miles southwest of Hanover near the little village of Gitt's Mill, however, Stuart's advance guard composed of troopers from the 13th Virginia Cavalry ran into and briefly skirmished with horsemen from the 18th Pennsylvania. The Confederates chased the Pennsylvanians into Hanover and the rear of Kilpatrick's column, sending panic into the Federal cavalry relaxing in Hanover.

When he got word of the enemy contact ahead at Hanover, Stuart decided to engage the Federals. He brought his artillery up along high ground south of the town and began shelling the enemy below. Regiments from Brig. Gen. Fitz Lee's and Col. John R.

Brig. Gen. Judson Kilpatrick
Image courtesy of Library of Congress

Chambliss' brigades engaged in a series of mounted charges and countercharges with Farnsworth's regiments on the southern streets of the town and in the town square itself. During several hours of vicious fighting, the terrified residents of Hanover hid inside their homes as men and horses galloped down the streets, fired pistols and carbines, and clashed with steel on steel.

Recalled from his position several miles north of Hanover, Custer turned his column around and joined the fighting in the early afternoon. Custer led his Michigan men in dismounted

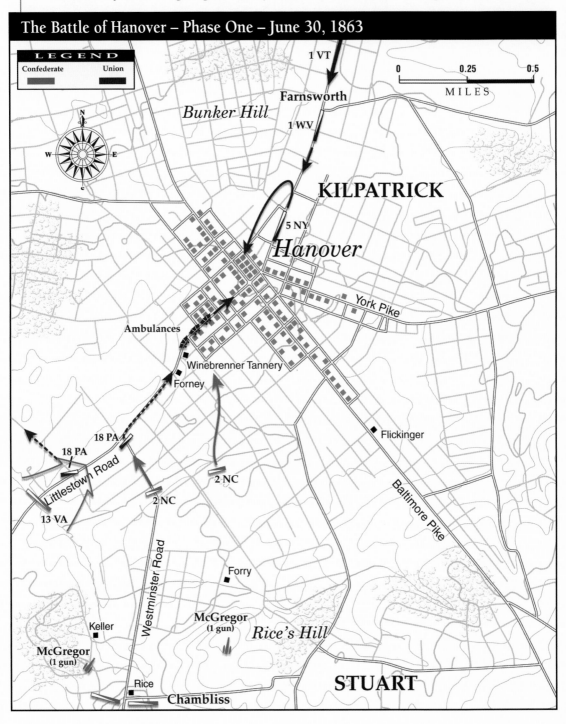

The Battle of Hanover – Phase One – June 30, 1863

fighting south of the town against Stuart's position along the high ground there, while Hampton's Confederates guarded the wagons captured two days earlier at Rockville. By the time darkness fell, Stuart was denied passage through the town and forced to withdraw under cover of darkness farther east and eventually continue riding north in his anxious search for Ewell and the rest of the Confederate army.

FEDERAL

ARMY OF THE POTOMAC
CAVALRY CORPS

THIRD CAVALRY DIVISION
[4,308] (13k, 4mw, 68w, 2w-c, 57c, 46m = 190) 4.4%
Brig. Gen. Hugh Judson Kilpatrick

HEADQUARTERS GUARDS AND ORDERLIES

1st Ohio Cavalry, Company A
[40] (No losses reported) 0.0%
Capt. Noah Jones

1st Ohio Cavalry, Company C
[37] (No losses reported) 0.0%
Capt. Samuel N. Stanford

FIRST BRIGADE
[2,074] (11k, 3mw, 59w, 1w-c, 41c, 34m = 149) 7.2%
Brig. Gen. Elon John Farnsworth

5th New York Cavalry
[460] (4k, 1mw, 25w, 12c, 9m = 51) 11.1%
Maj. John Hammond

18th Pennsylvania Cavalry
[585] (5k, 2mw, 27w, 1w-c, 21c, 6m = 62) 10.6%
Lt. Col. William Penn Brinton

1st Vermont Cavalry
[615] (0k, 1w, 2c, 7m = 10) 1.6%
Lt. Col. Addison Webster Preston

1st (West) Virginia Cavalry
[414] (2k, 6w, 6c, 12m = 26) 6.3%
Col. Nathaniel Pendleton Richmond

ATTACHED ARTILLERY
**4th United States Horse Artillery,
Battery E (Four 3-inch Ordnance Rifles)**
[62] (No losses reported) 0.0%
Lt. Samuel Sherer Elder

SECOND BRIGADE
[1,975] (1k, 1mw, 7w, 1w-c, 16c, 12m = 38) 1.9%
Brig. Gen. George Armstrong Custer

1st Michigan Cavalry
(Supported Pennington's battery)
[427] (0k, 1w-c, 1c, 2m = 4) 0.9%
Col. Charles Henry Town

5th Michigan Cavalry
[645] (1k, 5w = 6) 0.9%
Col. Russell Alexander Alger

6th Michigan Cavalry
[521] (0k, 1mw, 9c, 10m = 20) 3.8%
Col. George Gray

7th Michigan Cavalry
[382] (0k, 2w, 6c = 8) 2.1%
Col. William D'Alton Mann

ATTACHED ARTILLERY
**2nd United States Horse Artillery,
Battery M (Six 3-inch Ordnance Rifles)**
[120] (1k, 2w = 3) 2.5%
Lt. Alexander Cummings McWhorter Pennington, Jr.

CONFEDERATE

ARMY OF NORTHERN VIRGINIA
CAVALRY DIVISION
[5,353] (3k, 1mw, 9w, 5w-c, 23c, 2m = 43) 0.8%
Maj. Gen. James Ewell Brown Stuart

William Henry Fitzhugh Lee's Brigade
[1,351] (3k, 1mw, 8w, 2w-c, 22c, 1m = 37) 2.7%
Col. John Randolph Chambliss, Jr.

2nd North Carolina Cavalry
[163] (1k, 1mw = 2) 1.2%
Lt. Col. William Henry Fitzhugh Payne (c)
Capt. William A. Graham, Jr.

9th Virginia Cavalry
[574] (1k, 3w, 1w-c, 11c = 16) 2.8%
Col. Richard Lee Turberville Beale

10th Virginia Cavalry
[269] (1k, 1w, 2c = 4) 1.5%
Col. James Lucius Davis

13th Virginia Cavalry
[345] (0k, 4w, 1w-c, 9c, 1m = 15) 4.3%
Maj. Joseph Ezra Gillette (w)
Capt. Benjamin Franklin Winfield

Fitz Lee's Brigade
[1,857] (0k, 3w-c, 1c, 1m = 5) 0.3%
Brig. Gen. Fitzhugh Lee

1st Virginia Cavalry
[364] (0k, 3w-c, 1c, 1m = 5) 1.4%
Col. James Henry Drake

2nd Virginia Cavalry
[448] (No losses reported) 0.0%
Col. Thomas Taylor Munford

3rd Virginia Cavalry
[247] (No losses reported) 0.0%
Col. Thomas Howerton Owen

4th Virginia Cavalry
[628] (No losses reported) 0.0%
Col. Williams Carter Wickham

5th Virginia Cavalry
[170] (No losses reported) 0.0%
Col. Thomas Lafayette Rosser

Hampton's Brigade
(On the field but guarding wagons captured
at Rockville, Maryland on June 28)
[1,988] (0k, 1w = 1) 0.05%
Brig. Gen. Wade Hampton

1st North Carolina Cavalry
[466] (No losses reported) 0.0%
Col. Laurence Simmons Baker

1st South Carolina Cavalry
[383] (No losses reported) 0.0%
Lt. Col. John David Twiggs (?)
(Col. John Logan Black, wounded at Upperville,
later stated that Maj. William Walker
commanded the regiment at this time.)

2nd South Carolina Cavalry
[212] (No losses reported) 0.0%
Maj. Thomas Jefferson Lipscomb

Cobb's (Georgia) Legion Cavalry
[377] (0k, 1w = 1) 0.3%
Col. Pierce Manning Butler Young

Jeff Davis (Mississippi) Legion Cavalry
[281] (No losses reported) 0.0%
Lt. Col. Joseph Frederick Waring

Phillips' (Georgia) Legion Cavalry
[269] (No losses reported) 0.0%
Lt. Col. William Wofford Rich

Attached Artillery
**1st Stuart Horse Artillery, Breathed's (Virginia)
Battery (Four 3-inch Ordnance Rifles)**
[105] (No losses reported) 0.0%
Capt. James Williams Breathed

**2nd Stuart Horse Artillery, McGregor's (Virginia)
Battery (One Blakely, One unknown)**
[52] (No losses reported) 0.0%
Capt. William Morrell McGregor

The Battle of Hanover delayed Stuart's progress north by another full day. Stuart's troopers swung east and then north around Hanover and Kilpatrick's men to continue north. Ewell's Corps, however, had already begun moving south from the York and Carlisle areas toward Gettysburg to concentrate with other parts of the Army of Northern Virginia. While at Hanover, Stuart was only

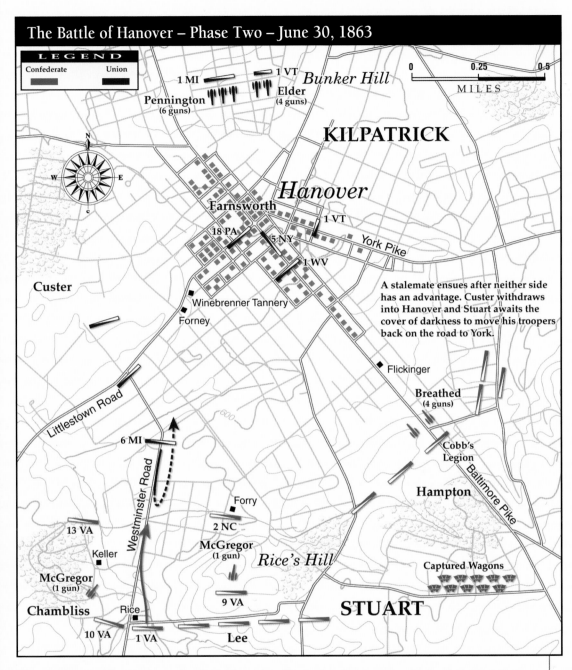

The Battle of Hanover – Phase Two – June 30, 1863

LEGEND
Confederate   Union

1 MI   1 VT   *Bunker Hill*

Pennington   Elder
(6 guns)   (4 guns)

0   0.25   0.5
MILES

KILPATRICK

Hanover

Farnsworth

1 VT

18 PA

5 NY

York Pike

1 WV

Custer

Winebrenner Tannery

Forney

A stalemate ensues after neither side has an advantage. Custer withdraws into Hanover and Stuart awaits the cover of darkness to move his troopers back on the road to York.

Flickinger

Breathed
(4 guns)

Cobb's Legion

6 MI

Hampton

Baltimore Pike

Forry

13 VA

2 NC

Keller

McGregor
(1 gun)

Rice's Hill

McGregor
(1 gun)

Captured Wagons

Chambliss   Rice

9 VA

STUART

10 VA   1 VA   Lee

Littlestown Road

Westminster Road

800

fifteen miles east of Gettysburg, but he had no idea that Lee's infantry was gathering in its vicinity. As his exhausted troopers tramped north, they actually moved farther away from their objective.

Although Stuart's withdrawal from Hanover was tailed that night for a time by a contingent of Regular cavalry that had hooked up with Kilpatrick that evening, Kilpatrick inexplicably allowed Stuart's troopers to slip away in the dark. Kilpatrick spent all of the next day (July 1) searching in vain for Stuart just north of Hanover. Not far to his west, however, the first day of the Battle of Gettysburg got underway.

CONFEDERATE CAVALRY NEAR HARRISBURG

THE SKIRMISH AT SPORTING HILL, PA.

JUNE 30, 1863

In obedience to Gen. Robert E. Lee's orders, Richard S. Ewell's Second Corps began moving south on the morning of June 30 near Carlisle and York toward Gettysburg. Lee's other two corps under James Longstreet and Ambrose P. Hill were concentrating between Chambersburg and Cashtown west of Gettysburg. **BRIGADIER GENERAL ALBERT G. JENKINS**' cavalry brigade, which served as Ewell's rearguard during his withdrawal, skirmished briefly with militia (the 22nd and 37th New York) on June 28 and 29 but was unable to dislodge the Federals. The following day Jenkins' troopers skirmished with the militia again on the west side of Camp Hill, Pennsylvania.

Brig. Gen. Albert Jenkins
Image courtesy of Library of Congress

Realizing the Confederates were withdrawing from the area, as Jenkins' men left Mechanicsburg, Brig. Gen. William F. Smith ordered his New York volunteers to reconnoiter in the direction of Camp Hill. Lieutenant Frank Stanwood and his small contingent of Regular Cavalry led the mission, which began about 10:00 a.m. just as the battle at Hanover was breaking out more than forty miles to the south between J.E.B. Stuart and Judson Kilpatrick. Stanwood encountered the 16th Virginia Cavalry posted atop Sporting Hill shortly after noon. When **BRIG. GEN. JOHN EWEN** (in command of the New Yorkers) hesitated, one of his staff officers, Lt. Rufus King, took control and ordered the 22nd and 37th New York to engage the Rebels. Two guns from Capt. Thomas E. Jackson's Virginia battery opened fire on the Federals. The two sides skirmished throughout the afternoon with little progress until about 5:00 p.m., when two artillery pieces from Landis' Philadelphia Militia Battery were brought up to hammer Jenkins' dismounted cavalrymen.

With the rear of Ewell's moving corps protected, Jenkins withdrew his men and artillery, but not before some sixteen of his troopers were killed and a couple dozen wounded. Eleven Federals were also wounded during the fluid skirmish.

FEDERAL

DEPARTMENT OF SUSQUEHANNA

FIRST DIVISION
[1,280] (0k, 11w = 11) 0.9%
New York Militia
[1,200] (0k, 11w = 11) est. 0.9%
Brig. Gen. John Ewen
Lt. Rufus King, Jr. (Tactical command)

11th New York Militia
(Not engaged)
Col. Joachim Maidhof

22nd New York Militia
[600] (est. 6w = 6) 1.0%
Lt. Col. John A. Elwell

37th New York Militia
[600] (est. 5w = 5) 0.8%
Col. Charles Roome

CAVALRY
3rd United States Cavalry "Stanwood Regulars"
(One company of new recruits)
[50 est.] (No losses reported) 0.0%
Lt. Frank Stanwood

ARTILLERY
(Henry) Landis' Philadelphia Independent Militia Battery, Light Artillery (Two 3-inch Ordnance Rifles)
[30] (No losses reported) 0.0%
Lt. Samuel C. Perkins

CONFEDERATE

ARMY OF NORTHERN VIRGINIA

CAVALRY DIVISION
[970] (16k est., 25w est. = 41 est.) 4.2%

JENKINS' BRIGADE
[863] (16k, 25w est. = 41 est.) 4.8%
Brig. Gen. Albert Gallatin Jenkins

14th Virginia Cavalry
[267] (No losses reported) 0.0%
Maj. Benjamin Franklin Eakle

16th Virginia Cavalry
[290] (12k est., 20w est. = 32 est.) 11.0%
Col. Milton James Ferguson

34th Virginia Battalion Cavalry
[172] (No losses reported) 0.0%
Lt. Col. Vincent Addison Witcher

36th Battalion Virginia Cavalry
[134] (4k est., 5w est. = 9 est.) 6.7%
Capt. Cornelius T. Smith

ATTACHED ARTILLERY
Jackson's Battery, Charlottesville (Virginia) Horse Artillery (Two 12-pounder Howitzers, Two 3-inch Ordnance Rifles)
(Only one section of two guns engaged)
[107] (No losses reported) 0.0%
Capt. Thomas Edwin Jackson

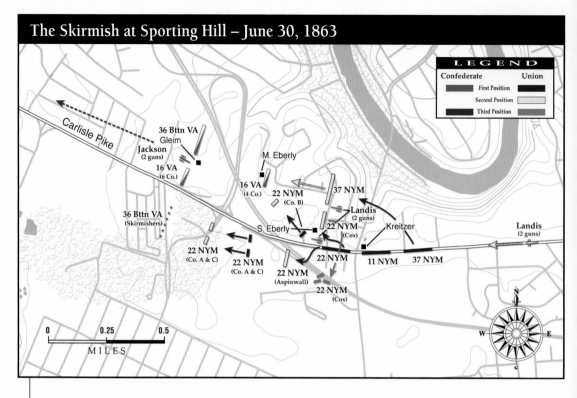

The Skirmish at Sporting Hill – June 30, 1863

The skirmish at Sporting Hill was the largest organized fighting near Harrisburg, Pennsylvania, during the entire Civil War, and the northernmost combat during the Gettysburg Campaign. Ewen's volunteers led by Lieutenant King outnumbered their adversaries and performed well against the experienced Virginia veterans. Ewen decided not to pursue Jenkins, who withdrew after the skirmishing to rejoin Ewell's Corps making for the Gettysburg area. For the rest of their lives the New Yorkers recalled with pride their participation in helping turn back the Rebel advance upon Harrisburg.

On the afternoon of June 30, two of the three brigades of Federal cavalry that made up Brig. Gen. John Buford's division screening the left portion of the Army of the Potomac's advance to Pennsylvania entered the town of Gettysburg. When a Confederate reconnaissance detail led by Brig. Gen. James J. Pettigrew was spotted just west of town, Buford's troopers pushed the probing Rebels back toward their camps near Cashtown. Pettigrew reported the encounter to A. P. Hill and emphasized that veteran Federal troops were in Gettysburg. Hill and one of his division commanders, Maj. Gen. Henry Heth, discounted the report and concluded the Federals were nothing more than militia. When Heth asked Hill if he had any objection if Heth were to march the next morning to Gettysburg, Hill replied, "none in the world."

STUART SEARCHES FOR THE ARMY

THE SIEGE OF CARLISLE, PA.

JULY 1-2, 1863

Following the unexpected battle with Judson Kilpatrick's Federal cavalry division at Hanover, Pennsylvania on June 30, **J.E.B. STUART** detoured his column to the east and then back north to Jefferson, where he rested his men and horses during the early morning hours of July 1. Stuart learned from local citizens and newspapers that part of Ewell's Corps had recently been at York farther north. What Stuart did not know was that Ewell and most of his men were now only a few hours away from Gettysburg. With the cumbersome captured wagons and 400 prisoners in tow, Stuart continued moving. The head of his column reached Dover, about seven miles east of York, later that morning. There, Stuart learned that Ewell's command vacated the area over the two previous days. Stuart dispatched couriers to search for

Maj. Gen. J.E.B. Stuart
Image courtesy of Library of Congress

Ewell's large column and led his brigades northwest toward Carlisle, Pennsylvania, the site of the Federal army barracks. Stuart was under the mistaken belief that most of Lee's army must be near Harrisburg, and Carlisle seemed a likely point to meet some portion of it.

When he reached Dillsburg, Stuart decided to leave Hampton's Brigade there with the captured wagons in an effort to speed up the march to Carlisle. When he heard the news that Confederate cavalry were riding toward Carlisle, **BRIG. GEN. WILLIAM F. "BALDY" SMITH** marched his 2,700 New York and Pennsylvania volunteer militia and a pair of guns from Landis' battery to Carlisle. Captain William H. Boyd's Company C of the 1st New York (Lincoln) Cavalry led Smith's column. The Federals arrived in Carlisle on the afternoon of July 1 and set up defensive

THE CAMPAIGN BEGINS
JUNE 3

THE BATTLE OF GETTYSBURG
JULY 1-3
SIEGE OF CARLISLE
JULY 1-2

LEE'S ARMY CROSSES THE POTOMAC RIVER
JULY 14

positions. When Stuart's troopers arrived later that evening they found Baldy Smith's men occupying the town instead of the Confederate infantry they were hoping to join.

Four local companies of militia skirmished on the eastern edge of town with troopers from Fitzhugh Lee's Brigade riding at the head of Stuart's column. The New Yorkers engaged Lee but were pushed back, leaving the army barracks vulnerable to the Rebels. Wishing to spare the town, Stuart sent a rider bearing a flag of truce who was escorted to General Smith. The bearer, Lt. Henry C. Lee (Fitzhugh Lee's younger brother) told Smith that if the town was not surrendered it would be shelled. Smith refused, sending the lieutenant back with the message, "Shell away and be damned!"

Rebuffed, Stuart deployed Capt. James W. Breathed's artillery on a ridge overlooking the town and asked once more that Smith surrender. When Smith refused a second time, Breathed's guns opened an intermittent shelling that lasted more than three hours. The cannon fire damaged several buildings, including the court house and a building on the campus of Dickinson College. During the shelling some of Stuart's men torched buildings at the army barracks and the gas works, which produced a bright flame visible for miles in every direction.

Shortly after midnight, Stuart received a welcomed and long-overdue message when his scouts returned with news that the Confederate army was at Gettysburg, a little more than twenty miles south, and a major battle had broken out there that day with elements of the Army of the Potomac.

FEDERAL

DEPARTMENT OF SUSQUEHANNA

FIRST DIVISION
[2,750 est.] (0k, 12w = 12) 0.04%
Brig. Gen. William Farrar Smith

FOURTH BRIGADE [1,189] (Losses unknown) *Brig. Gen. John Ewen*	**FIFTH BRIGADE** [1,400] (Losses unknown) *Col. William Brisbane*
22nd New York Militia [594] (Losses unknown) *Col. Lloyd Aspinwall*	**28th Pennsylvania** [700] (Losses unknown) *Col. James Chamberlin*
37th New York Militia [595] (Losses unknown) *Col. Charles Roome*	**33rd Pennsylvania** [700] (Losses unknown) *Col. William W. Taylor*

CAVALRY **1st New York (Lincoln) Cavalry, Company C** [31] (Losses unknown) *Capt. William H. Boyd*	**ARTILLERY** **(Henry) Landis' Philadelphia Independent Militia Battery, Light Artillery (Two 3-inch Ordnance Rifles)** [30] (Losses unknown) *Lt. Samuel C. Perkins*

LOCAL MILITIA
Four Companies
[100 est.] (Losses unknown)

CONFEDERATE

ARMY OF NORTHERN VIRGINIA
CAVALRY DIVISION
[1,957] (0k, 1w-c, 1c = 2) 0.1%
Maj. Gen. James Ewell Brown Stuart

FITZ LEE'S BRIGADE
[1,852] (0k, 1w-c, 1c = 2) 0.1%
Brig. Gen. Fitzhugh Lee

1st Virginia Cavalry
[359] (No losses reported) 0.0%
Col. James Henry Drake

2nd Virginia Cavalry
[448] (0k, 1c = 1) 0.2%
Col. Thomas Taylor Munford

3rd Virginia Cavalry
[247] (No losses reported) 0.0%
Col. Thomas Howerton Owen

4th Virginia Cavalry
[628] (0k, 1w-c = 1) 0.2%
Col. Williams Carter Wickham

5th Virginia Cavalry
[170] (No losses reported) 0.0%
Col. Thomas Lafayette Rosser

ATTACHED ARTILLERY

Breathed's Battery, 1st Stuart (Virginia)
Horse Artillery (Four 3-inch Ordnance Rifles)
[105] (No losses reported) 0.0%
Capt. James Williams Breathed

About 1:00 a.m. on July 2, Stuart began withdrawing his two brigades from Carlisle and sent word to Wade Hampton at Dillsburg to also ride for Gettysburg. Stuart's command faced yet another grueling all-night ride that further exhausted men and mounts alike. Stuart would not reach the Gettysburg battlefield until late on the afternoon of July 2. By that time the Army of Northern Virginia was deeply embroiled in a second day of bloody combat.

THE BATTLE OF GETTYSBURG

THE BATTLE OF GETTYSBURG, PA.

JULY 1-3, 1863

Late on the evening of June 30, Confederate cavalry leader J.E.B. Stuart and his three Confederate cavalry brigades were at Jefferson, Pennsylvania, on their way to Carlisle in the hopes of locating the Army of Northern Virginia. That same evening, **GEN. ROBERT E. LEE** and James Longstreet's First Corps and A. P. Hill's Third Corps were spread out east of Chambersburg, from just a few miles to about twenty miles from Gettysburg. Lieutenant General Richard S. Ewell's Second Corps, screened by Albert Jenkins', William French's, and Elijah White's cavalry, was operating north and northeast of Gettysburg within at most an easy day's march of that important crossroads town. **MAJOR GENERAL GEORGE G. MEADE**'s Federal Army of the

Gen. Robert E. Lee
Image courtesy of Library of Congress

Potomac, with its seven infantry corps and most of its cavalry corps, was widely dispersed from Hanover, Pennsylvania, about fifteen miles east of Gettysburg, all the way south to Taneytown and Emmitsburg, Maryland.

Two Federal cavalry brigades under Brig. Gen. John Buford had reached Gettysburg about midday on June 30 in time to blunt Brig. Gen. James J. Pettigrew's planned incursion into town. Once Pettigrew's Southerners retreated, Buford set up a ring of pickets to watch the roads running west and north out of Gettysburg. By the time the sun dropped below the horizon, scouts and locals had provided Buford with information concerning the general location of most

Maj. Gen. George G. Meade
Image courtesy of Library of Congress

The Fight for McPherson's Ridge – July 1: 9:30 to 11:30 a.m.

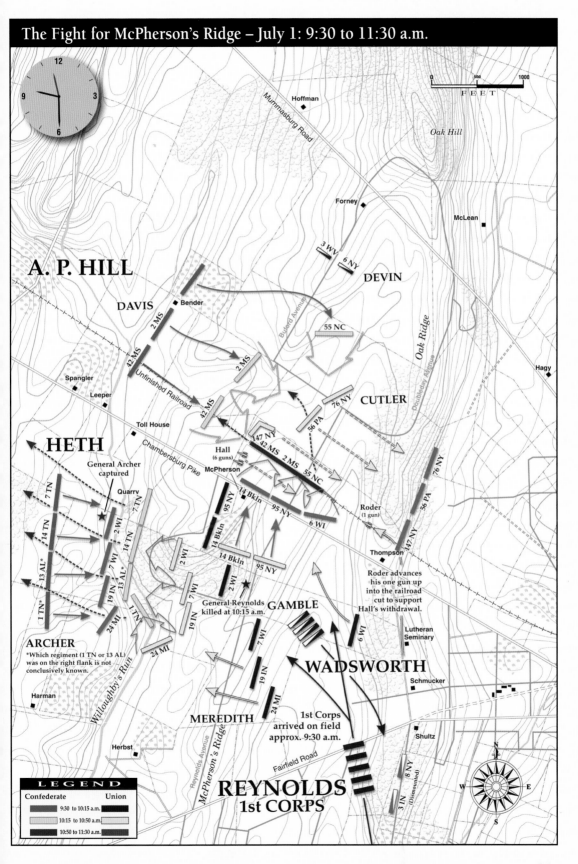

Hoffman

Oak Hill

Mummasburg Road

Forney

McLean

3 WV

6 NY

DEVIN

A. P. HILL

DAVIS

Bender

2 MS

Buford Avenue

55 NC

42 MS

Unfinished Railroad

2 MS

Oak Ridge

Doubleday Avenue

Hagy

Spangler

Leeper

42 MS

76 NY

CUTLER

Toll House

Chambersburg Pike

42 MS

56 PA

147 NY

HETH

General Archer
captured

Quarry

Hall
(6 guns)

McPherson

42 MS   2 MS

55 NC

76 NY

7 TN

2 WI

14 BkIn

95 NY

95 NY

6 WI

Roder
(1 gun)

56 PA

14 TN

14 TN

7 TN

95 NY

2 WI

14 BkIn

147 NY

13 AL*

7 WI

13 AL*

14 BkIn

95 NY

Thompson

Roder advances
his one gun up
into the railroad
cut to support
Hall's withdrawal.

2 WI

1 TN

1 TN*

19 IN

7 WI

2 WI

General Reynolds
killed at 10:15 a.m.

GAMBLE

7 WI

6 WI

Lutheran
Seminary

24 MI

ARCHER

24 MI

19 IN

WADSWORTH

*Which regiment (1 TN or 13 AL)
was on the right flank is not
conclusively known.

Harman

Willoughby's Run

19 IN

24 MI

Schmucker

Shultz

MEREDITH

1st Corps
arrived on field
approx. 9:30 a.m.

3 IN

8 NY
(Dismounted)

Herbst

McPherson's Ridge

Reynolds Avenue

Fairfield Road

REYNOLDS
1st CORPS

3 IN

N
W   E
S

LEGEND	
Confederate	Union
9:30 to 10:15 a.m.	
10:15 to 10:50 a.m.	
10:50 to 11:30 a.m.	

0   500   1000
FEET

of the Confederate army. Given the road network and Pettigrew's recent probe, Buford predicted to his officers that he and his troopers would be attacked the next day.

About 7:30 a.m. on July 1, one of Buford's pickets four miles west of town along the pike leading to Cashtown shattered the morning quiet with a single shot. The distant target was the approaching vanguard of Maj. Gen. Henry Heth's Division, part of Hill's Corps. Heth was on his way to Gettysburg with Hill's blessing to scatter any militia that might be there and search for supplies. Instead of the skittish militia they expected to find, however, Heth stumbled into Buford's veteran troopers. The large-scale, division-sized reconnaissance triggered a meeting engagement that would eventually swell into the Battle of Gettysburg.

For two hours Buford's dismounted cavalrymen fought a stubborn delaying action that slowed Heth's advance toward Gettysburg. By 10:00 a.m., Buford was making a stand atop McPherson's Ridge just west of town when leading elements of Maj. Gen. John Reynolds' I Corps began arriving from Emmitsburg, Maryland. Both sides deployed additional reinforcements. Reynolds was killed almost immediately as the fighting escalated into a major engagement along the ridge. Poor Confederate tactical arrangements and a stubborn defensive effort by the Federals threw back several Confederate attacks. Early that afternoon, however, Ewell's Corps began arriving from the north and more of A. P. Hill's Corps were preparing to enter the battle from the west. The Federal XI Corps under Maj. Gen. Oliver O. Howard also arrived, moving through town and fanning out north of Gettysburg to confront Ewell. As Howard soon discovered, he did not have enough men to defend the wide front assigned to him.

By late afternoon, determined attacks by Hill's and Ewell's soldiers swept against Cemetery Ridge, Oak Knoll, and across the undulating terrain on Howard's front, breaking the Federal defenses west and north of Gettysburg and routing the Yankees. The survivors clotted the town's streets and flooded across the fields in their effort to reach the higher ground east and south of town on Cemetery Hill and Cemetery Ridge. Although Lee offered Ewell the discretion to attack the defeated enemy, his corps commander decided the position was too strong and opted not to do so. Most of the rest of Meade's Federal infantry and artillery arrived on the battlefield that night and early the following morning. Using Cemetery Hill as the focal point, Meade and his generals worked tirelessly to establish a defensive line.

When dawn broke on July 2, the Union army was aligned in a strong position often described as a "fishhook." The sharp end of the hook — Meade's right flank — was anchored on Culp's Hill northeast of town, with the curve of the hook running through Cemetery Hill and the shank running south along Cemetery Ridge. Artillery studded the line, which also offered the advantage of interior lines. Lee moved Hill's Corps ahead to Seminary Ridge while Ewell assumed position outside town and beyond, confronting Culp's Hill. As a result, the Army of Northern Virginia's front was substantially longer than that of the Army of the Potomac. Lee's tenuous exterior line had the added disadvantage of running through Gettysburg itself.

James Longstreet's Corps (less Maj. Gen. George E. Pickett's Division) reached the field about 3:00 a.m. that morning and rested while Lee and Longstreet discussed how best to defeat the Union army. About 9:00 a.m. that morning, Lee instructed Longstreet to move his two available divisions south beyond A. P. Hill and attack and roll up the enemy's left flank. Although there is some debate on this issue, it appears that the plan was an *en echelon* attack, meaning that once

The Rest of the I Corps Arrives – July 1: 11:30 a.m. to 12:30 p.m.

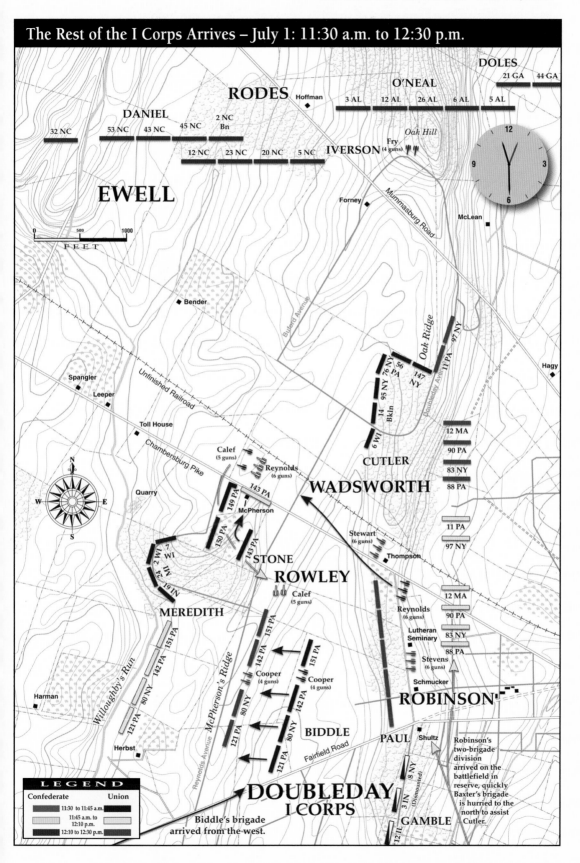

DOLES
21 GA 44 GA

O'NEAL
3 AL 12 AL 26 AL 6 AL 5 AL

RODES Hoffman

DANIEL
32 NC 53 NC 43 NC 45 NC 2 NC Bn

12 NC 23 NC 20 NC 5 NC IVERSON

Fry (4 guns) Oak Hill

EWELL McLean

Forney Mummasburg Road

Bender

Buford Avenue

Spangler Oak Ridge

Leeper 97 NY

Unfinished Railroad 56 PA 11 PA Hagy

Toll House 76 NY 147 NY

95 NY Doubleday Avenue

Chambersburg Pike 14 Bkln 12 MA

Calef (5 guns) 6 WI 90 PA

Reynolds (6 guns) CUTLER 83 NY

143 PA WADSWORTH 88 PA

Quarry 149 PA

McPherson 11 PA

150 PA 143 PA Stewart (6 guns) 97 NY

7 WI 2 WI Thompson

24 IN STONE 12 MA

19 IN ROWLEY Reynolds (6 guns) 90 PA

Calef (5 guns) 83 NY

MEREDITH Lutheran Seminary 88 PA

151 PA 151 PA Stevens (6 guns)

142 PA Schmucker

142 PA 151 PA ROBINSON

Cooper (4 guns) Cooper (4 guns)

80 NY

121 PA 80 NY 142 PA PAUL Shultz

Harman Robinson's two-brigade division arrived on the battlefield in reserve, quickly Baxter's brigade is hurried to the north to assist Cutler.

Herbst 121 PA BIDDLE

80 NY Fairfield Road

121 PA

DOUBLEDAY 8 NY (Dismounted)

I CORPS 3 IN

Biddle's brigade arrived from the west. GAMBLE

12 IL

LEGEND

Confederate   Union

11:30 to 11:45 a.m.
11:45 a.m. to 12:10 p.m.
12:10 to 12:30 p.m.

N W E S

0 500 1000
FEET

83

Longstreet was committed, Hill would attack one brigade at time, rolling the assault northward off Seminary Ridge. Ewell would join in, attacking Culp's Hill and Cemetery Hill.

The Union left, however, was not where Lee thought it was because Maj. Gen. Daniel Sickles, one of Meade's corps commanders, had marched most of his men forward from Cemetery Ridge to the Emmitsburg Road. Sickles' III Corps had barely formed into a long but weakly held bulging salient when Longstreet's artillery opened fire and his infantry attacked. The assault crushed the Peach Orchard bulge, captured rocky Devil's Den, and nearly occupied Little Round Top. Fighting swept through Rose's Wheatfield, broke the Union lines along the Emmitsburg Road, and in the process sucked in many thousands of Union troops from other parts of the line that Meade had stripped in an effort to save his endangered left flank.

A. P. Hill's attack also promised some success, gaining parts of lower Cemetery Ridge and tearing open a large hole in the line. The assault began breaking down about midway up Seminary Ridge, and fell apart about dusk when one of his division commanders was mortally wounded and his replacement did not continue the assault. Ewell, meanwhile, launched determined attacks against wooded and rocky Culp's Hill, driving back some of the defenders and capturing a portion of the line. An attack also captured East Cemetery Hill, but the second prong of the assault from the northwest failed to materialize and the victorious Rebels were thrown off the high ground in vicious nighttime fighting. Meade's line had held—just barely—but his casualties for the first two days of battle approached 20,000 men. Lee's casualties were also severe at some 13,000.

The third day of the battle on July 3 opened just before dawn with a Union-spoiling attack that drove Ewell's men away from the valuable ground they had won the previous evening and back down the slope. After hours of heavy fighting Meade re-established his lines and solidified his right flank. Having tried and failed against both flanks, Lee determined to make one final large-scale attack against the Federal center on Cemetery Ridge. The core of the assault was built around George Pickett's fresh, three-brigade Virginia division (Longstreet's Corps), which had reached the field late the previous evening. Other troops from A. P. Hill's Corps more than doubled the number Pickett contributed, although history has come to call the attack "Pickett's Charge." Lee ordered a giant concentric circle of artillery to soften the enemy defense before the infantry moved out. The artillery bombardment that opened about 1:00 p.m. was thunderous and a grand sight to behold, but overshot the enemy lines and did little damage to Meade's waiting infantry. The gray infantry that followed, approximately 13,000 men, moved forward smartly across nearly a mile of open ground. The Federals easily beat back the assault, although a small number of men managed to pierce the line at a place now known as "The Angle." Pickett's Charge contributed the majority of the estimated 10,000 additional casualties the Confederates suffered on July 3 (including Ewell's losses on Culp's Hill). Federal losses that day were about 3,000 from all causes.

Unbeknownst to many readers, sharp cavalry fighting took place on July 2 and 3 on both flanks of the Union army. These swirling, fluid actions added another 1,500 casualties to the butcher's bill. A rainstorm broke out that night after the fighting ended, adding to the misery of the wounded covering the expansive field. Soon after the repulse of his grand attack that afternoon, Lee decided to withdraw his army south of the Potomac River to end his campaign.

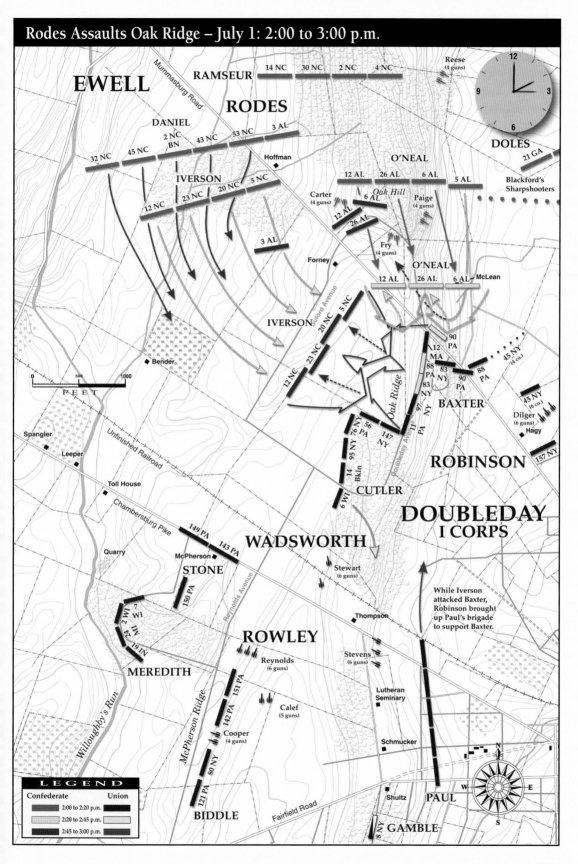

Rodes Assaults Oak Ridge – July 1: 2:00 to 3:00 p.m.

EWELL

RAMSEUR

14 NC · 30 NC · 2 NC · 4 NC

Reese
(4 guns)

Mummasburg Road

RODES

DOLES

DANIEL

2 NC BN · 43 NC · 53 NC · 3 AL

21 GA

32 NC · 45 NC

IVERSON

Hoffman

O'NEAL

12 AL · 26 AL · 6 AL · 5 AL

Blackford's
Sharpshooters

12 NC · 23 NC · 20 NC · 5 NC

Carter
(4 guns)

6 AL

Oak Hill

Paige
(4 guns)

3 AL

12 AL

26 AL

Forney

Fry
(4 guns)

O'NEAL

IVERSON

20 NC · 5 NC

12 AL · 26 AL · 6 AL · McLean

Bender

23 NC

90 PA

12 MA

45 NY
(4 co.)

12 NC

Oak Ridge

88 PA · 83 NY

83 NY

90 PA

88 PA

45 NY
(6 co.)

BAXTER

97 PA

11 PA

Spangler

Leeper

Unfinished Railroad

56 PA · 76 PA

147 NY

Dilger
(6 guns)

Hagy

ROBINSON

157 NY

95 NY

Toll House

14 Bkln

ROBINSON

Chambersburg Pike

6 WI

CUTLER

DOUBLEDAY
I CORPS

Quarry

149 PA · 143 PA

WADSWORTH

150 PA

McPherson

STONE

Stewart
(6 guns)

While Iverson
attacked Baxter,
Robinson brought
up Paul's brigade
to support Baxter.

Reynolds Avenue

7 WI · 2 WI

24 WI · 19 IN

MEREDITH

ROWLEY

Thompson

151 PA

Reynolds
(6 guns)

Stevens
(6 guns)

142 PA

Calef
(5 guns)

Lutheran
Seminary

McPherson Ridge

Cooper
(4 guns)

80 NY

Schmucker

121 PA

Willoughby's Run

BIDDLE

Fairfield Road

Shultz

PAUL

GAMBLE

8 NY

LEGEND

Confederate	Union	
		2:00 to 2:20 p.m.
		2:20 to 2:45 p.m.
		2:45 to 3:00 p.m.

N · E · W · S

The Fight on Barlow's Knoll – July 1: 2:45 to 4:30 p.m.

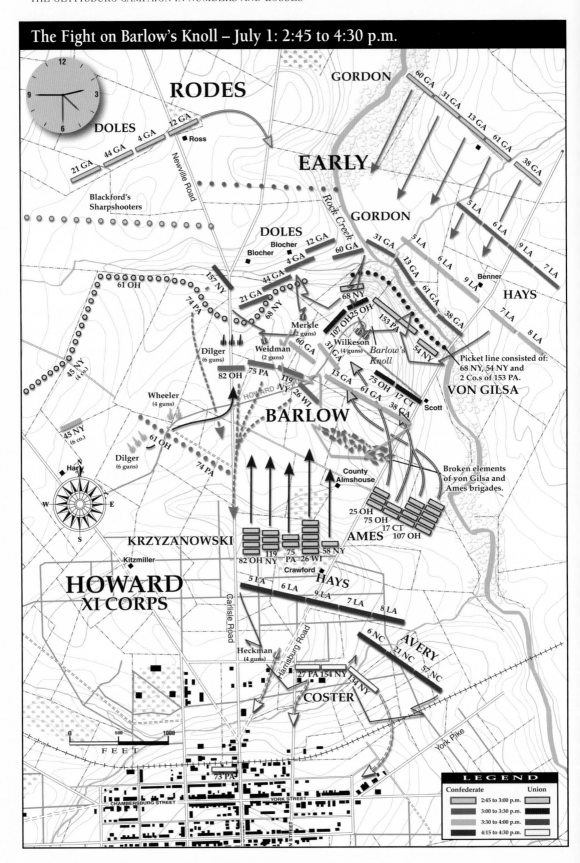

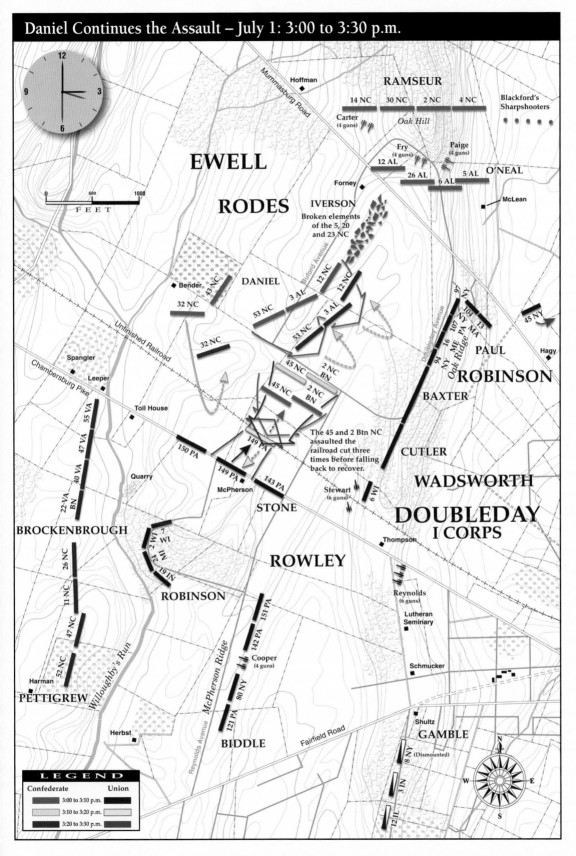

Daniel Continues the Assault – July 1: 3:00 to 3:30 p.m.

RAMSEUR

14 NC   30 NC   2 NC   4 NC   Blackford's Sharpshooters

Hoffman

Carter (4 guns)   Oak Hill

Fry (4 guns)   Paige (4 guns)

12 AL   26 AL   6 AL   5 AL   O'NEAL

McLean

EWELL

RODES

Forney

IVERSON

Broken elements of the 5, 20 and 23 NC

Bender   43 NC   DANIEL   12 NC   12 NC   97 NY   45 NY

32 NC   53 NC   3 AL   101 NY   13

16 NY   107   PA   NY

32 NC   53 NC   3 AL   94   ME   Hagy

53 NC   2 NC   BN   PAUL

45 NC   2 NC   BN   ROBINSON

Spangler   45 NC   BAXTER

Leeper

Toll House   The 45 and 2 Btn NC assaulted the railroad cut three times before falling back to recover.   CUTLER

55 VA   149 PA   WADSWORTH

47 VA   150 PA   149 PA   143 PA   Stewart (6 guns)   6 WI   DOUBLEDAY

Quarry   McPherson   I CORPS

40 VA   STONE   Thompson

22 VA BN   7   WI

26 NC   2   WI   ROWLEY   Reynolds (6 guns)

BROCKENBROUGH   24 WI   19 IN

11 NC   ROBINSON   Lutheran Seminary

47 NC   151 PA

52 NC   142 PA   Schmucker

Harman   Cooper (4 guns)

PETTIGREW   80 NY   Shultz

Herbst   121 PA   GAMBLE

BIDDLE   Fairfield Road   (Dismounted)

8 NY

3 IN

12 IL

LEGEND

Confederate | Union
3:00 to 3:10 p.m.
3:10 to 3:20 p.m.
3:20 to 3:30 p.m.

Mummasburg Road   Buford Avenue   Doubleday Avenue   Oak Ridge   Chambersburg Pike   Unfinished Railroad   McPherson Ridge   Reynolds Avenue   Willoughby's Run

FEET   0   500   1000

N W S E

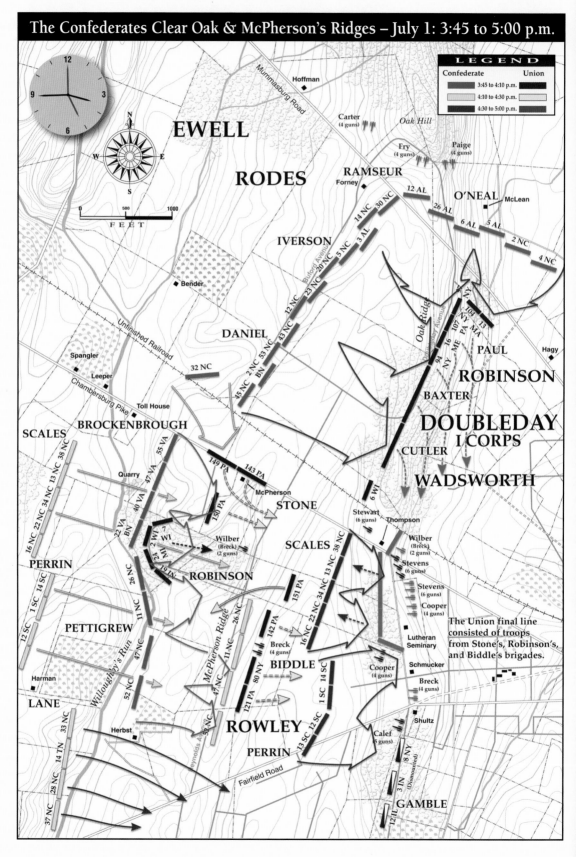

The Confederates Clear Oak & McPherson's Ridges – July 1: 3:45 to 5:00 p.m.

LEGEND

Confederate   Union

3:45 to 4:10 p.m.
4:10 to 4:30 p.m.
4:30 to 5:00 p.m.

The Union final line consisted of troops from Stone's, Robinson's, and Biddle's brigades.

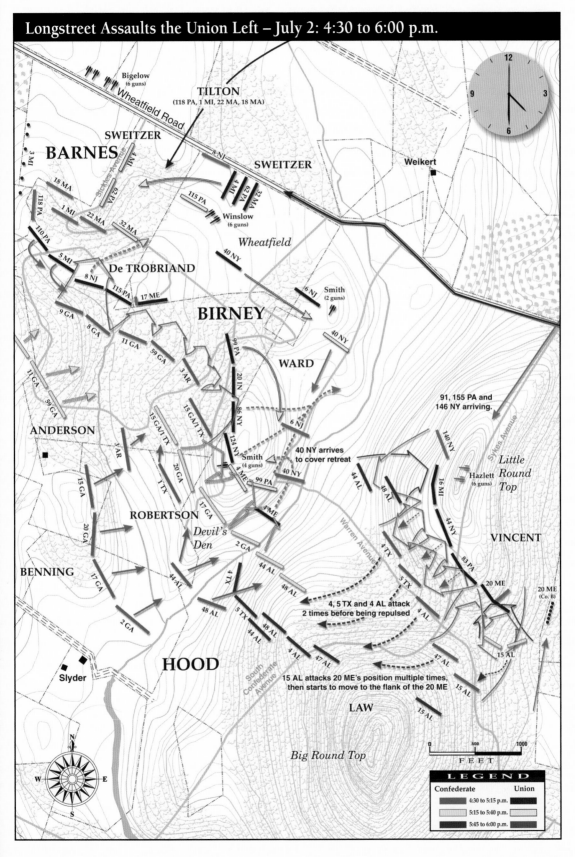

Longstreet Assaults the Union Left – July 2: 4:30 to 6:00 p.m.

Bigelow
(6 guns)

Wheatfield Road

TILTON
(118 PA, 1 MI, 22 MA, 18 MA)

SWEITZER

BARNES

SWEITZER

Weikert

8 NJ

4 MI

62 PA

22 MA

115 PA

Winslow
(6 guns)

18 MA

1 MI

22 MA

32 MA

Wheatfield

110 PA

5 MI

8 NJ

De TROBRIAND

115 PA

17 ME

40 NY

6 NJ

Smith
(2 guns)

9 GA

8 GA

11 GA

59 GA

BIRNEY

40 NY

WARD

91, 155 PA and
146 NY arriving.

11 GA

59 GA

99 PA

20 IN

86 NY

124 NY

6 NJ

140 NY

Little
Round
Top

ANDERSON

15 GA/1 TX

15 GA/1 TX

Smith
(4 guns)

40 NY

40 NY arrives
to cover retreat

4 ME

99 PA

44 AL

48 AL

16 MI

Hazlett
(6 guns)

3 AR

3 AR

15 GA

20 GA

1 TX

17 GA

4 ME

44 NY

Warren Avenue

83 PA

VINCENT

ROBERTSON

20 GA

Devil's
Den

2 GA

44 AL

4 TX

44 AL

48 AL

4 TX

5 TX

4 AL

20 ME

20 ME
(Co. B)

BENNING

17 GA

48 AL

5 TX

44 AL

48 AL

4, 5 TX and 4 AL attack
2 times before being repulsed

47 AL

15 AL

2 GA

HOOD

4 AL

47 AL

15 AL attacks 20 ME's position multiple times,
then starts to move to the flank of the 20 ME

47 AL

15 AL

Slyder

South Confederate Avenue

LAW

15 AL

N
W   E
S

Big Round Top

0   500   1000

FEET

LEGEND

Confederate	Union
4:30 to 5:15 p.m.	
5:15 to 5:40 p.m.	
5:45 to 6:00 p.m.	

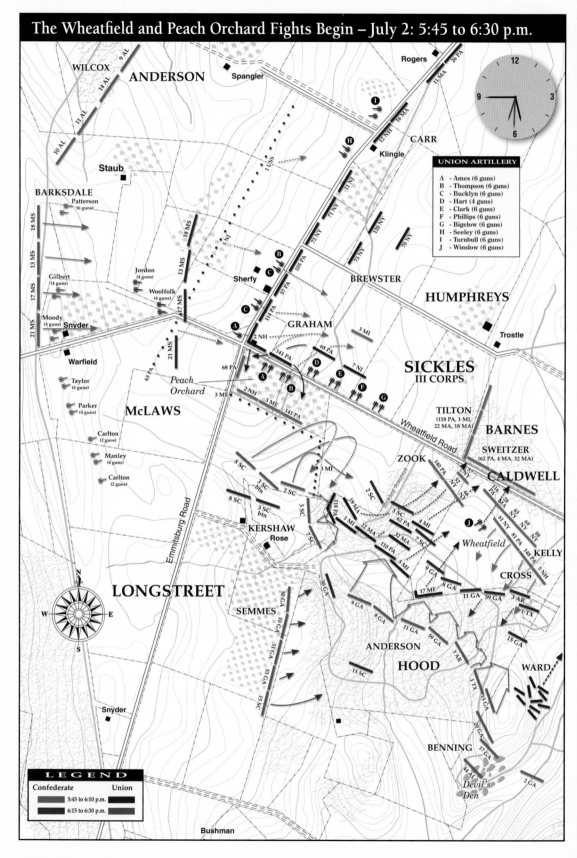

The Wheatfield and Peach Orchard Fights Begin – July 2: 5:45 to 6:30 p.m.

UNION ARTILLERY

A - Ames (6 guns)
B - Thompson (6 guns)
C - Bucklyn (6 guns)
D - Hart (4 guns)
E - Clark (6 guns)
F - Phillips (6 guns)
G - Bigelow (6 guns)
H - Seeley (6 guns)
I - Turnbull (6 guns)
J - Winslow (6 guns)

LEGEND

Confederate   Union

5:45 to 6:10 p.m.

6:15 to 6:30 p.m.

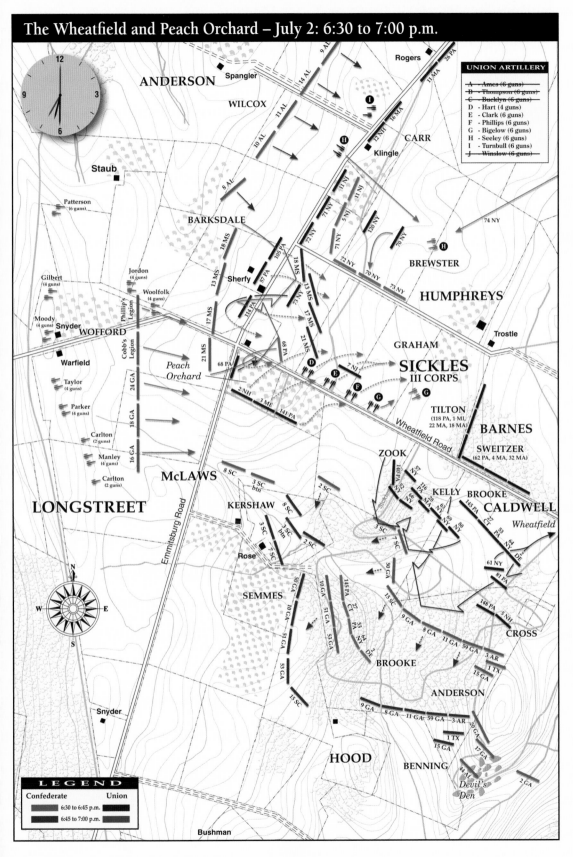

The Wheatfield and Peach Orchard – July 2: 6:30 to 7:00 p.m.

UNION ARTILLERY

A	Ames (6 guns)
B	Thompson (6 guns)
C	Bucklyn (6 guns)
D	Hart (4 guns)
E	Clark (6 guns)
F	Phillips (6 guns)
G	Bigelow (6 guns)
H	Seeley (6 guns)
I	Turnbull (6 guns)
J	Winslow (6 guns)

ANDERSON

Spangler

WILCOX

Rogers

26 PA

9 AL

14 AL

7 AL

11 AL

10 AL

I

11 MA

12 NH 16 MA

CARR

8 AL

Klingle

H

Staub

Patterson
(6 guns)

BARKSDALE

18 MS

105 PA

13 MS

Sherfy

57 PA

18 MS

13 MS

17 MS

16 MA

11 NJ

11 MA

5 NJ

11 NJ

6 NJ

120 NY

71 NY

70 NY

72 NY

74 NY

70 NY

73 NY

H

BREWSTER

HUMPHREYS

Gilbert
(4 guns)

Jordon
(4 guns)

Woolfolk
(4 guns)

Moody
(4 guns)

Snyder

WOFFORD

Phillip's
Legion

Cobb's
Legion

17 MS

21 MS

114 PA

68 PA

13 MS

17 MS

21 MS

68 PA

D

E

7 NJ

F

G

GRAHAM

SICKLES
III CORPS

Trostle

Warfield

Taylor
(4 guns)

Parker
(4 guns)

Carlton
(2 guns)

Manley
(4 guns)

Carlton
(2 guns)

Peach
Orchard

24 GA

18 GA

16 GA

2 NH

3 ME

141 PA

Wheatfield Road

TILTON
(118 PA, 1 MI,
22 MA, 18 MA)

BARNES

SWEITZER
(62 PA, 4 MA, 32 MA)

McLAWS

LONGSTREET

8 SC

3 SC
btn

KERSHAW

8 SC

3 SC
btn

Rose

7 SC

3 SC

2 SC

2 SC

2 SC

7 SC

3 SC

ZOOK

140 PA

57
NY

52
NY

116
PA

66
NY

64
NY

KELLY

140 PA

27
CT

145 PA

BROOKE

CALDWELL

Wheatfield

61 NY

81 PA

Enmitsburg Road

SEMMES

50 GA

10 GA

51 GA

10 GA

51 GA

53 GA

53 GA

15 SC

145 PA

27
CT

53
PA

2
DE

30 GA

9 GA

15 SC

8 GA

11 GA

148 PA

5 NH

59 GA

CROSS

3 AR

1 TX

15 GA

BROOKE

ANDERSON

Snyder

9 GA

8 GA

11 GA

59 GA

3 AR

30 GA

1 TX

15 GA

17 GA

HOOD

BENNING

44 AL

Devil's
Den

2 GA

LEGEND

Confederate	Union
6:30 to 6:45 p.m.	
6:45 to 7:00 p.m.	

Bushman

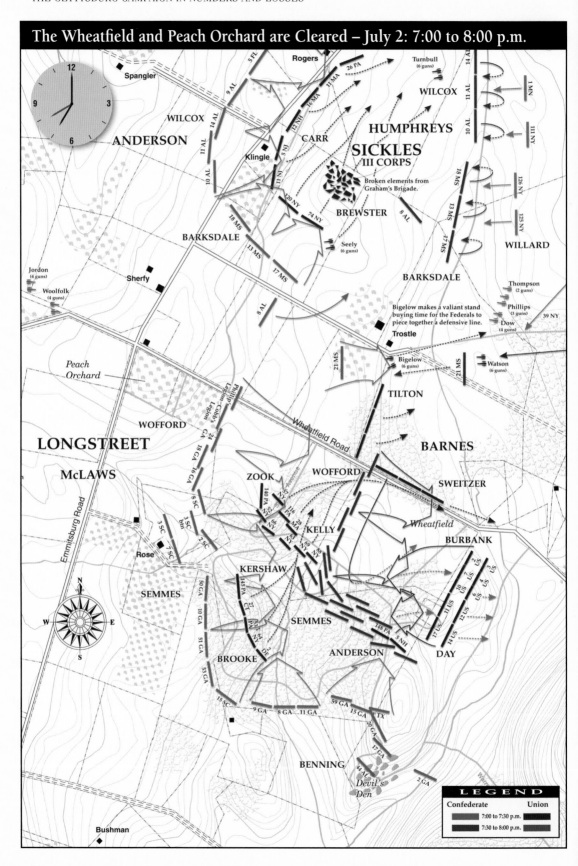

The Wheatfield and Peach Orchard are Cleared – July 2: 7:00 to 8:00 p.m.

Spangler

WILCOX

ANDERSON

Klingle

BARKSDALE

Jordon
(4 guns)

Woolfolk
(4 guns)

Sherfy

Peach
Orchard

WOFFORD

LONGSTREET

McLAWS

Rose

SEMMES

KERSHAW

BROOKE

Rogers

5 FL

9 AL

14 AL

14 AL

10 AL

5 NJ

11 NJ

20 NY

18 MS

13 MS

17 MS

8 AL

ZOOK

3 SC
btn

3 SC

7 SC

2 SC

50 GA

10 GA

51 GA

53 GA

15 SC

Turnbull
(6 guns)

26 PA

21 MA

12 NH

16 MA

11 MA

CARR

74 NY

WILCOX

HUMPHREYS

SICKLES
III CORPS

Broken elements from
Graham's Brigade.

BREWSTER

Seely
(6 guns)

Bigelow makes a valiant stand
buying time for the Federals to
piece together a defensive line.

Trostle

Bigelow
(6 guns)

TILTON

Wheatfield Road

Legion-Cobb's
Legion

Phillips
Legion

24
GA

18 GA

16 GA

8 SC

140
PA

57
NY

66
NY

52
PA

116
PA

28
MA

53
PA

27
CT

145PA

147
NY

KELLY

64
NY

61
NY

148 PA

SEMMES

ANDERSON

WOFFORD

Wheatfield

BARNES

SWEITZER

BURBANK

DAY

5 NH

14 AL

11 AL

10 AL

18 MS

13 MS

17 MS

21 MS

21 MS

8 AL

1 MN

111 NY

126 NY

125 NY

WILLARD

Thompson
(2 guns)

Phillips
(3 guns)

Dow
(4 guns)

39 NY

Watson
(6 guns)

10
US

7
US

2
US

4
US

6
US

3
US

11 US

12 US

17 US

14 US

9 GA

8 GA

11 GA

59 GA

15 GA

20 GA

17 GA

44 AL

2 GA

BENNING

Devil's
Den

Bushman

LEGEND

Confederate	Union
7:00 to 7:30 p.m.	7:00 to 7:30 p.m.
7:30 to 8:00 p.m.	7:30 to 8:00 p.m.

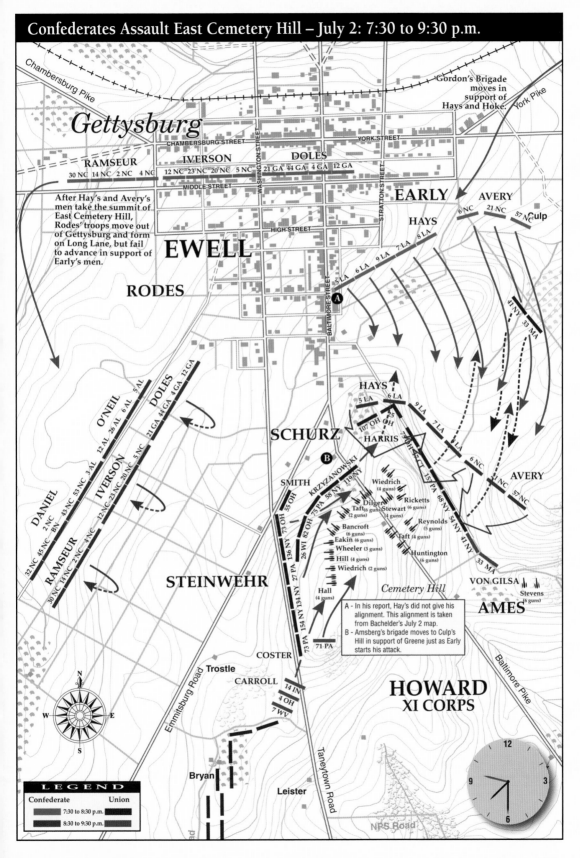

Confederates Assault East Cemetery Hill – July 2: 7:30 to 9:30 p.m.

Chambersburg Pike

York Pike

Gordon's Brigade moves in support of Hays and Hoke.

Gettysburg

CHAMBERSBURG STREET
YORK STREET

RAMSEUR
30 NC 14 NC 2 NC 4 NC

IVERSON
12 NC 23 NC 20 NC 5 NC

DOLES
21 GA 44 GA 4 GA 12 GA

EARLY

AVERY
6 NC   21 NC   57 NC   Culp

MIDDLE STREET

WASHINGTON STREET

STRATTON STREET

After Hay's and Avery's men take the summit of East Cemetery Hill, Rodes' troops move out of Gettysburg and form on Long Lane, but fail to advance in support of Early's men.

HAYS

HIGH STREET

EWELL

5 LA 6 LA 9 LA 7 LA 8 LA

BALTIMORE STREET

A

RODES

5 LA 6 LA

41 NY 33 MA

O'NEIL
5 AL 6 AL 26 AL 12 AL

DOLES
21 GA 44 GA 4 GA 12 GA

HAYS
5 LA   6 LA   9 LA 7 LA 8 LA

IVERSON
12 NC 23 NC 20 NC 5 NC 3 NC

107 OH 25 OH
75 OH

SCHURZ

HARRIS

6 NC

AVERY

21 NC   57 NC

B

DANIEL
2 NC 45 NC 43 BN 53 NC 3 NC

RAMSEUR
30 NC 14 NC 2 NC 4 NC

32 NC

SMITH

55 OH

73 OH

KRZYZANOWSKI

58 NY 119 NY

Wiedrich
(4 guns)

Ricketts
(6 guns)

15 PA 69 NY 54 NY 41 NY

STEINWEHR

82 OH 26 WI 136 NY 75 PA

27 PA 27 PA 134 NY

73 PA

71 PA

Dilger
(6 guns)
Taft
(2 guns)

Stewart
(4 guns)

Bancroft
(6 guns)

Eakin
(6 guns)

Wheeler (3 guns)

Hill (4 guns)

Wiedrich (2 guns)

Reynolds
(5 guns)

Taft (4 guns)

Huntington
(6 guns)

33 MA

VON GILSA
Stevens
(6 guns)

AMES

Hall
(4 guns)

Cemetery Hill

A - In his report, Hay's did not give his alignment. This alignment is taken from Bachelder's July 2 map.
B - Amsberg's brigade moves to Culp's Hill in support of Greene just as Early starts his attack.

COSTER

Trostle

CARROLL

14 IN
4 OH
7 WV

HOWARD
XI CORPS

Emmitsburg Road

Taneytown Road

Baltimore Pike

Bryan

Leister

NPS Road

N
W — E
S

LEGEND

Confederate	Union
7:30 to 8:30 p.m.	
8:30 to 9:30 p.m.	

12
9   3
6

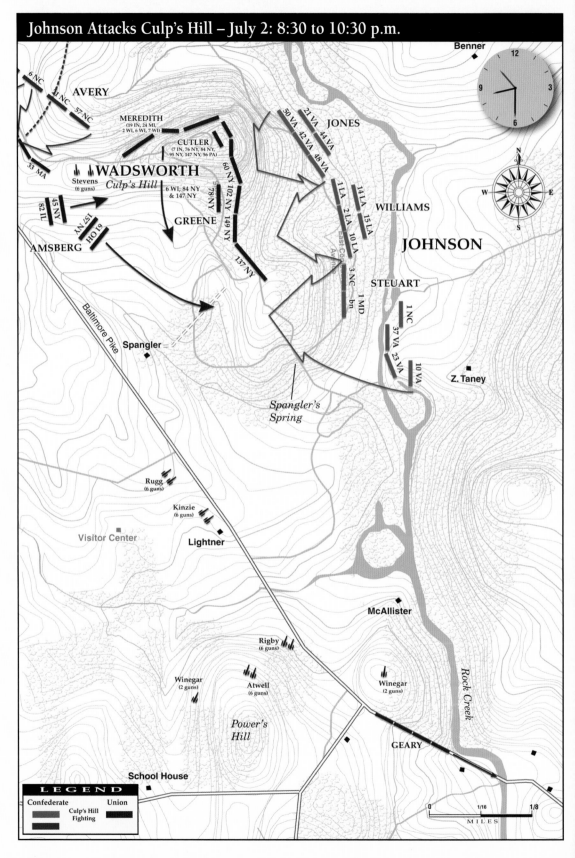

Johnson Attacks Culp's Hill – July 2: 8:30 to 10:30 p.m.

Benner

6 NC
4 NC
57 NC
AVERY

MEREDITH
(19 IN, 24 MI,
2 WI, 6 WI, 7 WI)

CUTLER
(7 IN, 76 NY, 84 NY,
95 NY, 147 NY, 56 PA)

50 VA 21 VA 44 VA
42 VA 48 VA
JONES

33 MA

WADSWORTH
Culp's Hill

Stevens
(6 guns)

6 WI, 84 NY
& 147 NY

60 NY 102 NY
149 NY

78 NY

1 LA 14 LA
2 LA 15 LA
10 LA
WILLIAMS

82 IL
45 NY
157 NY

19 IND

GREENE

137 NY

3 NC
1 MD
bn

JOHNSON

STEUART

AMSBERG

Baltimore Pike

Spangler

East Co...
A Avin...

1 NC
37 VA
23 VA
10 VA

Z. Taney

*Spangler's
Spring*

Rugg
(6 guns)

Kinzie
(6 guns)

Visitor Center

Lightner

McAllister

Rigby
(6 guns)

Winegar
(2 guns)

Atwell
(6 guns)

Winegar
(2 guns)

Rock Creek

*Power's
Hill*

GEARY

School House

LEGEND

Confederate	Union
	Culp's Hill Fighting

0   1/16   1/8
MILES

Johnson Resumes the Attack on Culp's Hill – July 3: 5:00 to 8:00 a.m.

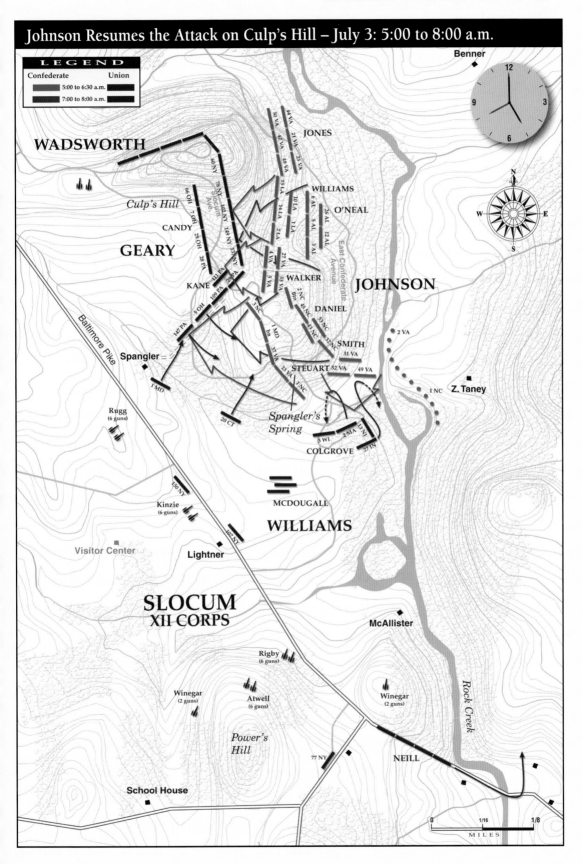

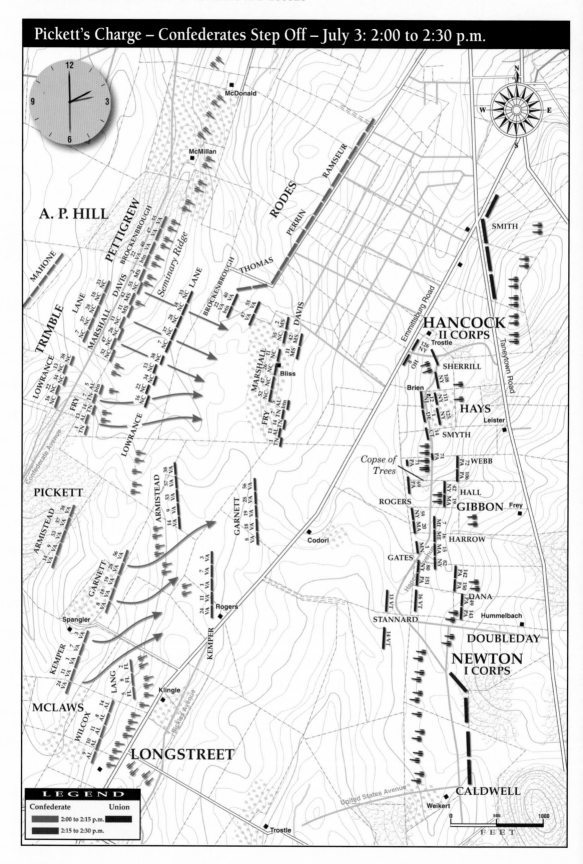

Pickett's Charge – Confederates Step Off – July 3: 2:00 to 2:30 p.m.

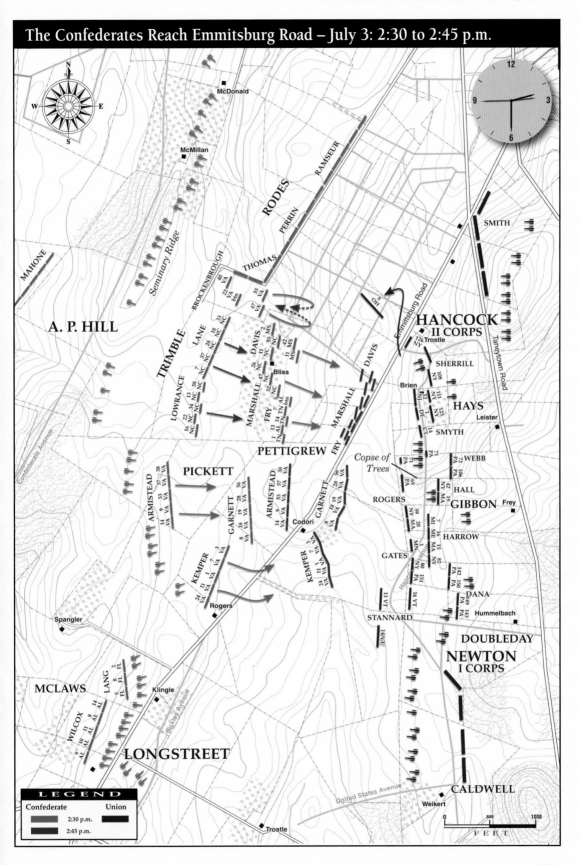

The Confederates Reach Emmitsburg Road – July 3: 2:30 to 2:45 p.m.

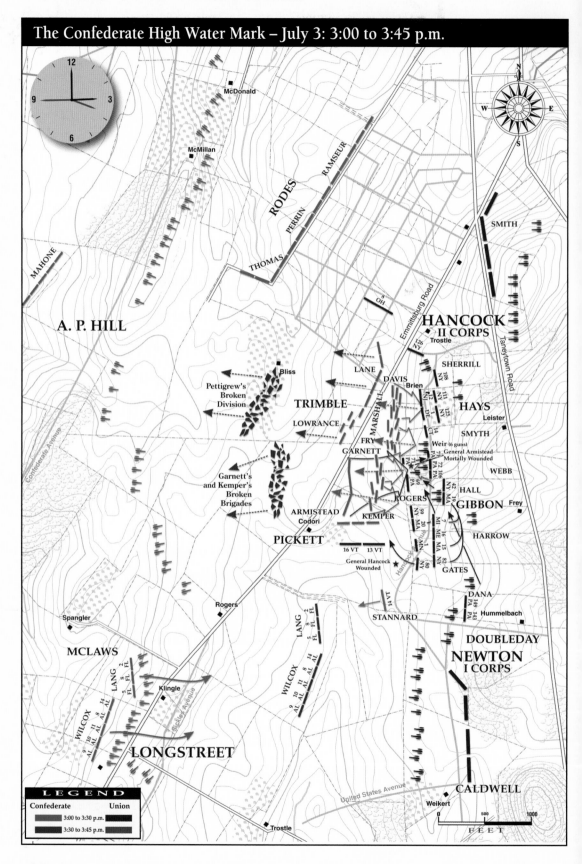

The Confederate High Water Mark – July 3: 3:00 to 3:45 p.m.

McDonald

McMillan

RODES

RAMSEUR

PERRIN

THOMAS

MAHONE

A. P. HILL

SMITH

8
OH

HANCOCK
II CORPS
Trostle

126
NY

SHERRILL

Bliss

LANE

DAVIS

Brien

108
NY

111
NY

Pettigrew's
Broken
Division

TRIMBLE

MARSHALL

DE

125
NY

HAYS

Leister

LOWRANCE

FRY

SMYTH

GARNETT

Weir (6 guns)
General Armistead
Mortally Wounded

WEBB

Garnett's
and Kemper's
Broken
Brigades

72 106
PA PA

69
PA

42 NY
MA 19

HALL

GIBBON   Frey

ARMISTEAD
Codori

ROGERS

KEMPER

59
NY

20
MA

16 7
ME ME
MI MA

1
MN

HARROW

PICKETT

16 VT   13 VT

80
NY

82
NY

GATES

General Hancock
Wounded

Hancock Avenue

DANA

14 VT

STANNARD

149 143
PA PA

Hummelbach

LANG
5 FL FL

Rogers

DOUBLEDAY

Spangler

NEWTON
I CORPS

MCLAWS

LANG
2
8 FL
5 FL

WILCOX
9 14
AL 11 AL
10 AL
AL

Klingle

Sickles Avenue

WILCOX
11 8
AL AL
10 AL
9 AL

LONGSTREET

CALDWELL

United States Avenue

Weikert

LEGEND

Confederate	Union
3:00 to 3:30 p.m.	
3:30 to 3:45 p.m.	

0   500   1000
FEET

Trostle

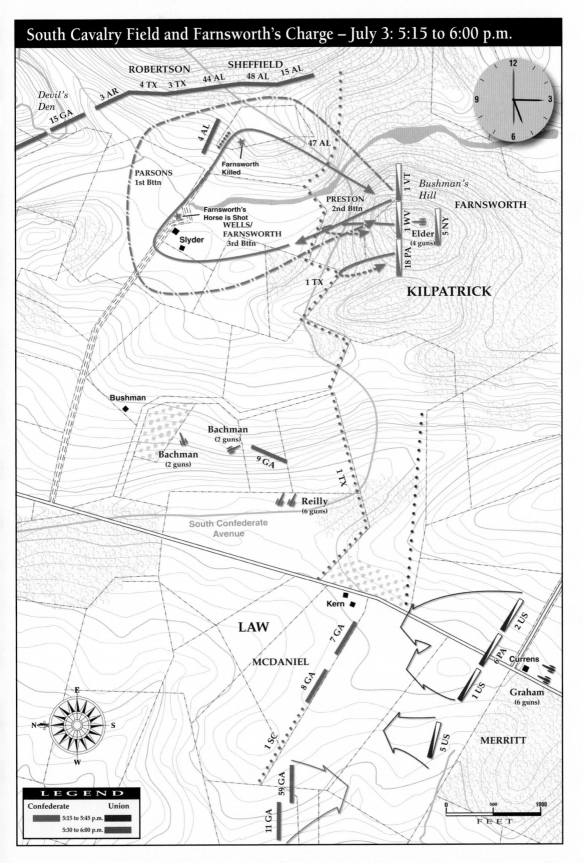

South Cavalry Field and Farnsworth's Charge – July 3: 5:15 to 6:00 p.m.

Devil's Den

15 GA

3 AR

ROBERTSON

4 TX   3 TX

SHEFFIELD

44 AL   48 AL   15 AL

4 AL

47 AL

Farnsworth Killed

PARSONS
1st Bttn

Farnsworth's
Horse is Shot

WELLS/
FARNSWORTH
3rd Bttn

Slyder

PRESTON
2nd Bttn

1 VT

Bushman's
Hill

FARNSWORTH

1 WV

18 PA

Elder
(4 guns)

5 NY

1 TX

KILPATRICK

Bushman

Bachman
(2 guns)

Bachman
(2 guns)

9 GA

1 TX

Reilly
(6 guns)

South Confederate
Avenue

Kern

LAW

MCDANIEL

7 GA

8 GA

1 SC

59 GA

11 GA

2 US

6 PA

Currens

1 US

Graham
(6 guns)

5 US

MERRITT

E

N   S

W

LEGEND

Confederate	Union
5:15 to 5:45 p.m.	
5:30 to 6:00 p.m.	

12
9   3
6

0   500   1000

FEET

FEDERAL

ARMY OF THE POTOMAC

[94,954] (3,179k, 2,124mw, 12,981w, 453w-c, 970c, 3,794m = 23,501) 24.7%
Maj. Gen. George Gordon Meade, Commanding

ARMY HEADQUARTERS

Maj. Gen. Daniel Adams Butterfield, Chief of Staff (w)
Brig. Gen. Gouverneur Kemble Warren, Chief of Engineers (w)
Brig. Gen. Henry Jackson Hunt, Chief of Artillery
Brig. Gen. Seth Williams, Assistant Adjutant General
Lt. Col. Joseph Dickinson, Adjutant General staff (w)
Brig. Gen. Rufus Ingalls, Chief Quartermaster
Col. Edmund Schriver, Inspector General
Dr. Jonathan Letterman, Medical Director
Col. George Henry Sharpe, Bureau of Military Information
Lt. John R. Edie, Acting Chief Ordnance Officer

PROVOST MARSHAL
Brig. Gen. Marsena Rudolph Patrick

PROVOST GUARD
[2,049] (0k, 2m = 2) 0.1%

93rd New York Infantry Battalion
[412] (No losses reported) 0.0%
Col. John S. Crocker

8th United States Infantry (8 Companies)
[est. 290] (No losses reported) 0.0%
Capt. Edwin W. H. Read

1st Pennsylvania Cavalry (7 Companies)
[301] (0k, 2m = 2) 0.7%
Col. John P. Taylor

2nd Pennsylvania Cavalry
[575] (No losses reported) 0.0%
Col. Richard Butler Price

6th Pennsylvania Cavalry, Companies E and I
[50] (No losses reported) 0.0%
Capt. James H. Starr
Company E: Capt. Emlen N. Carpenter
Company I: Capt. James H. Starr

1st, 2nd, 5th, and 6th Regiments
United States Cavalry (detachments)
[421] (No losses reported) 0.0%

HEADQUARTERS GUARDS AND ORDERLIES

Oneida (New York) Cavalry
[49] (No losses reported) 0.0%
Capt. Daniel P. Mann

SIGNAL CORPS
[45] (0k, 2w = 2) 4.4%
Capt. Lemuel B. Norton

ENGINEER BRIGADE
[946] (Not on battlefield – at Beaver Dam Creek,
MD on July 1 then ordered to Washington)
Brig. Gen. Henry Washington Benham

15th New York Engineers Battalion (3 Companies)
Maj. Walter L. Cassin

50th New York Engineers
Col. William H. Pettes

United States Engineer Battalion
Capt. George H. Mendell

I ARMY CORPS

[12,066] (691k, 390mw, 2,822w, 255w-c, 2,061m = 6,189) 51.2%
Maj. Gen. John F. Reynolds (k)
Maj. Gen. Abner Doubleday (w) (relieved from corps command)
Maj. Gen. John Newton

HEADQUARTERS GUARDS AND ORDERLIES

1st Maine Cavalry, Company L
[57] (0k, 2w = 2) 3.5%
Capt. Constantine Taylor

FIRST DIVISION

[3,814] (302k, 140mw, 1,118w, 57w-c, 539m = 2,156) 56.5%
Brig. Gen. James Samuel Wadsworth

FIRST BRIGADE ("IRON BRIGADE")

[1,814] (178k, 72mw, 659w, 39w-c, 235m = 1,183) 65.2%
Brig. Gen. Solomon Meredith (w)
Col. William W. Robinson

19th Indiana
[308] (26k, 7mw, 126w, 2w-c, 52m = 213) 69.2%
Col. Samuel J. Williams

24th Michigan
[496] (71k, 25mw, 186w, 13w-c, 76m = 371) 74.8%
Col. Henry A. Morrow (w)
Capt. Albert M. Edwards

2nd Wisconsin
[302] (29k, 16mw, 135w, 18w-c, 42m = 240) 79.5%
Col. Lucius Fairchild (w)
Maj. John Mansfield (w)
Capt. George H. Otis

6th Wisconsin
[344] (31k, 8mw, 110w, 3w-c, 22m = 174) 50.6%
Lt. Col. Rufus R. Dawes

7th Wisconsin
[364] (21k, 16mw, 102w, 3w-c, 43m = 185) 50.8%
Col. William W. Robinson
Lt. Col. John B. Callis (w-c)
Maj. Mark Finnicum

SECOND BRIGADE

[2,000] (124k, 68mw, 459w, 18w-c, 304m = 973) 48.7%
Brig. Gen. Lysander Cutler

7th Indiana
[434] (1k, 1mw, 4w, 3m = 9) 2.1%
Col. Ira G. Grover

76th New York
[375] (34k, 19mw, 122w, 6w-c, 35m = 216) 57.6%
Maj. Andrew J. Grover (k)
Capt. John E. Cook

84th New York (14th Brooklyn)
[318] (13k, 12mw, 94w, 2w-c, 97m = 218) 68.6%
Col. Edward B. Fowler

95th New York
[241] (9k, 2mw, 63w, 1w-c, 42m = 117) 48.6%
Col. George H. Biddle (w)
Maj. Edward Pye

147th New York
[380] (53k, 27mw, 124w, 9w-c, 71m = 284) 74.7%
Lt. Col. Francis C. Miller (w)
Maj. George Harney

56th Pennsylvania (9 Companies)
[252] (14k, 7mw, 52w, 56m = 129) 51.2%
Col. J. William Hofmann

SECOND DIVISION

[2,994] (117k, 76mw, 531w, 60w-c, 948m = 1,732) 57.8%
Brig. Gen. John Cleveland Robinson

FIRST BRIGADE

[1,547] (66k, 53mw, 275w, 47w-c, 601m = 1,042) 67.4%
Brig. Gen. Gabriel Rene Paul (w)
Col. Samuel H. Leonard (w)
Col. Adrian R. Root (w-c)
Col. Peter Lyle
Col. Richard Coulter (w) (final command of brigade)

16th Maine
[298] (16k, 9mw, 46w, 13w-c, 157m = 241) 80.9%
Col. Charles W. Tilden (c)
Maj. Archibald D. Leavitt

13th Massachusetts
[298] (12k, 12mw, 60w, 7w-c, 105m = 196) 65.8%
Col. Samuel H. Leonard (w)
Lt. Col. N. Walter Batchelder

94th New York
[411] (11k, 6mw, 38w, 21w-c, 164m = 240) 58.4%
Col. Adrian R. Root (w-c)
Maj. Samuel A. Moffett

104th New York
[285] (16k, 16mw, 73w, 5w-c, 84m = 194) 68.1%
Col. Gilbert G. Prey

107th Pennsylvania
[255] (11k, 10mw, 58w, 1w-c, 91m = 171) 67.1%
Lt. Col. James MacThomson (w)
Capt. Emanuel D. Roath

SECOND BRIGADE
[1,447] (51k, 23mw, 256w, 13w-c, 347m = 690) 47.7%
Brig. Gen. Henry Baxter

12th Massachusetts
[261] (8k, 5mw, 45w, 3w-c, 66m = 127) 48.7%
Col. James L. Bates (w)
Lt. Col. David Allen, Jr.

83rd New York (9th New York Militia)
[199] (6k, 1mw, 21w, 2w-c, 62m = 92) 46.2%
Lt. Col. Joseph A. Moesch

97th New York
[236] (15k, 4mw, 34w, 5w-c, 77m = 135) 57.2%
Col. Charles Wheelock (w-c, escaped)
Maj. Charles Northrup

11th Pennsylvania
(Transferred to First Brigade evening of July 1)
[270] (8k, 5mw, 62w, 3w-c, 58m = 136) 50.4%
Col. Richard Coulter (w)
Capt. Benjamin F. Haines (w)
Capt. John B. Overmyer

88th Pennsylvania
[273] (6k, 4mw, 52w, 48m = 110) 40.3%
Maj. Benezet F. Foust (w)
Capt. Edmund A. Mass (c)
Capt. Henry Whiteside

90th Pennsylvania
[208] (8k, 4mw, 42w, 36m = 90) 43.3%
Col. Peter Lyle (final command of regiment after
temporarily commanding First Brigade)
Maj. Alfred J. Sellers

THIRD DIVISION
[4,612] (265k, 168mw, 1,091w, 137w-c, 534m = 2,195) 47.6%
Maj. Gen. Abner Doubleday (w) (final command after being relieved of corps command)
Brig. Gen. Thomas Algeo Rowley

FIRST BRIGADE
[1,353] (124k, 69mw, 421w, 117w-c, 233m = 964) 71.2%
Col. Chapman Biddle (w) (final command of brigade)
Brig. Gen. Thomas Algeo Rowley

80th New York (20th New York Militia)
[287] (31k, 7mw, 88w, 22w-c, 32m = 180) 62.7%
Col. Theodore B. Gates

121st Pennsylvania
[263] (18k, 11mw, 89w, 5w-c, 51m = 174) 66.2%
Col. Chapman Biddle (w)
Maj. Alexander Biddle

142nd Pennsylvania
[336] (22k, 24mw, 105w, 4w-c, 68m = 223) 66.4%
Col. Robert P. Cummins (mw)
Lt. Col. A. B. McCalmont

151st Pennsylvania
[467] (53k, 27mw, 139w, 86w-c, 82m = 387) 82.9%
Lt. Col. George F. McFarland (w)
Capt. Walter L. Owens
Col. Harrison Allen

SECOND BRIGADE
[1,315] (100k, 63mw, 433w, 20w-c, 239m = 855) 65.0%
Col. Roy Stone (w)
Col. Langhorne Wister (w)
Col. Edmund L. Dana

143rd Pennsylvania
[465] (17k, 23mw, 106w, 105m = 251) 54.0%
Col. Edmund L. Dana
Lt. Col. John D. Musser

149th Pennsylvania
[450] (51k, 16mw, 181w, 5w-c, 59m = 312) 69.3%
Lt. Col. Walton Dwight (w)
Capt. James Glenn

150th Pennsylvania
[400] (32k, 24mw, 146w, 15w-c, 75m = 292) 73.0%
Col. Langhorne Wister (w)
Lt. Col. Henry S. Huidekoper (w)
Capt. Cornelius C. Widdis

THIRD BRIGADE
[1,944] (41k, 36mw, 237w, 62m = 376) 19.3%
Brig. Gen. George Jerrison Stannard (w)
Col. Francis V. Randall

12th Vermont
(detached as train guard)
Col. Asa P. Blunt

13th Vermont
[636] (9k, 13mw, 85w, 24m = 131) 20.6%
Col. Francis V. Randall
Lt. Col. William D. Munson (final command of regiment)
Maj. Joseph J. Boynton

14th Vermont
[647] (17k, 13mw, 70w, 18m = 118) 18.2%
Col. William T. Nichols

15th Vermont
(detached as train guard)
Col. Redfield Proctor

16th Vermont
[661] (15k, 10mw, 82w, 20m = 127) 19.2%
Col. Wheelock G. Veazey

ARTILLERY BRIGADE

[589] (7k, 6mw, 80w, 1w-c, 10m = 104) 17.7%
Col. Charles Sheils Wainright

**2nd Maine Light Artillery, Battery B
(Six 3-inch Ordnance Rifles)**
[117] (0k, 17w, 1m = 18) 15.4%
Capt. James A. Hall

**5th Maine Light Artillery,
Battery E (Six Napoleons)**
[119] (3k, 1mw, 12w, 6m = 22) 18.5%
Capt. Greenleaf T. Stevens (w)
Lt. Edward N. Whittier

**1st New York Light Artillery, Batteries L and E
(Six 3-inch Ordnance Rifles)**
[124] (1k, 1mw, 14w = 16) 12.9%
Capt. Gilbert H. Reynolds (w)
Lt. George Breck

**1st Pennsylvania Light Artillery, Battery B
(Four 3-inch Ordnance Rifles)**
[106] (1k, 2mw, 9w = 12) 11.3%
Capt. James H. Cooper

**4th United States Light Artillery,
Battery B (Six Napoleons)**
[123] (2k, 2mw, 28w, 1w-c, 3m = 36) 29.3%
Lt. James Stewart

II ARMY CORPS

[11,306] (725k, 509mw, 2,930w, 40w-c, 284m = 4,488) 40.7%
Maj. Gen. Winfield Scott Hancock (w)
Brig. Gen. John Gibbon (w)
Brig. Gen. John C. Caldwell
Brig. Gen. William Hays

HEADQUARTERS GUARDS AND ORDERLIES

6th New York Cavalry
[64] (0k, 4w, 3m = 7) 10.9%

Company D
[34] (0k, 3w, 3m = 6) 17.6%

Company K
[30] (0k, 1w = 1) 3.3%
Lt. Henry A. Wetmore

FIRST DIVISION

[3,201] (183k, 129mw, 820w, 24w-c, 148m = 1,304) 40.7%
Brig. Gen. John C. Caldwell

PROVOST GUARD

Lt. William M. Hobart (116th Pennsylvania), Provost Marshal
**116th Pennsylvania, Company B
53rd Pennsylvania, Companies A, B, and K**

FIRST BRIGADE

[850] (60k, 31mw, 244w, 2w-c, 7m = 344) 40.5%
Col. Edward Everett Cross (mw)
Col. H. Boyd McKeen

5th New Hampshire
[179] (26k, 7mw, 50w = 83) 46.4%
Lt. Col. Charles E. Hapgood

61st New York
[104] (9k, 7mw, 46w = 62) 59.6%
Lt. Col. K. Oscar Broady

81st Pennsylvania
[175] (9k, 3mw, 46w, 4m = 62) 35.4%
Col. H. Boyd McKeen
Lt. Col. Amos Stroh

148th Pennsylvania
[392] (16k, 14mw, 102w, 2w-c, 3m = 137) 34.9%
Lt. Col. Robert McFarlane

SECOND BRIGADE ("IRISH BRIGADE")

[530] (21k, 21mw, 122w, 9w-c, 48m = 221) 41.7%
Col. Patrick Kelly

28th Massachusetts
[224] (10k, 3mw, 58w, 5w-c, 30m = 106) 47.3%
Col. Richard Byrnes

63rd New York (Companies A and B)
[75] (4k, 4mw, 8w, 1w-c, 5m = 22) 29.3%
Lt. Col. Richard C. Bentley (w)
Capt. Thomas Touhy

69th New York (Companies A and B)
[75] (2k, 2mw, 19w, 1w-c, 4m = 28) 37.3%
Capt. Richard Moroney (w)
Lt. James J. Smith

88th New York (Companies A and B)
[90] (5k, 1mw, 17w, 1w-c, 4m = 28) 31.1%
Capt. Denis F. Burke

116th Pennsylvania (Companies A, B, C, and D)
[66] (0k, 11mw, 20w, 1w-c, 5m = 37) 56.1%
Maj. St. Clair Augustine Mulholland

Third Brigade

[971] (48k, 29mw, 212w, 10w-c, 51m = 350) 36.0%
Brig. Gen. Samuel K. Zook (mw)
Lt. Col. John Fraser

52nd New York
[134] (2k, 3mw, 23w, 1w-c, 8m = 37) 27.6%
Lt. Col. Charles G. Freudenberg (w)
Capt. William Scherrer

57th New York
[175] (3k, 2mw, 26w, 3w-c, 1m = 35) 20.0%
Lt. Col. Alford B. Chapman

66th New York
[147] (4k, 3mw, 31w, 10m = 48) 32.7%
Col. Orlando H. Morris (w)
Lt. Col. John S. Hammell (w)
Maj. Peter Nelson

140th Pennsylvania
[515] (39k, 21mw, 132w, 6w-c, 32m = 230) 44.7%
Col. Richard P. Roberts (k)
Lt. Col. John Fraser

Fourth Brigade

[850] (54k, 48mw, 242w, 3w-c, 42m = 389) 45.8%
Col. John Rutter Brooke (w)

27th Connecticut (2 Companies, remnants of 8 Companies)
[75] (12k, 9mw, 13w, 2w-c, 3m = 39) 52.0%
Lt. Col. Henry Czar Merwin (k)
Maj. James H. Coburn

2nd Delaware
[234] (9k, 8mw, 55w, 12m = 84) 35.9%
Col. William P. Baily
Capt. Charles H. Christman

64th New York
[204] (14k, 10mw, 60w, 18m = 102) 50.0%
Col. Daniel G. Bingham (w)
Maj. Leman W. Bradley

53rd Pennsylvania
[135] (10k, 4mw, 62w, 1w-c, 2m = 79) 58.5%
Lt. Col. Richard McMichael

145th Pennsylvania
[202] (9k, 17mw, 52w, 7m = 85) 42.1%
Col. Hiram L. Brown (w)
Capt. John W. Reynolds (w)
Capt. Moses W. Oliver

SECOND DIVISION

[3,518] (305k, 213mw, 1,097w, 9w-c, 78m = 1,702) 48.4%
Brig. Gen. John Oliver Gibbon (w)
Brig. Gen. William Harrow

Provost Guard

1st Minnesota, Company C

First Brigade

[1,343] (124k, 110mw, 518w, 3w-c, 38m = 794) 60.4%
Brig. Gen. William Harrow
Col. Francis E. Heath

19th Maine
[439] (29k, 37mw, 145w = 211) 48.1%
Col. Francis E. Heath
Lt. Col. Henry W. Cunningham

15th Massachusetts
[239] (21k, 14mw, 80w, 1w-c, 28m = 144) 60.3%
Col. George H. Ward (mw)
Lt. Col. George C. Joslin

1st Minnesota
[297] (36k, 39mw, 161w, 1w-c = 237) 79.8%
2nd Company Minnesota Sharpshooters (attached)
[33] (1k, 2w = 3) 9.1%
Col. William Colvill, Jr. (w)
Capt. Nathan S. Messick (k)
Capt. Henry C. Coates

82nd New York (2nd New York Militia)
[335] (38k, 20mw, 130w, 1w-c, 10m = 199) 59.4%
Lt. Col. James Huston (k)
Capt. John Darrow

Second Brigade

[1,205] (100k, 56mw, 314w, 2w-c, 36m = 508) 42.2%
Brig. Gen. Alexander Stewart Webb (w)

69th Pennsylvania
[284] (40k, 15mw, 73w, 16m = 144) 50.7%
Col. Dennis O'Kane (mw)
Capt. William Davis

71st Pennsylvania
[261] (17k, 8mw, 57w, 1w-c, 19m = 102) 39.1%
Col. Richard Penn Smith

72nd Pennsylvania
[380] (39k, 26mw, 132w = 197) 51.8%
Col. De Witt C. Baxter (w)
Lt. Col. Theodore Hesser

106th Pennsylvania
[280] (4k, 7mw, 52w, 1w-c, 1m = 65) 23.2%
Lt. Col. William L. Curry

THIRD BRIGADE
[970] (80k, 47mw, 265w, 4w-c, 4m = 400) 41.2%
Col. Norman Jonathan Hall

19th Massachusetts
[163] (10k, 5mw, 65w, 1m = 81) 49.7%
Col. Arthur F. Devereux

20th Massachusetts
[243] (30k, 13mw, 80w, 3w-c, 2m = 128) 52.7%
Col. Paul J. Revere (mw)
Lt. Col. George N. Macy (w)
Capt. Henry L. Abbott

7th Michigan
[165] (19k, 6mw, 42w = 67) 40.6%
Lt. Col. Amos E. Steele, Jr. (k)
Maj. Sylvanus W. Curtis

42nd New York
[197] (15k, 13mw, 47w, 1w-c = 76) 38.6%
Col. James E. Mallon

59th New York (4 Companies)
[152] (4k, 8mw, 27w, 1m = 40) 26.3%
Lt. Col. Max A. Thoman (mw)
Capt. William McFadden

UNATTACHED (OPERATED WITH BRIGADE)

1st Massachusetts Sharpshooters
[50] (2k, 2mw, 4w = 8) 16.0%
Capt. William Plumer
Lt. Emerson L. Bicknell

THIRD DIVISION
[3,506] (209k, 155mw, 890w, 7w-c, 50m = 1,311) 37.4%
Brig. Gen. Alexander Hays

PROVOST GUARD

10th New York Battalion (4 Companies)
[82] (1k, 1mw, 2w = 4) 4.9%
Maj. George F. Hopper

FIRST BRIGADE
[933] (29k, 29mw, 147w, 8m = 213) 22.8%
Col. Samuel Sprigg Carroll

14th Indiana
[191] (5k, 4mw, 22w = 31) 16.2%
Col. John Coons

4th Ohio
[299] (8k, 4mw, 15w, 6m = 33) 11.0%
Lt. Col. Leonard W. Carpenter

8th Ohio
[209] (12k, 16mw, 76w, 1m = 105) 50.2%
Lt. Col. Franklin Sawyer

7th West Virginia
[234] (4k, 5mw, 34w, 1m = 44) 18.8%
Lt. Col. Jonathan H. Lockwood

SECOND BRIGADE
[1,067] (48k, 27mw, 270w, 1w-c, 26m = 372) 34.9%
Col. Thomas Alfred Smyth (w)
Lt. Col. Francis E. Pierce

14th Connecticut
[172] (8k, 6mw, 50w, 1w-c, 4m = 69) 40.1%
Maj. Theodore G. Ellis

1st Delaware
[251] (8k, 7mw, 49w, 13m = 77) 30.7%
Lt. Col. Edward P. Harris
Capt. Thomas B. Hizar (w)
Lt. William Smith (mw)
Lt. John T. Dent

12th New Jersey
[444] (16k, 11mw, 81w, 9m = 117) 26.4%
Maj. John T. Hill

108th New York
[200] (16k, 3mw, 90w = 109) 54.5%
Lt. Col. Francis E. Pierce

THIRD BRIGADE
[1,506] (132k, 99mw, 473w, 6w-c, 16m = 726) 48.2%
Col. George Lamb Willard (k)
Col. Eliakim Sherrill (mw)
Col. Clinton D. MacDougall (w)
Lt. Col. James L. Bull

39th New York (4 Companies)
[269] (11k, 14mw, 68w, 1w-c = 94) 34.9%
Maj. Hugo Hildebrandt (w)

111th New York
[390] (54k, 46mw, 145w, 1w-c, 4m = 250) 64.1%
Col. Clinton D. MacDougall (w)
Lt. Col. Isaac M. Lusk (w)
Capt. Aaron P. Seeley

125th New York
[392] (28k, 13mw, 98w, 1w-c, 8m = 148) 37.8%
Lt. Col. Levin Crandell

126th New York
[455] (39k, 26mw, 162w, 3w-c, 4m = 234) 51.4%
Col. Eliakim Sherrill (mw)
Lt. Col. James L. Bull
Capt. Morris Brown

ARTILLERY BRIGADE
[601] (27k, 11mw, 113w, 2m = 153) 25.5%
Capt. John Gardner Hazard

**1st New York Light Artillery, Battery B and 14th
New York Light Artillery (Four 10-Pounder Parrotts)**
[117] (11k, 15w = 26) 22.2%
Lt. Albert S. Sheldon (w)
Capt. James McKay Rorty (k)
Lt. Robert E. Rogers

**1st Rhode Island Light Artillery, Battery A
(Six 3-inch Ordnance Rifles)**
[117] (3k, 2mw, 29w = 34) 29.1%
Capt. William A. Arnold

**1st Rhode Island Light Artillery, Battery B
(Six 3-inch Ordnance Rifles)**
[129] (5k, 2mw, 18w, 2m = 27) 20.9%
Lt. T. Fred Brown (w)
Lt. Walter S. Perrin

**1st United States Light Artillery,
Battery I (Six Napoleons)**
[112] (2k, 3mw, 20w = 25) 22.3%
Lt. George A. Woodruff (mw)
Lt. Tully McCrea

**4th United States Light Artillery, Battery A
(Six 3-inch Ordnance Rifles)**
[126] (6k, 4mw, 31w = 41) 32.5%
Lt. Alonzo H. Cushing (k)
Sgt. Frederick Fuger

III ARMY CORPS

[10,750] (618k, 447mw, 2,659w, 53w-c, 546m = 4,323) 40.2%
Maj. Gen. Daniel Edgar Sickles (w)
Maj. Gen. David Bell Birney

HEADQUARTERS GUARD AND ORDERLIES

6th New York Cavalry, Company A
[36] (1k = 1) 2.8%

9th New York Cavalry, Companies F and K (attached July 2 only)
[125] (Losses included in regimental totals)
Capt. Timothy Hanley

FIRST DIVISION

[5,082] (279k, 227mw, 1,196w, 31w-c, 328m = 2,061) 40.6%
Maj. Gen. David Bell Birney
Brig. Gen. John Henry Hobart Ward

FIRST BRIGADE

[1,515] (80k, 75mw, 435w, 7w-c, 137m = 734) 48.4%
Brig. Gen. Charles Kinnaird Graham (w-c)
Col. Andrew H. Tippin

57th Pennsylvania (8 Companies)
[207] (12k, 6mw, 41w, 2w-c, 54m = 115) 55.6%
Col. Peter Sides (w)
Capt. Alanson H. Nelson

63rd Pennsylvania
[246] (1k, 2mw, 29w, 3m = 35) 14.2%
Maj. John A. Danks

68th Pennsylvania
[320] (16k, 30mw, 94w, 1w-c, 10m = 151) 47.2%
Col. Andrew H. Tippin
Capt. Milton S. Davis

105th Pennsylvania
[274] (12k, 8mw, 106w, 1w-c, 4m = 131) 47.8%
Col. Calvin A. Craig

114th Pennsylvania (Collis' Zouaves)
[259] (13k, 7mw, 74w, 1w-c, 54m = 149) 57.5%
Lt. Col. Frederick F. Cavada (c)
Capt. Edward R. Bowen

141st Pennsylvania
[209] (26k, 22mw, 91w, 2w-c, 12m = 153) 73.2%
Col. Henry J. Madill

SECOND BRIGADE

[2,180] (127k, 84mw, 414w, 21w-c, 170m = 816) 37.4%
Brig. Gen. John Henry Hobart Ward
Col. Hiram Berdan

20th Indiana
[400] (30k, 10mw, 98w, 22m = 160) 40.0%
Col. John Wheeler (k)
Lt. Col. William C. L. Taylor (w)

3rd Maine
[210] (20k, 11mw, 52w, 3w-c, 40m = 126) 60.0%
Col. Moses B. Lakeman

4th Maine
[287] (10k, 14mw, 47w, 7w-c, 67m = 145) 50.5%
Col. Elijah Walker (w)
Capt. Edwin Libby

86th New York
[287] (10k, 10mw, 44w, 1w-c, 5m = 70) 24.4%
Lt. Col. Benjamin L. Higgins

124th New York
[238] (28k, 7mw, 58w, 2w-c, 2m = 97) 40.8%
Col. Augustus Van Horne Ellis (k)
Lt. Col. Francis Markoe Cummins (w)
(final command of regiment)
Capt. Charles Weygant

99th Pennsylvania
[277] (20k, 24mw, 60w, 3w-c, 7m = 114) 41.2%
Maj. John W. Moore

1st United States Sharpshooters
[312] (5k, 5mw, 34w, 3w-c, 10m = 57) 18.3%
Col. Hiram Berdan
Lt. Col. Casper Trepp

2nd United States Sharpshooters (8 Companies)
[169] (4k, 3mw, 21w, 2w-c, 17m = 47) 27.8%
Maj. Homer R. Stoughton

THIRD BRIGADE
[1,387] (72k, 68mw, 347w, 3w-c, 21m = 511) 36.8%
Col. Philippe Regis Denis de Keredern de Trobriand

17th Maine
[350] (19k, 22mw, 93w, 1w-c, 1m = 136) 38.9%
Lt. Col. Charles B. Merrill

3rd Michigan
[238] (6k, 6mw, 25w, 6m = 43) 18.1%
Col. Byron R. Pierce (w)
Lt. Col. Edwin S. Pierce

5th Michigan
[216] (16k, 14mw, 74w, 1w-c, 7m = 112) 51.9%
Lt. Col. John Pulford (w)
Maj. Salmon S. Matthews (w)
Lt. Charles T. Bissell

40th New York
[431] (23k, 16mw, 121w, 1w-c, 7m = 168) 39.0%
Col. Thomas W. Egan (w)

110th Pennsylvania (6 Companies)
[152] (8k, 10mw, 34w = 52) 34.2%
Lt. Col. David M. Jones (w)
Maj. Isaac Rogers

SECOND DIVISION
[4,913] (330k, 213mw, 1,390w, 21w-c, 201m = 2,155) 43.9%
Brig. Gen. Andrew Atkinson Humphreys

FIRST BRIGADE
[1,716] (136k, 83mw, 536w, 3w-c, 101m = 859) 50.1%
Brig. Gen. Joseph Bradford Carr

1st Massachusetts
[321] (24k, 11mw, 77w, 32m = 144) 44.9%
Lt. Col. Clark B. Baldwin (w)

11th Massachusetts
[286] (24k, 14mw, 91w, 17m = 146) 51.0%
Lt. Col. Porter D. Tripp

16th Massachusetts
[245] (16k, 4mw, 50w, 1w-c, 21m = 92) 37.6%
Lt. Col. Waldo Merriam (w)
Capt. Matthew Donovan

12th New Hampshire
[224] (15k, 11mw, 60w, 1w-c, 19m = 106) 47.3%
Capt. John F. Langley

11th New Jersey
[275] (23k, 15mw, 112w, 6m = 156) 56.7%
Col. Robert McAllister (w)
Capt. Luther Martin (w)
Lt. John Schoonover (w) (final command of regiment)
Capt. William H. Lloyd (w)
Capt. Samuel T. Sleeper

26th Pennsylvania
[365] (34k, 28mw, 146w, 1w-c, 6m = 215) 58.9%
Maj. Robert L. Bodine

84th Pennsylvania
(detached, guarding Corps trains)
Lt. Col. Milton Opp

SECOND BRIGADE
[1,834] (129k, 75mw, 537w, 4w-c, 37m = 782) 42.6%
Col. William Root Brewster

70th New York
[288] (24k, 18mw, 79w = 121) 42.0%
Col. J. Egbert Farnum

71st New York
[243] (12k, 5mw, 66w, 9m = 92) 37.9%
Col. Henry L. Potter (w)

72nd New York
[305] (7k, 8mw, 85w, 1w-c, 10m = 111) 36.4%
Col. John S. Austin (w)
Lt. Col. John Leonard

73rd New York
[349] (34k, 25mw, 88w, 1w-c, 8m = 156) 44.7%
Maj. Michael W. Burns

74th New York
[266] (12k, 10mw, 68w, 2w-c = 92) 34.6%
Lt. Col. Thomas Holt

120th New York
[383] (40k, 9mw, 151w, 10m = 210) 54.8%
Lt. Col. Cornelius D. Westbrook (w)
Maj. John R. Tappen

THIRD BRIGADE
[1,363] (65k, 55mw, 317w, 14w-c, 63m = 514) 37.7%
Col. George Childs Burling

2nd New Hampshire
[354] (23k, 24mw, 104w, 12w-c, 30m = 193) 54.5%
Col. Edward L. Bailey

5th New Jersey
[206] (15k, 7mw, 59w, 1w-c, 11m = 93) 45.1%
Col. William J. Sewell (w)
Capt. Thomas C. Godfrey
Capt. Henry H. Woolsey (w) (final command of regiment)

6th New Jersey
[207] (2k, 4mw, 29w, 6m = 41) 19.8%
Lt. Col. Stephen R. Gilkyson

7th New Jersey
[275] (14k, 10mw, 78w, 12m = 114) 41.5%
Col. Louis R. Francine (mw)
Maj. Frederick Cooper

8th New Jersey
[170] (8k, 7mw, 31w, 1w-c, 1m = 48) 28.2%
Col. John Ramsey (w)
Capt. John G. Langston

115th Pennsylvania
[151] (3k, 3mw, 16w, 3m = 25) 16.6%
Maj. John P. Dunne

ARTILLERY BRIGADE
[594] (8k, 7mw, 73w, 1w-c, 17m = 106) 17.8%
Capt. George E. Randolph (w)
Capt. A. Judson Clark

1st New Jersey Light Artillery, 2nd Battery (B)
(Six 10-pounder Parrotts)
[131] (2k, 1mw, 14w, 3m = 20) 15.3%
Capt. A. Judson Clark
Lt. Robert Sims

1st New York Light Artillery,
Battery D (Six Napoleons)
[116] (0k, 1mw, 9w, 8m = 18) 15.5%
Capt. George B. Winslow

New York Light Artillery, 4th Battery
(Six 10-pounder Parrotts)
[126] (1k, 1mw, 10w, 1m = 13) 10.3%
Capt. James E. Smith

1st Rhode Island Light Artillery,
Battery E (Six Napoleons)
[108] (2k, 3mw, 23w, 1w-c, 1m = 30) 27.8%
Lt. John K. Bucklyn (w)
Lt. Benjamin Freeborn (w)

4th United States Light Artillery,
Battery K (Six Napoleons)
[113] (3k, 1mw, 17w, 4m = 25) 22.1%
Lt. Francis W. Seeley (w)
Lt. Robert James
Maj. Isaac Rogers

V ARMY CORPS
[10,917] (347k, 261mw, 1,422w, 14w-c, 5c, 173m = 2,222) 20.4%
Maj. Gen. George Sykes

PROVOST GUARD
12th New York Infantry (Companies D and E)
[117] (No losses reported) 0.0%
Capt. Henry W. Rider

HEADQUARTERS GUARD AND ORDERLIES
17th Pennsylvania Cavalry (Companies D and H)
[95] (No losses reported) 0.0%
Capt. William Thompson

FIRST DIVISION
[3,411] (156k, 98mw, 544w, 12w-c, 130m = 940) 27.6%
Brig. Gen. James Barnes (w)
Brig. Gen. Charles Griffin

FIRST BRIGADE
[654] (13k, 14mw, 79w, 1w-c, 17m = 124) 19.0%
Col. William Stowell Tilton

18th Massachusetts
[139] (1k, 1mw, 14w, 1w-c, 3m = 20) 14.4%
Col. Joseph Hayes (w)

22nd Massachusetts, 2nd Company Massachusetts
Sharpshooters (attached to regiment)
[137] (3k, 8mw, 23w, 3m = 37) 27.0%
Lt. Col. Thomas Sherwin, Jr.

1st Michigan
[145] (5k, 3mw, 33w, 6m = 47) 32.4%
Col. Ira C. Abbott (w)
Lt. Col. William A. Throop (w)

118th Pennsylvania
[233] (4k, 2mw, 9w, 5m = 20) 8.6%
Lt. Col. James Gwyn

SECOND BRIGADE
[1,422] (69k, 35mw, 236w, 9w-c, 103m = 452) 31.8%
Col. Jacob Bowman Sweitzer

9th Massachusetts (8 Companies)
[412] (2k, 11w, 2m = 15) 3.6%
Col. Patrick R. Guiney

32nd Massachusetts (9 Companies)
[242] (10k, 12mw, 62w, 1w-c, 3m = 88) 36.4%
Col. George Lincoln Prescott

4th Michigan
[342] (30k, 13mw, 61w, 7w-c, 67m = 178) 52.0%
Col. Harrison H. Jeffords (mw)
Lt. Col. George W. Lumbard

62nd Pennsylvania
[426] (27k, 10mw, 102w, 1w-c, 31m = 171) 40.1%
Lt. Col. James C. Hull

THIRD BRIGADE
[1,335] (74k, 49mw, 229w, 2w-c, 10m = 364) 27.3%
Col. Strong Vincent (mw)
Col. James C. Rice

20th Maine
[386] (20k, 23mw, 88w, 1w-c, 4m = 136) 35.2%
Col. Joshua Lawrence Chamberlain

**16th Michigan, 1st Company Michigan
Sharpshooters (attached to regiment)**
[263] (21k, 5mw, 32w, 4m = 62) 23.6%
Lt. Col. Norval E. Welch

44th New York
[391] (26k, 11mw, 74w, 1w-c, 2m = 114) 29.2%
Col. James C. Rice
Lt. Col. Freeman Conner

83rd Pennsylvania
[295] (7k, 10mw, 35w = 52) 17.6%
Capt. Orpheus S. Woodward

SECOND DIVISION
[4,003] (163k, 133mw, 677w, 40m = 1,013) 25.3%
Brig. Gen. Romeyn Beck Ayers

FIRST BRIGADE
[1,551] (51k, 56mw, 261w, 15m = 383) 24.7%
Col. Hannibal Day

3rd United States (6 Companies)
[300] (15k, 9mw, 50w = 74) 24.7%
Capt. Henry W. Freedley
Capt. Richard G. Lay

4th United States (4 Companies)
[173] (10k, 7mw, 23w = 40) 23.1%
Capt. Julius W. Adams, Jr.

6th United States (5 Companies)
[150] (4k, 7mw, 33w = 44) 29.3%
Capt. Levi C. Bootes

12th United States (8 Companies)
[415] (7k, 7mw, 67w, 12m = 93) 22.4%
Capt. Thomas S. Dunn

14th United States (8 Companies)
[513] (15k, 26mw, 88w, 3m = 132) 25.7%
Maj. Grotius R. Giddings

SECOND BRIGADE
[952] (75k, 58mw, 288w, 23m = 444) 46.6%
Col. Sidney Burbank

2nd United States (6 Companies)
[197] (6k, 10mw, 48w, 4m = 68) 34.5%
Maj. Arthur T. Lee (w)
Capt. Samuel A. McKee

7th United States (4 Companies)
[116] (11k, 9mw, 31w, 2m = 53) 45.7%
Capt. David P. Hancock

10th United States (3 Companies)
[93] (18k, 3mw, 26w, 3m = 50) 53.8%
Capt. William Clinton

11th United States (6 Companies)
[286] (16k, 22mw, 76w, 8m = 122) 42.7%
Maj. DeLancey Floyd-Jones

17th United States (7 Companies)
[260] (24k, 14mw, 107w, 6m = 151) 58.1%
Lt. Col. J. Durell Greene

THIRD BRIGADE
[1,500] (37k, 19mw, 128w, 2m = 186) 12.4%
Brig. Gen. Stephen Hinsdale Weed (k)
Col. Kenner Garrard

140th New York
[453] (26k, 14mw, 76w, 1m = 117) 25.8%
Col. Patrick H. O'Rorke (k)
Lt. Col. Louis Ernst

146th New York
[460] (2k, 3mw, 18w = 23) 5.0%
Col. Kenner Garrard
Lt. Col. David T. Jenkins

91st Pennsylvania
[222] (3k, 2mw, 17w = 22) 9.9%
Lt. Col. Joseph H. Sinex

155th Pennsylvania
[365] (6k, 17w, 1m = 24) 6.6%
Lt. Col. John H. Cain

THIRD DIVISION
[2,862] (25k, 22mw, 172w, 1w-c, 3c, 2m = 225) 7.9%
Brig. Gen. Samuel Wylie Crawford

FIRST BRIGADE
[1,245] (20k, 19mw, 124w, 1w-c, 1c, 2m = 167) 13.4%
Col. William McCandless

1st Pennsylvania Reserves (30th Pennsylvania)
[382] (7k, 6mw, 32w = 45) 11.8%
Col. William C. Talley

**2nd Pennsylvania Reserves
(31st Pennsylvania) (9 Companies)**
[235] (4k, 7mw, 28w = 39) 16.6%
Lt. Col. George A. Woodward

6th Pennsylvania Reserves (35th Pennsylvania)
[327] (2k, 1mw, 21w = 24) 7.3%
Lt. Col. Wellington H. Ent

13th Pennsylvania Reserves (42nd Pennsylvania)
[301] (7k, 5mw, 43w, 1w-c, 1c, 2m = 59) 19.6%
Col. Charles F. Taylor (k)
Maj. William R. Hartshorne

Third Brigade
[1,617] (5k, 3mw, 48w, 2c = 58) 3.6%
Col. Joseph Washington Fisher

5th Pennsylvania Reserves
(34th Pennsylvania) (3 Companies)
[288] (0k, 2w, 1c = 3) 1.0%
Lt. Col. George Dare

9th Pennsylvania Reserves
(38th Pennsylvania) (3 Companies)
[325] (0k, 5w = 5) 1.5%
Lt. Col. James McK. Snodgrass

10th Pennsylvania Reserves
(39th Pennsylvania) (4 Companies)
[401] (1k, 1mw, 3w = 5) 1.2%
Col. Adoniram J. Warner

11th Pennsylvania Reserves (40th Pennsylvania)
[327] (3k, 2mw, 37w = 42) 12.8%
Col. Samuel M. Jackson

12th Pennsylvania Reserves
(41st Pennsylvania) (3 Companies)
[276] (1k, 1w, 1c = 3) 1.1%
Col. Martin D. Hardin

Artillery Brigade
[429] (3k, 8mw, 29w, 1w-c, 2c, 1m = 44) 10.3%
Capt. Augustus Pearl Martin

Massachusetts Light Artillery,
3rd Battery (C) (Six Napoleons)
[115] (0k, 6w = 6) 5.2%
Lt. Aaron F. Walcott

1st New York Light Artillery, Battery C
(Four 3-inch Ordnance Rifles)
[62] (No losses reported) 0.0%
Capt. Almont Barnes

1st Ohio Light Artillery, Battery L (Six Napoleons)
[113] (0k, 3w = 3) 2.7%
Capt. Frank C. Gibbs

5th United States Light Artillery,
Battery D (Six 10-pounder Parrotts)
[68] (2k, 5mw, 6w = 13) 19.1%
Lt. Charles E. Hazlett (k)
Lt. Benjamin F. Rittenhouse

5th United States Light Artillery,
Battery I (Four 3-inch Ordnance Rifles)
[71] (1k, 3mw, 14w, 1w-c, 2c, 1m = 22) 31.0%
Lt. Malbone F. Watson (w)
Lt. Charles C. MacConnell

VI ARMY CORPS
[14,330] (26k, 28mw, 210w, 5c, 22m = 291) 2.0%
Maj. Gen. John Sedgwick

Provost Guard

1st Massachusetts Cavalry
[292] (0k, 2w = 2) 0.7%
Lt. Greely Stevenson Curtis

Headquarters Guards and Orderlies

1st New Jersey Cavalry, Company L
[32] (Losses unknown)
Capt. William H. Hick

1st Pennsylvania Cavalry, Company H
[42] (1k = 1) 2.4%
Capt. William S. Craft (Command of the detachment)

FIRST DIVISION
[4,400] (1k, 3mw, 31w = 35) 0.8%
Brig. Gen. Horatio Gouverneur Wright

Provost Guard

4th New Jersey (3 Companies)
[est. 115] (No losses reported) 0.0%
Capt. William R. Maxwell

FIRST BRIGADE
[1,357] (0k, 2mw, 9w = 11) 0.8%
Brig. Gen. Alfred T. Archimedes Torbert

1st New Jersey
[292] (No losses reported) 0.0%
Lt. Col. William Henry, Jr.

2nd New Jersey
[357] (0k, 1mw, 5w = 6) 1.7%
Lt. Col. Charles Wiebecke

3rd New Jersey
[295] (0k, 2w = 2) 0.7%
Col. Henry W. Brown

15th New Jersey
[413] (0k, 1mw, 2w = 3) 0.7%
Col. William H. Penrose

SECOND BRIGADE
[1,382] (1k, 1mw, 20w = 22) 1.6%
Brig. Gen. Joseph Jackson Bartlett

5th Maine (2 Companies)
[307] (0k, 1mw, 2w = 3) 1.0%
Col. Clark S. Edwards

121st New York (6 Companies)
[429] (0k, 13w = 13) 3.0%
Col. Emory Upton

95th Pennsylvania (1 Company)
[323] (1k, 2w = 3) 0.9%
Lt. Col. Edward Carroll

96th Pennsylvania (2 Companies)
[323] (0k, 3w = 3) 0.9%
Maj. William H. Lessig

THIRD BRIGADE
[1,546] (0k, 2w = 2) 0.1%
Brig. Gen. David Allen Russell

6th Maine
[395] (No losses reported) 0.0%
Col. Hiram Burnham

49th Pennsylvania (4 Companies)
[289] (No losses reported) 0.0%
Lt. Col. Thomas M. Hulings

119th Pennsylvania
[423] (0k, 2w = 2) 0.5%
Col. Peter C. Ellmaker

5th Wisconsin
[439] (No losses reported) 0.0%
Col. Thomas S. Allen

SECOND DIVISION
[3,712] (3k, 4mw, 12w, 3c = 22) 0.6%
Brig. Gen. Albion Parris Howe

SECOND BRIGADE
[1,900] (0k, 1mw = 1) 0.05%
Col. Lewis Addison Grant

2nd Vermont
[465] (No losses reported) 0.0%
Col. James Hicks Walbridge

3rd Vermont
[381] (No losses reported) 0.0%
Col. Thomas Orville Seaver

4th Vermont
[399] (0k, 1mw = 1) 0.3%
Col. Charles B. Stoughton

5th Vermont
[309] (No losses reported) 0.0%
Lt. Col. John R. Lewis

6th Vermont
[346] (No losses reported) 0.0%
Col. Elisha L. Barney

THIRD BRIGADE
[1,812] (3k, 3mw, 12w, 3c = 21) 1.2%
Brig. Gen. Thomas Hewson Neill

7th Maine (6 Companies)
[216] (1k, 2mw, 5w, = 8) 3.7%
Lt. Col. Selden Connor

43rd New York
[370] (2k, 1mw, 2w, 2c = 7) 1.9%
Lt. Col. John Wilson

49th New York
[376] (0k, 4w = 4) 1.1%
Col. Daniel D. Bidwell

33rd New York (attached to 49th New York)
[79] (No losses reported) 0.0%
Capt. Henry J. Gifford

77th New York
[385] (No losses reported) 0.0%
Lt. Col. Winsor B. French

61st Pennsylvania
[386] (0k, 1w, 1c = 2) 0.5%
Lt. Col. George F. Smith

THIRD DIVISION
[4,918] (17k, 20mw, 157w, 2c, 22m = 218) 4.4%
Maj. Gen. John Newton
Brig. Gen. Frank Wheaton

FIRST BRIGADE
[1,833] (12k, 7mw, 61w, 2m = 82) 4.5%
Brig. Gen. Alexander Shaler

65th New York
[290] (4k, 8w = 12) 4.1%
Col. Joseph E. Hamblin

67th New York
[349] (0k, 1m = 1) 0.3%
Col. Nelson Cross

122nd New York
[414] (7k, 7mw, 34w, 1m = 49) 11.8%
Col. Silas Titus

23rd Pennsylvania
[489] (1k, 13w = 14) 2.9%
Lt. Col. John F. Glenn

82rd Pennsylvania
[291] (0k, 6w = 6) 2.1%
Col. Isaac C. Bassett

SECOND BRIGADE
[1,668] (4k, 5mw, 44w, 20m = 73) 4.4%
Col. Henry Lawrence Eustis

7th Massachusetts
[335] (0k, 6w = 6) 1.8%
Lt. Col. Franklin P. Harlow

10th Massachusetts
[378] (0k, 1mw, 7w, 2m = 10) 2.6%
Lt. Col. Joseph B. Parsons

37th Massachusetts
[591] (3k, 4mw, 26w, 17m = 50) 8.5%
Col. Oliver Edwards

2nd Rhode Island
[364] (1k, 5w, 1m = 7) 1.9%
Col. Horatio Rogers, Jr.

THIRD BRIGADE
[1,417] (1k, 8mw, 52w, 2c = 63) 4.4%
Brig. Gen. Frank Wheaton
Col. David J. Nevin

62nd New York
[237] (1k, 1mw, 16w = 18) 7.6%
Col. David J. Nevin
Lt. Col. Theodore B. Hamilton

93rd Pennsylvania
[245] (0k, 1mw, 9w = 10) 4.1%
Maj. John I. Nevin

98th Pennsylvania
[368] (0k, 2mw, 10w = 12) 3.3%
Maj. John B. Kohler

102nd Pennsylvania
[103] (No losses reported) 0.0%
(detached guarding wagons at Westminster, MD)
Col. John W. Patterson

139th Pennsylvania
[464] (0k, 4mw, 17w, 2c = 23) 5.0%
Col. Frederick H. Collier (w)
Lt. Col. William H. Moody

ARTILLERY BRIGADE
[934] (4k, 1mw, 8w = 13) 1.4%
Col. Charles Henry Tompkins

Massachusetts Light Artillery,
1st Battery (A) (Six Napoleons)
[135] (No losses reported) 0.0%
Capt. William H. McCartney

New York Light Artillery, 1st Battery
(Six 3-inch Ordnance Rifles)
[103] (4k, 1mw, 7w = 12) 11.7%
Capt. Andrew Cowan

New York Light Artillery, 3rd Battery
(Six 10-pounder Parrotts)
[111] (No losses reported) 0.0%
Capt. William A. Harn

1st Rhode Island Light Artillery, Battery C
(Six 3-inch Ordnance Rifles)
[116] (0k, 1w = 1) 0.9%
Capt. Richard Waterman

1st Rhode Island Light Artillery, Battery G
(Six 10-pounder Parrotts)
[126] (No losses reported) 0.0%
Capt. George W. Adams

2nd United States Light Artillery,
Battery D (Six Napoleons)
[126] (No losses reported) 0.0%
Lt. Edward B. Williston

2nd United States Light Artillery,
Battery G (Six Napoleons)
[101] (No losses reported) 0.0%
Lt. John H. Butler

5th United States Light Artillery, Battery F
(Six 10-pounder Parrotts)
[116] (No losses reported) 0.0%
Lt. Leonard Martin

XI ARMY CORPS

[9,268] (480k, 279mw, 1,745w, 83w-c, 896c, 489m = 3,972) 42.9%
Maj. Gen. Oliver Otis Howard (final command of corps)
Maj. Gen. Carl Schurz

HEADQUARTERS GUARDS AND ORDERLIES

1st Indiana Cavalry, Companies I and K
[95] (0k, 1c, 2m = 3) 3.2%
Capt. Abram Sharra

17th Pennsylvania Cavalry, Company K
[50] (Unknown losses)
Capt. Richard Fitzgerald

8th New York Infantry Independent Company
[50] (Unknown losses)
Lt. Hermann Foerster

FIRST DIVISION

[2,471] (155k, 104mw, 631w, 28w-c, 300c, 183m = 1,401) 56.7%
Brig. Gen. Francis Channing Barlow (w-c)
Brig. Gen. Adelbert Ames

FIRST BRIGADE
[1,138] (70k, 39mw, 307w, 10w-c, 95c, 77m = 598) 52.5%
Col. Leopold Von Gilsa

41st New York (9 Companies)
[218] (15k, 7mw, 54w, 2m = 78) 35.8%
Lt. Col. Detleo von Einsiedel

54th New York
[189] (7k, 3mw, 43w, 28c, 20m = 101) 53.4%
Maj. Stephen Kovacs (c)
Lt. Ernst Both

68th New York
[232] (12k, 2mw, 65w, 5w-c, 16c, 50m = 150) 64.7%
Col. Gotthilf Bourry

153rd Pennsylvania
[499] (36k, 27mw, 145w, 5w-c, 51c, 5m = 269) 53.9%
Maj. John F. Frueauff

SECOND BRIGADE
[1,333] (85k, 65mw, 324w, 18w-c, 205c, 106m = 803) 60.2%
Brig. Gen. Adelbert Ames
Col. Andrew L. Harris

17th Connecticut
[386] (24k, 14mw, 69w, 12w-c, 78c = 197) 51.0%
Lt. Col. Douglas Fowler (k)
Maj. Allen G. Brady

25th Ohio
[220] (16k, 4mw, 99w, 1w-c, 1c, 69m = 190) 86.4%
Lt. Col. Jeremiah Williams (c)
Capt. Nathaniel J. Manning (w)
Lt. William Maloney
Lt. Israel White

75th Ohio
[269] (24k, 13mw, 60w, 3w-c, 60c, 31m = 191) 71.0%
Col. Andrew L. Harris
Capt. George B. Fox

107th Ohio
[458] (21k, 34mw, 96w, 2w-c, 66c, 6m = 225) 49.1%
Col. Seraphim Meyer (w)
Capt. John M. Lutz

SECOND DIVISION

[2,892] (128k, 81mw, 427w, 18w-c, 220c, 101m = 975) 33.7%
Brig. Gen. Adolph Wilhelm von Steinwehr

PROVOST GUARD

29th New York Independent Company
[33] (7k, 2w = 9) 27.3%

FIRST BRIGADE
[1,215] (73k, 33mw, 202w, 18w-c, 205c, 98m = 629) 51.8%
Col. Charles R. Coster

134th New York
[400] (48k, 22mw, 130w, 6w-c, 24c, 45m = 275) 68.8%
Lt. Col. Allan H. Jackson

154th New York
[240] (5k, 6mw, 22w, 12w-c, 162c, 2m = 209) 87.1%
Lt. Col. Daniel B. Allen

27th Pennsylvania
[284] (13k, 4mw, 24w, 19c, 51m = 111) 39.1%
Lt. Col. Lorenz Cantador

73rd Pennsylvania
[291] (7k, 1mw, 26w = 34) 11.7%
Capt. Daniel F. Kelley

SECOND BRIGADE
[1,644] (48k, 48mw, 223w, 15c, 3m = 337) 20.5%
Col. Orland Smith

33rd Massachusetts
[493] (7k, 2mw, 35w = 44) 8.9%
Col. Adin Ballou Underwood

136th New York
[484] (15k, 12mw, 80w, 2c, 1m = 110) 22.7%
Col. James Wood, Jr.

55th Ohio
[329] (7k, 4mw, 26w, 12c = 49) 14.9%
Col. Charles B. Gambee

73rd Ohio
[338] (19k, 30mw, 82w, 1c, 2m = 134) 39.6%
Lt. Col. Richard Long

THIRD DIVISION
[3,107] (190k, 84mw, 639w, 37w-c, 371c, 199m = 1,520) 48.9%
Maj. Gen. Carl Schurz (final command of division)
Brig. Gen. Alexander Schimmelfennig (m)

FIRST BRIGADE
[1,683] (59k, 22mw, 299w, 13w-c, 268c, 161m = 822) 48.8%
Brig. Gen. Alexander Schimmelfennig (m)
Col. George von Amsberg

82nd Illinois
[318] (7k, 1mw, 17w, 83c, 1m = 109) 34.3%
Lt. Col. Edward S. Salomon

45th New York
[375] (9k, 7mw, 36w, 3w-c, 84c, 88m = 227) 60.5%
Col. George von Amsberg
Lt. Col. Adolphus Dobke

157th New York
[409] (31k, 2mw, 170w, 8w-c, 93c, 10m = 314) 76.8%
Col. Philip B. Brown, Jr.

61st Ohio
[247] (3k, 5mw, 40w, 2w-c, 4c, 8m = 62) 25.1%
Col. Stephen J. McGroarty

74th Pennsylvania
[334] (9k, 7mw, 36w, 4c, 54m = 110) 32.9%
Col. Adolph von Hartung (w)
Lt. Col. Alexander von Mitzel (c)
Capt. Gustav Schleiter
Capt. Henry Krauseneck

SECOND BRIGADE
[1,424] (131k, 62mw, 340w, 24w-c, 103c, 38m = 698) 49.0%
Col. Wladimir Krzyzanowski

58th New York
[195] (2k, 2mw, 14w, 2c, 2m = 22) 11.3%
Lt. Col. August Otto
Capt. Emil Koenig

119th New York
[263] (43k, 17mw, 56w, 1w-c, 18c, 15m = 150) 57.0%
Col. John T. Lockman (w)
Lt. Col. Edward F. Lloyd

82nd Ohio
[312] (26k, 11mw, 70w, 8w-c, 39c, 18m = 172) 55.1%
Col. James S. Robinson (w)
Lt. Col. David Thomson

75th Pennsylvania
[208] (17k, 16mw, 70w, 8w-c, 1c, 2m = 114) 54.8%
Col. Francis Mahler (mw)
Maj. August Ledig

26th Wisconsin
[446] (43k, 16mw, 130w, 7w-c, 43c, 1m = 240) 53.8%
Lt. Col. Hans Boebel (w)
Capt. John W. Fuchs

ARTILLERY BRIGADE
[603] (7k, 10mw, 48w, 4c, 4m = 73) 12.1%
Maj. Thomas Ward Osborn

1st New York Light Artillery, Battery I
(Six 3-inch Ordnance Rifles)
[141] (3k, 1mw, 10w = 14) 9.9%
Capt. Michael Wiedrich

New York Light Artillery, 13th Battery
(Four 3-inch Ordnance Rifles)
[110] (0k, 8w, 3m = 11) 10.0%
Lt. William Wheeler

1st Ohio Light Artillery,
Battery I (Six Napoleons)
[127] (0k, 6mw, 9w = 15) 11.8%
Capt. Hubert Dilger

1st Ohio Light Artillery,
Battery K (Four Napoleons)
[110] (3k, 2mw, 10w, 1m = 16) 14.5%
Capt. Lewis Heckman

4th United States Light Artillery,
Battery G (Six Napoleons)
[115] (1k, 1mw, 11w, 4c = 17) 14.8%
Lt. Bayard Wilkeson (mw-c)
Lt. Eugene A. Bancroft

XII ARMY CORPS

[9,823] (174k, 126mw, 744w, 4w-c, 31c, 55m = 1,134) 11.5%
Maj. Gen. Henry Warner Slocum
Brig. Gen. Alpheus Starkey Williams

PROVOST GUARD

10th Maine Battalion (3 Companies)
[170] (No losses reported) 0.0%
Capt. John Davis Beardsley

HEADQUARTERS GUARDS AND ORDERLIES

9th New York Cavalry, Companies D and L
[78] (No losses reported) 0.0%
Capt. Joseph G. Weld

FIRST DIVISION

[5,230] (82k, 61mw, 396w, 2w-c, 13c, 19m = 573) 11.0%
Brig. Gen. Alpheus S. Williams
Brig. Gen. Thomas H. Ruger

FIRST BRIGADE

[1,834] (12k, 6mw, 54w, 9c, 1m = 82) 4.5%
Col. Archibald L. McDougall

5th Connecticut
[221] (0k, 3w, 8c = 11) 5.0%
Col. Warren W. Packer

20th Connecticut
[321] (5k, 4mw, 19w = 28) 8.7%
Lt. Col. William B. Wooster

3rd Maryland
[290] (1k, 7w = 8) 2.8%
Col. Joseph M. Sudsburg

123rd New York
[495] (3k, 1mw, 9w, 1c = 14) 2.8%
Lt. Col. James C. Rogers

145th New York
[245] (1k, 1mw, 8w = 10) 4.1%
Col. Edward L. Price

46th Pennsylvania
[262] (2k, 8w, 1m = 11) 4.2%
Col. James L. Selfridge

SECOND BRIGADE

[1,815] (29k, 13mw, 117w, 1c, 17m = 177) 9.8%
Brig. Gen. Henry Hayes Lockwood

1st Maryland (Potomac Home Brigade)
[674] (18k, 9mw, 78w, 1m = 106) 15.7%
Col. William P. Maulsby

1st Maryland (Eastern Shore)
[532] (5k, 2mw, 16w, 2m = 25) 4.7%
Col. James Wallace

150th New York
[609] (6k, 2mw, 23w, 1c, 14m = 46) 7.6%
Col. John H. Ketcham

THIRD BRIGADE

[1,581] (41k, 42mw, 225w, 2w-c, 3c, 1m = 314) 19.9%
Brig. Gen. Thomas H. Ruger
Col. Silas Colgrove

27th Indiana
[339] (16k, 18mw, 105w = 139) 41.0%
Col. Silas Colgrove
Lt. Col. John R. Fesler

2nd Massachusetts
[316] (22k, 22mw, 89w, 2w-c, 3c, 1m = 139) 44.0%
Lt. Col. Charles Redington Mudge (k)
Maj. Charles F. Morse

13th New Jersey
[347] (1k, 1mw, 19w = 21) 6.1%
Col. Ezra Ayres Carman

107th New York
[319] (0k, 1mw, 2w = 3) 0.9%
Col. Nirom M. Crane

3rd Wisconsin
[260] (2k, 10w = 12) 4.6%
Col. William Hawley

SECOND DIVISION
[3,948] (92k, 63mw, 344w, 2w-c, 18c, 36m = 555) 14.1%
Brig. Gen. John White Geary

PROVOST GUARD

28th Pennsylvania, Company B
[34] (Unknown losses)
Lt. George W. Newmeyer

FIRST BRIGADE
[1,796] (12k, 21mw, 100w, 1c = 134) 7.5%
Col. Charles Candy

5th Ohio
[299] (2k, 4mw, 11w = 17) 5.7%
Col. John H. Patrick

7th Ohio
[282] (1k, 1mw, 16w = 18) 6.4%
Col. William R. Creighton

29th Ohio
[315] (5k, 4mw, 30w = 39) 12.4%
Capt. Wilbur F. Stevens (w)
Capt. Edward Hayes

66th Ohio
[299] (0k, 3mw, 15w = 18) 6.0%
Lt. Col. Eugene Powell

28th Pennsylvania
[303] (2k, 4mw, 21w, 1c = 28) 9.2%
Capt. John H. Flynn (w)

147th Pennsylvania (8 Companies)
[298] (2k, 5mw, 7w = 14) 4.7%
Lt. Col. Ario Pardee, Jr.

SECOND BRIGADE
[697] (22k, 7mw, 65w, 2c, 22m = 118) 16.9%
Col. George A. Cobham, Jr. (final command of regiment)
Brig. Gen. Thomas Leiper Kane

29th Pennsylvania
[357] (14k, 5mw, 42w, 2c, 13m = 76) 21.3%
Col. William Rickards, Jr.

109th Pennsylvania
[149] (4k, 6w, 8m = 18) 12.1%
Capt. Frederick L. Gimber

111th Pennsylvania (7 Companies)
[191] (4k, 2mw, 17w, 1m = 24) 12.6%
Lt. Col. Thomas L. Walker (final command of regiment)
Col. George A. Cobham, Jr.

THIRD BRIGADE
[1,421] (58k, 35mw, 179w, 2w-c, 15c, 14m = 303) 21.3%
Brig. Gen. George Sears Greene

60th New York
[273] (12k, 7mw, 33w, 1w-c = 53) 19.4%
Col. Abel Godard

78th New York
[198] (5k, 2mw, 22w, 2c = 31) 15.7%
Lt. Col. Herbert von Hammerstein

102nd New York
[230] (1k, 6mw, 16w, 1c, 8m = 32) 13.9%
Col. James C. Lane (w)
Capt. Lewis R. Stegman

137th New York
[423] (33k, 16mw, 76w, 1w-c, 12c, 6m = 144) 34.0%
Col. David Ireland

149th New York
[297] (7k, 4mw, 32w = 43) 14.5%
Col. Henry A. Barnum (final command of regiment)
Lt. Col. Charles B. Randall (w)
Capt. Nicholas Grumbach

ARTILLERY BRIGADE
[397] (0k, 2mw, 4w = 6) 1.5%
Lt. Edward Duchman Muhlenberg

1st New York Light Artillery, Battery M
(Four 10-pounder Parrotts)
[97] (No losses reported) 0.0%
Lt. Charles E. Winegar

Pennsylvania Light Artillery, Battery E
(Six 10-pounder Parrotts)
[139] (0k, 1mw, 2w = 3) 2.2%
Lt. Charles A. Atwell

4th United States Light Artillery,
Battery F (Six Napoleons)
[89] (0k, 1w = 1) 1.1%
Lt. Sylvanus T. Rugg

5th United States Light Artillery,
Battery K (Four Napoleons)
[72] (0k, 1mw, 1w = 2) 2.8%
Lt. David H. Kinzie

CAVALRY CORPS

[11,328] (82k, 53mw, 287w, 4w-c, 31c, 154m = 611) 5.4%
Maj. Gen. Alfred Pleasonton

STAFF

Chief of Staff and Assistant Adjutant General
Lt. Col. Alexander J. Alexander

Commissary of Musters
Col. George A. H. Blake (1st United States Cavalry)

Commissary of Subsistence
Lt. Col. A. S. Austin

Ordnance Officer
Lt. Col. Charles Ross Smith (6th Pennsylvania Cavalry)

Inspector General
Lt. Col. William H. Crocker
Capt. John Green, Asst. (2nd United States Cavalry)
Capt. Frederick C. Newhall, Asst. (6th Pennsylvania Cavalry)

Medical Department
Surgeon George L. Pancoast, Director
Surgeon G. M. McGill, Asst.

Topographical Engineer (Acting)
Capt. V. E. von Koerber

Assistant Quartermaster (Acting)
1st Lt. John W. Spangler (6th United States Cavalry)

Ambulance Department
1st Lt. W. M. Taylor (8th Illinois Cavalry)

Aides-de-Camp
1st Lt. Clifford Thomson (1st New York Cavalry)
1st Lt. L. Walker (5th United States Cavalry)
1st Lt. G. W. Yates (4th Michigan Infantry)

Acting Aides-de-Camp
Capt. George A. Crocker (6th New York Cavalry)
1st Lt. C. B. McClellan (6th United States Cavalry)
1st Lt. G. H. Thompson (1st Rhode Island Cavalry)
2nd Lt. E. B. Parsons (8th New York Cavalry)
1st Lt. James G. Birney (7th Michigan Cavalry)
1st Lt. Daniel W. Littlefield (7th Michigan Cavalry)

PROVOST GUARD AND ORDERLIES

6th United States Cavalry, Companies D and K
[110] (No losses reported) 0.0%
Lt. James F. Wade

4th Pennsylvania Cavalry
[258] (1k = 1) 0.4%
Lt. Col. William Emile Doster

FIRST DIVISION

[4,217] (22k, 21mw, 86w, 8c, 53m = 190) 4.5%
Brig. Gen. John Buford

UNITED STATES SIGNAL CORPS (DETACHMENT)
[1] (No losses reported) 0.0%
Lt. Aaron Brainard Jerome

FIRST BRIGADE
[1,596] (14k, 12mw, 45w, 7c, 24m = 102) 6.4%
Col. William Gamble

8th Illinois Cavalry
[470] (0k, 4w, 1m = 5) 1.1%
Maj. John Lourie Beveridge

12th Illinois Cavalry (8 Companies)
[233] (5k, 3mw, 7w, 5m = 20) 8.6%

3rd Indiana Cavalry (6 Companies)
[313] (8k, 5mw, 14w, 5m = 32) 10.2%
Col. George Henry Chapman
(Capt. George Washington Shears had subordinate command of the 12th Illinois)

8th New York Cavalry
[580] (1k, 4mw, 20w, 7c, 13m = 45) 7.8%
Lt. Col. William L. Markell

ATTACHED ARTILLERY

2nd United States Horse Artillery, Battery A
(Six 3-inch Ordnance Rifles)
[81] (0k, 12w = 12) 14.8%
Lt. John Haskell Calef

SECOND BRIGADE
[1,108] (2k, 3mw, 1w, 1c, 18m = 25) 2.3%
Col. Thomas Casimer Devin

PROVOST GUARD

6th New York Cavalry, Company L
[36] (0k, 1c = 1) 2.8%
Capt. Harrison White

6th New York Cavalry (5 Companies)
[182] (0k, 2mw, 7w = 9) 5.0%
Maj. William Elliott Beardsley

9th New York Cavalry
[367] (2k, 1mw, 1w, 4m = 8) 202.%
Col. William Sackett

17th Pennsylvania Cavalry
[464] (0k, 3m = 3) 0.6%
Col. Josiah Holcomb Kellogg

3rd West Virginia Cavalry (Companies A and C)
[59] (0k, 4m = 4) 6.8%
Capt. Seymour Beach Conger

RESERVE BRIGADE
[1,317] (6k, 6mw, 27w, 11m = 50) 3.8%
Brig. Gen. Wesley Merritt

6th Pennsylvania Cavalry (10 Companies)
[242] (1k, 11w, 1m = 13) 5.4%
Maj. James H. Haseltine

1st United States Cavalry
[362] (1k, 4mw, 8w, 3m = 16) 4.4%
Capt. Richard S. C. Lord

2nd United States Cavalry
[407] (4k, 2mw, 4w, 6m = 16) 3.9%
Capt. Theophilus F. Rodenbough

5th United States Cavalry
[306] (0k, 4w, 1m = 5) 1.6%
Capt. Julius Wilmot Mason

6th United States Cavalry
(Not on battlefield; engagement at
Fairfield, July 3 – see page 145)

ATTACHED ARTILLERY
1st United States Horse Artillery, Battery K
(Six 3-inch Ordnance Rifles)
[114] (0k, 1w = 1) 0.9%
Capt. William Montrose Graham, Jr.
(Attached July 3 only)

SECOND DIVISION
[2,442] (6k, 4mw, 34w, 12m = 56) 2.3%
First and Third Brigades fought at Brinkerhoff's Ridge (July 2 – see page 143)
and East Cavalry Field (July 3 – see page 148)
Brig. Gen. David McMurtrie Gregg

SECOND BRIGADE
Not on battlefield; at Westminster, MD guarding trains during battle; engaged at
Monterey Pass (July 4 – see page 155) and Smithsburg (July 5 – see page 161)
Col. Pennock Huey

THIRD DIVISION
[3,927] (51k, 28mw, 162w, 4w-c, 23c, 89m = 357) 9.0%
Brig. Gen. Hugh Judson Kilpatrick

HEADQUARTERS GUARDS AND ORDERLIES

1st Ohio Cavalry, Company A
[40] (No losses reported) 0.0%
Capt. Noah Jones

1st Ohio Cavalry, Company C
[40] (No losses reported) 0.0%
Capt. Samuel N. Stanford
(Capt. Jones had command of the squadron)

FIRST BRIGADE
[1,924] (19k, 4mw, 39w, 4w-c, 23c, 11m = 100) 5.2%
Brig. Gen. Elon John Farnsworth (k)
Col. Nathaniel Pendleton Richmond

5th New York Cavalry
[420] (1k, 1w, 4c, 1m = 7) 1.7%
Maj. John Hammond

18th Pennsylvania Cavalry
[509] (2k, 1mw, 4w, 1w-c, 1c, 5m = 14) 2.8%
Lt. Col. William Penn Brinton

1st Vermont Cavalry
[600] (13k, 2mw, 28w, 3w-c, 17c, 2m = 65) 10.8%
Lt. Col. Addison Webster Preston

1st West Virginia Cavalry
[395] (3k, 1mw, 6w, 1c, 3m = 14) 3.5%
Col. Nathaniel Pendleton Richmond
Maj. Charles E. Capehart

ATTACHED ARTILLERY
4th United States Horse Artillery, Battery E
(Four 3-inch Ordnance Rifles)
[61] (1k = 1) 1.6%
Lt. Samuel Sherer Elder

SECOND BRIGADE
[1,923] (32k, 24mw, 123w, 78m = 257) 13.4%
Engaged at Hunterstown (July 2 – see page 139) and
East Cavalry Field (July 3 – see page 148)
Brig. Gen. George Armstrong Custer

HORSE ARTILLERY

FIRST HORSE ARTILLERY BRIGADE
[313] (1k, 5w = 6) 1.9%
Capt. James M. Robertson
(Batteries not otherwise attached, in reserve on field)

9th Michigan Light Battery
(Six 3-inch Ordnance Rifles)
[111] (1k, 4w = 5) 4.5%
Capt. Jabez J. Daniels

6th Independent New York Light Artillery
(Six 3-inch Ordnance Rifles)
[103] (0k, 1w = 1) 1.0%
Capt. Joseph W. Martin

2nd United States Light Artillery, Batteries B and L
(Six 3-inch Ordnance Rifles)
[99] (No losses reported) 0.0%
Lt. Edward Heaton

SECOND HORSE ARTILLERY BRIGADE
Capt. John Caldwell Tidball
(All batteries attached to cavalry units)

ARTILLERY RESERVE
[2,404] (36k, 31mw, 162w, 2c, 8m = 239) 9.9%
Brig. Gen. Robert Ogden Tyler
(Injured during fall from horse on July 3)
Capt. James M. Robertson

HEADQUARTERS GUARD

32nd Massachusetts Infantry, Company C
[27] (No losses reported) 0.0%
Capt. Josiah C. Fuller

TRAINS AND PROVOST GUARD

4th New Jersey Infantry (7 Companies)
[386] (No losses reported) 0.0%
Maj. Charles Ewing

FIRST REGULAR BRIGADE
[443] (13k, 7mw, 47w, 2m = 69) 15.6%
Capt. Dunbar Richard Ransom (w)

1st United States Light Artillery,
Battery H (Six Napoleons)
[129] (1k, 1mw, 7w, 1m = 10) 7.8%
Lt. Chandler P. Eakin (w)
Lt. Philip D. Mason

3rd United States Light Artillery,
Batteries F and K (Six Napoleons)
[115] (9k, 2mw, 12w, 1m = 24) 20.9%
Lt. John G. Turnbull

4th United States Light Artillery,
Battery C (Six Napoleons)
[95] (1k, 2mw, 15w = 18) 18.9%
Lt. Evan Thomas

5th United States Light Artillery,
Battery C (Six Napoleons)
[104] (2k, 2mw, 13w = 17) 16.3%
Lt. Gulian V. Weir

FIRST VOLUNTEER BRIGADE
[383] (15k, 12mw, 58w, 1c, 3m = 89) 23.2%
Lt. Col. Freeman McGilvery

5th Massachusetts Light Artillery,
Battery E (Six 3-inch Ordnance Rifles)
[104] (4k, 3mw, 11w = 18) 17.3%
Capt. Charles A. Phillips

9th Massachusetts Light Artillery
(Six Napoleons)
[104] (7k, 4mw, 18w, 1c = 30) 28.8%
Capt. John Bigelow (w)
Lt. Richard Sweet Milton

15th New York Independent Light Battery
(Four Napoleons)
[70] (3k, 1mw, 10w = 14) 20.0%
Capt. Patrick Hart (w)

1st Pennsylvania Light Artillery, Independent
Batteries C and F (Six 3-inch Ordnance Rifles)
[105] (1k, 4mw, 19w, 3m = 27) 25.7%
Capt. James Thompson

SECOND VOLUNTEER BRIGADE
[239] (0k, 3mw, 4w, 2m = 9) 3.8%
Capt. Elijah D. Taft

**1st Connecticut Heavy Artillery,
Battery B (Four 4.5-inch Rifles)**
(Not on the field – at Westminster, MD)
Capt. Albert F. Brooker

**1st Connecticut Heavy Artillery,
Battery M (Four 4.5-inch Rifles)**
(Not on the field – at Westminster, MD)
Capt. Franklin A. Pratt

**2nd Connecticut Light Artillery (Four 14-pounder
James Rifles, Two 12-pounder Howitzers)**
[93] (0k, 3w, 2m = 5) 5.4%
Capt. John W. Sterling

**5th New York Independent Light Battery
(Six 20-pounder Parrotts)**
[146] (0k, 3mw, 1w = 4) 2.7%
Capt. Elijah D. Taft

THIRD VOLUNTEER BRIGADE
[429] (6k, 8mw, 21w, 1c, 1m = 37) 8.6%
Capt. James F. Huntington

**1st New Hampshire Light Artillery,
Battery A (Four 3-inch Ordnance Rifles)**
[86] (0k, 2w = 2) 2.3%
Capt. Frederick M. Edgell

**1st Ohio Light Artillery, Battery H
(Six 3-inch Ordnance Rifles)**
[99] (0k, 3mw, 7w = 10) 10.1%
Lt. George W. Norton

**1st Pennsylvania Light Artillery, Batteries F and G
(Six 3-inch Ordnance Rifles)**
[144] (4k, 5mw, 10w, 1c, 1m = 21) 14.6%
Capt. Robert Bruce Ricketts

**1st West Virginia Light Artillery,
Battery C (Four 10-pounder Parrotts)**
[100] (2k, 2w = 4) 4.0%
Capt. Wallace Hill

FOURTH VOLUNTEER BRIGADE
[497] (2k, 1mw, 32w = 35) 7.0%
Capt. Robert Hughes Fitzhugh

**6th Maine Light Artillery, Battery F
(Four Napoleons)**
[87] (0k, 13w = 13) 14.9%
Lt. Edwin B. Dow

**1st Maryland Light Artillery, Battery A
(Six 3-inch Ordnance Rifles)**
[106] (No losses reported) 0.0%
Capt. James H. Rigby

**1st New Jersey Light Artillery, Battery A
(Six 10-pounder Parrotts)**
[98] (2k, 6w = 8) 8.2%
Lt. Augustin N. Parsons

**1st New York Light Artillery, Battery G
(Six Napoleons)**
[84] (0k, 1mw, 6w = 7) 8.3%
Capt. Nelson Ames

**1st New York Light Artillery, Battery K
(Six 3-inch Ordnance Rifles)**
[122] (0k, 7w = 7) 5.7%
Capt. Robert H. Fitzhugh

CONFEDERATE

ARMY OF NORTHERN VIRGINIA
[71,429] (4,675k, 12,266w, 5,597m = 22,538) 31.6%

Field and Staff — All Units
[422] (33k, 165w, 132m = 330) 78.2%

Totals reported for the Army
[71,851] (4,708k, 12,431w, 5,729m = 22,868) 31.8%
Gen. Robert Edward Lee, commanding

ARMY HEADQUARTERS
Col. Robert Hall Chilton, Chief of Staff and Inspector General
Brig. Gen. William Nelson Pendleton, Chief of Artillery
Col. Armistead Lindsay Long, Military Secretary and Acting Asst. Chief of Artillery
Lt. Col. Briscoe G. Baldwin, Chief of Ordnance
Lt. Col. Robert C. Cole, Chief of Commissary
Lt. Col. James Lawrence Corely, Chief Quartermaster
Maj. Henry Edward Young, Judge Advocate General
Maj. Walter Herron Taylor, Aide-de-Camp and Assistant Adjutant General
Maj. Charles Marshall, Aide-de-Camp and Assistant Military Secretary
Maj. Charles Venable, Aide-de-Camp and Assistant Inspector General
Capt. Samuel Richards Johnston, Engineer

Escort and Couriers

39th Virginia Cavalry Battalion, Pifer's Company and Brown's Company
Maj. John H. Richardson (w)

Pifer's Company
[60 est.] (No losses reported) 0.0%
Capt. Augustus P. Pifer

Brown's Company
[60 est.] (No losses reported) 0.0%
Capt. Samuel B. Brown

(During the reorganization of the battalion in the fall of 1863, Pifer's Company became Company A, and Brown's Company became Company C.)

LONGSTREET'S CORPS
[20,795] (1,597k, 4,094w, 1,852m+ = 7,543+) 36.3%+
Lt. Gen. James Longstreet

McLAWS' DIVISION
[7,127] (462k, 1,331w, 471m+ = 2,264+) 31.8%+
Maj. Gen. Lafayette McLaws

Kershaw's Brigade
[2,179] (179k, 439w, 51m = 669) 30.7%
Brig. Gen. Joseph Brevard Kershaw

2nd South Carolina
[412] (53k, 100w, 17m = 170) 41.3%
Col. John Doby Kennedy (w)
Lt. Col. Franklin Gaillard

3rd South Carolina
[407] (22k, 59w, 6m = 87) 21.4%
Maj. Robert Clayton Maffett
Col. James Drayton Nance

3rd South Carolina Battalion
[203] (14k, 31w, 3m = 48) 23.6%
Lt. Col. William George Rice

7th South Carolina
[408] (29k, 79w, 7m = 115) 28.2%
Col. David Wyatt Aiken

8th South Carolina
[300] (31k, 74w = 105) 35.0%
Col. John Williford Henagan

15th South Carolina
[449] (30k, 96w, 18m = 144) 32.1%
Col. William DeSaussure (mw)
Maj. William Murena Gist

SEMMES' BRIGADE
[1,331] (79k, 239w, 73m = 391) 29.4%
Brig. Gen. Paul Jones Semmes (mw)
Col. Goode Bryan

10th Georgia
[303] (17k, 73w, 11m = 101) 33.3%
Col. John B. Weems (w)

50th Georgia
[303] (17k, 65w, 14m = 96) 31.7%
Col. William Richard Manning

51st Georgia
[303] (15k, 40w, 40m = 95) 31.4%
Col. Edward Ball

53rd Georgia
[422] (30k, 61w, 8m = 99) 23.5%
Col. James Phillip Simms

BARKSDALE'S BRIGADE
[1,615] (141k, 470w, 178m = 789) 48.9%
Brig. Gen. William Barksdale (mw-c)
Col. Benjamin Grubb Humphreys

13th Mississippi
[481] (39k, 171w, 33m = 243) 50.5%
Col. James William Carter (k)
Lt. Col. Kennon McElroy (w)
Maj. John M. Bradley (mw)
Lt. Absalom H. Farrar (w-c)

17th Mississippi
[468] (64k, 108w, 98m = 270) 57.7%
Col. William Dunbar Holder (w)
Lt. Col. John Calvin Fizer (w)
Maj. Andrew Jackson Pulliam (w-c)
Maj. Richard E. Jones (k)
Capt. Gwen R. Cherry

18th Mississippi
[242] (20k, 81w, 36m = 137) 56.6%
Col. Thomas Milton Griffin (w)
Lt. Col. William Henry Luse (c)
Maj. George Bruce Gerald

21st Mississippi
[424] (18k, 110w, 11m = 139) 32.8%
Col. Benjamin Grubb Humphreys

WOFFORD'S BRIGADE
[1,628] (48k, 146w, 132m+ = 326+) 20.0+%
Brig. Gen. William Tatum Wofford

16th Georgia
[303] (20k, 41w, 43m = 104) 34.3%
Col. Goode Bryan

18th Georgia
[303] (3k, 16w, 17m = 36) 11.9%
Lt. Col. Solon Zachry Ruff

24th Georgia
[303] (10k, 29w, 46m = 85) 28.1%
Col. Robert McMillan

Cobb's (Georgia) Legion
[213] (6k, 16w, ?m = 22+) 10.3+%
Lt. Col. Luther Judson Glenn

Phillips' (Georgia) Legion
[273] (6k, 41w, 19m = 66) 24.2%
Lt. Col. Elihu Stuart Barclay, Jr.

3rd Georgia Battalion Sharpshooters
[233] (3k, 3w, 7m = 13) 5.6%
Lt. Col. Nathan Louis Hutchins, Jr.

ARTILLERY BATTALION (McLAWS' DIVISION)
[374] (15k, 37w = 52) 13.9%
Col. Henry Coalter Cabell

Manly's Battery, 1st North Carolina Artillery, Battery A (Two Napoleons, Two 3-inch Ordnance Rifles)
[131] (3k, 10w = 13) 9.9%
Capt. Basil Charles Manly

Fraser's Battery, Pulaski (Georgia) Artillery (Two 3-inch Ordnance Rifles, Two 10-pounder Parrotts)
[63] (7k, 12w = 19) 30.2%
Capt. John C. Fraser (mw)
Lt. William J. Furlong

McCarthy's Battery, 1st Richmond Howitzers (Two Napoleons, Two 3-inch Ordnance Rifles)
[90] (3k, 10w = 13) 14.4%
Capt. Edward S. McCarthy (w)
Lt. Robert M. Anderson

Carlton's Battery, Troup County (Georgia) Artillery (Two 12-pounder Howitzers, Two 10-pounder Parrotts)
[90] (2k, 5w = 7) 7.8%
Capt. Henry H. Carlton (w)
Lt. Columbus W. Motes

PICKETT'S DIVISION
[5,442] (621k, 1,290w, 840m = 2,751) 50.6%
Brig. Gen. George Edward Pickett

GARNETT'S BRIGADE
[1,455] (230k, 391w, 324m = 945) 65.0%
Brig. Gen. Richard Brooke Garnett (k)
Maj. Charles Stephens Peyton (w)

8th Virginia
[193] (39k, 79w, 60m = 178) 92.2%
Col. Eppa Hunton (w)
Lt. Col. Norbonne Berkeley (w-c)
Maj. Edmund Berkeley (w)
Lt. John Gray

18th Virginia
[312] (54k, 134w, 57m = 245) 78.5%
Lt. Col. Henry A. Carrington (w-c)
Capt. Henry T. Owen

19th Virginia
[328] (42k, 41w, 68m = 151) 46.0%
Col. Henry Gantt (w)
Lt. Col. John T. Ellis (mw)
Maj. Charles Stephens Peyton (w)

28th Virginia
[333] (44k, 65w, 73m = 182) 54.7%
Col. Robert C. Allen (k)
Lt. Col. William Watts

56th Virginia
[289] (51k, 72w, 66m = 189) 65.4%
Col. William D. Stuart (mw)
Lt. Col. Philip Peyton Slaughter

KEMPER'S BRIGADE
[1,630] (169k, 365w, 165m = 699) 42.9%
Brig. Gen. James Lawson Kemper (w-c, rescued)
Col. Joseph Mayo, Jr. (final command of brigade)

1st Virginia
[209] (27k, 73w, 13m = 113) 54.1%
Col. Lewis Burwell Williams, Jr. (mw)
Lt. Col. Frederick Gustavus Skinner

3rd Virginia
[332] (30k, 41w, 57m = 128) 38.6%
Col. Joseph Mayo, Jr.
Lt. Col. Alexander Daniel Callcote (k)
Maj. William Hamlin Pryor

7th Virginia
[335] (31k, 82w, 36m = 149) 44.5%
Col. Waller Tazewell Patton (mw-c)
Lt. Col. Charles Conway Flowerree

11th Virginia
[359] (34k, 86w, 26m = 146) 40.7%
Maj. Kirkwood Otey (w)
Capt. James Risque Hutter (w-c)
Capt. John H. Smith

24th Virginia
[395] (47k, 83w, 33m = 163) 41.3%
Col. William Richard Terry (w)
Maj. Joseph Adam Hambrick (w)
Capt. William Weldon Bentley

ARMISTEAD'S BRIGADE
[1,946] (213k, 523w, 347m = 1,083) 55.7%
Brig. Gen. Lewis Addison Armistead (mw-c)
Lt. Col. William White (w)
Maj. Joseph Robert Cabell
Col. William Roane Aylett (w)
(final command of brigade)

9th Virginia
[257] (24k, 70w, 83m = 177) 68.9%
Maj. John Crowder Owens (mw)
Capt. James J. Phillips

14th Virginia
[422] (58k, 104w, 88m = 250) 59.2%
Col. James G. Hodges (k)
Lt. Col. William White (w)
Maj. Robert H. Moore (mw)

38th Virginia
[356] (40k, 112w, 42m = 194) 54.5%
Col. Edward Claxton Edmonds (k)
Lt. Col. Powhatan Bolling Whittle (mw)
Maj. Joseph Robert Cabell

53rd Virginia
[435] (34k, 101w, 78m = 213) 49.0%
Col. William Roane Aylett (w)
Lt. Col. Rawley Martin (mw-c)
Maj. John Timberlake (c)
Capt. Henry Edmunds

57th Virginia
[476] (57k, 136w, 56m = 249) 52.3%
Col. John Bowie Magruder (mw-c)
Lt. Col. Benjamin H. Wade (mw)
Maj. Clement Royster Fontaine (w)

ARTILLERY BATTALION (PICKETT'S DIVISION)
[411] (9k, 11w, 4m = 24) 5.8%
Maj. James Dearing

**Stribling's Battery, Fauquier (Virginia) Artillery
(Four Napoleons, Two 20-pounder Parrotts)**
[135] (1k, 4w = 5) 3.7%
Capt. Robert M. Stribling

**Caskie's Battery, Richmond "Hampden" (Virginia)
Artillery (Two Napoleons, One 10-pounder Parrott,
One 3-inch Ordnance Rifle)**
[90] (0k, 3w, 1m = 4) 4.4%
Capt. William H. Caskie

**Macon's Battery, Richmond "Fayette" Artillery
(Two Napoleons, Two 10-pounder Parrotts)**
[90] (3k, 1w, 1m = 5) 5.6%
Capt. Miles C. Macon

**Blount's Battery, Lynchburg (Virginia) Artillery
(Four Napoleons)**
[96] (5k, 3w, 2m = 10) 10.4%
Capt. Joseph G. Blount

HOOD'S DIVISION
[7,330] (484k, 1,351w, 526m = 2,361+) 32.2%+
Maj. Gen. John Bell Hood (w)
Brig. Gen. Evander McIvor Law

LAW'S BRIGADE
[1,929] (79k, 287w, 137m = 503) 26.1%
Brig. Gen. Evander McIvor Law
Col. James Lawrence Sheffield

4th Alabama
[346] (18k, 55w, 19m = 92) 26.6%
Col. Lawrence Houston Scruggs

15th Alabama
[499] (18k, 77w, 83m = 178) 35.7%
Col. William Calvin Oates
Capt. Blanton Abram Hill

44th Alabama
[363] (25k, 58w, 5m = 88) 24.2%
Col. William Flake Perry

47th Alabama
[347] (10k, 46w, 13m = 69) 19.9%
Lt. Col. Michael Jefferson Bulger (w-c)
Maj. James McDonald Campbell

48th Alabama
[374] (8k, 51w, 17m = 76) 20.3%
Col. James Lawrence Sheffield
Capt. Thomas J. Eubanks (w)
Lt. Col. William McTyiere Hardwick (w)
Maj. Columbus B. St. John (w)
Capt. Jeremiah Edwards (c)
Lt. Francis M. Burk
Lt. Reuben T. Ewing

ROBERTSON'S BRIGADE
[1,729] (152k, 312w, 138m = 602) 34.8%
Brig. Gen. Jerome Bonaparte Robertson (w)

3rd Arkansas
[479] (41k, 101w, 40m = 182) 38.0%
Col. Vannoy Hartrog Manning (w)
Lt. Col. Robert Samuel Taylor

1st Texas
[426] (29k, 46w, 22m = 97) 22.8%
Col. Phillip Alexander Work
Maj. Frederick Samuel Bass

4th Texas
[415] (28k, 53w, 31m = 112) 27.0%
Col. John Cotlett Garrett Key (w)
Lt. Col. Benjamin Franklin Carter (mw)
Maj. John Pierson Bane

5th Texas
[409] (54k, 112w, 45m = 211) 51.6%
Col. Robert Michael Powell (w-c)
Lt. Col. Kindallis (King) Bryan (w)
Maj. Jefferson Carroll Rogers

ANDERSON'S BRIGADE
[1,862] (152k, 467w, 102m = 721) 38.7%
Brig. Gen. George Thomas Anderson (w)
Lt. Col. William M. Luffman (w)
Col. William Wilkinson White

7th Georgia
[377] (5k, 10w, 6m = 21) 5.6%
Col. William Wilkinson White
Lt. Col. George Hunter Carmical

8th Georgia
[311] (36k, 103w, 29m = 168) 54.0%
Col. John Reed Towers (w)
Maj. George Oscar Dawson (w)
Capt. Dunlap Scott

9th Georgia
[340] (34k, 123w, 32m = 189) 55.6%
Lt. Col. John Clark Mounger (k)
Maj. William Mays Jones (w)
Capt. James M. D. King (mw)
Capt. George Hillyer

11th Georgia
[309] (40k, 156w, 5m = 201) 65.0%
Col. Francis Hamilton Little (w)
Lt. Col. William M. Luffman (w)
Maj. Henry Dickerson McDaniel
(final command of regiment)
Capt. William Mitchell

59th Georgia
[525] (37k, 75w, 30m = 142) 27.0%
Col. William Andrew Jackson (Jack) Brown (w-c)
Maj. Bolivar Hopkins Gee (w)
Capt. Maston Green Bass

BENNING'S BRIGADE
[1,416] (96k, 274w, 149m = 519) 36.7%
Brig. Gen. Henry Lewis Benning

2nd Georgia
[348] (26k, 66w, 11m = 103) 29.6%
Lt. Col. William Terrell Harris (k)
Maj. William Smythe Shepherd

15th Georgia
[368] (14k, 58w, 99m = 171) 46.5%
Col. Dudley McIver DuBose

17th Georgia
[350] (31k, 66w, 11m = 108) 30.9%
Col. Wesley Clarke Hodges

20th Georgia
[350] (25k, 84w, 28m = 137) 39.1%
Col. John Abraham Jones (k)
Lt. Col. James Daniel Waddell

ARTILLERY BATTALION (HOOD'S DIVISION)
[394] (5k, 11w = 16+) 4.1+%
Maj. Mathis Winston Henry

**Latham's Battery, "Branch" (North Carolina)
Artillery (Three Napoleons,
One 12-pounder Howitzer, One 6-pounder Gun)**
[112] (1k, 2w = 3) 2.7%
Capt. Alexander C. Latham

**Bachman's Battery, "German" Charleston
(South Carolina) Artillery (Four Napoleons)**
[71] (Unknown losses)
Capt. William K. Bachman

**Garden's Battery, Palmetto (South Carolina)
Light Artillery (Two Napoleons,
Two 10-pounder Parrotts)**
[63] (2k, 5w = 7) 11.1%
Capt. Hugh R. Garden

**Reilly's Battery, Rowan (North Carolina) Artillery
(Two Napoleons, Two 3-inch Ordnance Rifles,
Two 10-pounder Parrotts)**
[148] (2k, 4w = 6) 4.1%
Capt. James Reilly

ARTILLERY RESERVE (LONGSTREET'S CORPS)
[896] (30k, 122w, 15m = 167) 18.6%
Col. James Burdge Walton

ALEXANDER'S BATTALION
[567] (22k, 111w, 4m = 137) 24.2%
Col. Edward Porter Alexander

**Woolfolk's Battery, Ashland (Virginia) Artillery
(Two Napoleons, Two 20-pounder Parrotts)**
[103] (3k, 24w, 1m = 28) 27.2%
Capt. Pichegru Woolfolk, Jr. (w)
Lt. James Woolfolk

**Jordan's Battery, Bedford (Virginia) Artillery
(Four 3-inch Ordnance Rifles)**
[78] (1k, 7w, 1m = 9) 11.5%
Capt. Tyler Calhoun Jordan

**Gilbert's Battery, Brooks (South Carolina) Artillery
(Four 12-pounder Howitzers)**
[71] (7k, 29w = 36) 50.7%
Lt. Stephen Capers Gilbert

**Moody's Battery, Madison (Louisiana) "Tipperarys"
Light Artillery (Four 24-pounder Howitzers)**
[135] (4k, 29w = 33) 24.4%
Capt. George V. Moody

**Parker's Battery, Virginia (Richmond) Battery
(Three 3-inch Ordnance Rifles,
One 10-pounder Parrott)**
[90] (3k, 14w, 1m = 18) 20.0%
Capt. William W. Parker

**Taylor's Battery, Virginia (Bath) Artillery
(Four Napoleons)**
[90] (4k, 8w, 1m = 13) 14.4%
Capt. Osmond B. Taylor

WASHINGTON (LOUISIANA)
ARTILLERY BATTALION
[329] (8k, 11w, 11m = 30) 9.1%
Maj. Benjamin Franklin Eshleman

1st Company (One Napoleon)
[77] (1k, 3w = 4) 5.2%
Capt. Charles W. Squires

**2nd Company (Two Napoleons,
One 12-pounder Howitzer)**
[80] (2k, 3w, 1m = 6) 7.5%
Capt. John B. Richardson

3rd Company (Three Napoleons)
[92] (5k, 2w, 3m = 10) 10.9%
Capt. Merritt B. Miller

**4th Company (Two Napoleons,
One 12-pounder Howitzer)**
[80] (0k, 6w, 4m = 10) 12.5%
Capt. Joseph Norcom (w)
Lt. Harry A. Battles

EWELL'S CORPS
[20,917] (1,297k, 3,578w, 1,757m = 6,632) 31.7%
Lt. Gen. Richard Stoddert Ewell

ESCORT AND ORDERLIES
39th Virginia Cavalry Battalion, Randolph's Company
[31] (0k, 6m = 6) 19.4%
Capt. William F. Randolph

PROVOST GUARD
1st North Carolina Battalion Sharpshooters, Companies A and B
[94] (No losses reported) 0.0%
Maj. Rufus Watson Wharton (?)

EARLY'S DIVISION
[5,897] (311k, 830w, 404m = 1,545) 26.2%
Maj. Gen. Jubal Anderson Early

ESCORT
35th Virginia Cavalry Battalion (attached)
[232] (0k, 8m = 8) 3.5%
Lt. Col. Elijah Viers White

17th Virginia Cavalry (attached)
[241] (0k, 2w, 6m = 8) 3.3%
Lt. Col. William Henderson French

HAYS' BRIGADE
[1,292] (61k, 187w, 86m = 334) 25.9%
Brig. Gen. Harry Thompson Hays

5th Louisiana
[196] (7k, 30w, 30m = 67) 34.2%
Maj. Alexander Hart (w)
Capt. Thomas H. Briscoe

6th Louisiana
[218] (8k, 32w, 21m = 61) 28.0%
Lt. Col. Joseph Hanlon

7th Louisiana
[235] (13k, 40w, 5m = 58) 24.7%
Col. Davidson Bradfute Penn

8th Louisiana
[296] (14k, 50w, 11m = 75) 25.3%
Col. Trevanion Dudley Lewis (k)
Lt. Col. Alcibiades de Blanc (w)
Maj. German Albert Lester

9th Louisiana
[347] (19k, 35w, 19m = 73) 21.0%
Col. Leroy Augustus Stafford

SMITH'S BRIGADE
[802] (46k, 115w, 52m = 213) 26.6%
Brig. Gen. William Smith
(The 13th and 58th Virginia were left behind at Winchester following the battle of June 13-15 to process prisoners and collect supplies. They rejoined the brigade following the Gettysburg battle.)

31st Virginia
[267] (19k, 16w, 24m = 59) 22.1%
Col. John Stringer Hoffman

49th Virginia
[281] (18k, 73w, 9m = 100) 35.6%
Lt. Col. Jonathan Catlett Gibson

52nd Virginia
[254] (9k, 26w, 19m = 54) 21.3%
Lt. Col. James Henry Skinner (w)
Maj. John DeHart Ross

HOKE'S BRIGADE
[1,242] (90k, 223w, 120m = 433) 34.9%
Col. Isaac Erwin Avery (mw)
Col. Archibald Campbell Godwin
(The 1st North Carolina Battalion and 54th North Carolina were left behind at Winchester following the battle of June 13-15 to process prisoners and collect supplies. They rejoined the brigade following the Gettysburg battle.)

6th North Carolina
[509] (47k, 118w, 43m = 208) 40.9%
Maj. Samuel McDowell Tate

21st North Carolina
[436] (27k, 76w, 36m = 139) 31.9%
Col. William Whedbee Kirkland

57th North Carolina
[297] (16k, 29w, 41m = 86) 29.0%
Col. Archibald Campbell Godwin
Lt. Col. Hamilton Chamberlain Jones

GORDON'S BRIGADE
[1,807] (112k, 297w, 128m = 537) 29.7%
Brig. Gen. John Brown Gordon

13th Georgia
[312] (37k, 75w, 25m = 137) 43.9%
Col. James Milton Smith

26th Georgia
[315] (2k, 13w, 17m = 32) 10.2%
Col. Edmund Nathan Atkinson

31st Georgia
[252] (13k, 44w, 8m = 65) 25.8%
Col. Clement Anselm Evans (w)

38th Georgia
[341] (18k, 62w, 53m = 133) 39.0%
Capt. William L. McLeod (k)
Lt. John Oglesby (k)
Lt. William F. Goodwin (k)

60th Georgia
[299] (12k, 28w, 19m = 59) 19.7%
Capt. Walter Burrus Jones

61st Georgia
[288] (30k, 75w, 6m = 111) 38.5%
Col. John Hill Lamar

ARTILLERY BATTALION (EARLY'S DIVISION)
[281] (2k, 6w, 4m = 12) 4.3%
Lt. Col. Hilary Pollard Jones

Carrington's Battery, Charlottesville (Virginia) Artillery (Four Napoleons)
[71] (0k, 2m = 2) 2.8%
Capt. James McD. Carrington

Tanner's Battery, "Courtney" (Virginia) Artillery (Four Napoleons)
[90] (0k, 2m = 2) 2.2%
Capt. William A. Tanner

Green's Battery, Louisiana Guard Artillery (Two 3-inch Ordnance Rifles, Two 10-pounder Parrotts)
[60] (2k, 5w = 7) 11.7%
Capt. Charles A. Green
(One section of two guns under Green detached to Wade
Hampton's cavalry brigade on the afternoon of July 2
where they fought at Hunterstown;
guns remained with the cavalry through July 3
and served that day at East Cavalry Field.)

Garber's Battery, Staunton (Virginia) Artillery (Four Napoleons)
[60] (0k, 1w = 1) 1.7%
Capt. Asher W. Garber

RODES' DIVISION
[7,940] (594k, 1,644w, 881m+ = 3,119+) 39.3+%
Maj. Gen. Robert Emmett Rodes

DANIEL'S BRIGADE
[2,157] (233k, 593w, 171m+ = 997+) 46.2+%
Brig. Gen. Junius Daniel

32nd North Carolina
[465] (39k, 111w, 31m = 181) 38.9%
Col. Edmund Crey Brabble

43rd North Carolina
[583] (40k, 116w, 31m = 187) 32.1%
Col. Thomas Stephens Kenan (w-c)
Lt. Col. William Gaston Lewis

45th North Carolina
[460] (63k, 156w, ?m = 219+) 47.6+%
Lt. Col. Samuel Hill Boyd (w-c)
Maj. John Reynolds Winston (w-c)
Capt. Alexander H. Gallaway (w)
Capt. James A. Hopkins

53rd North Carolina
[409] (45k, 132w, 34m = 211) 51.6%
Col. William Allison Owens

2nd North Carolina Battalion
[240] (46k, 78w, 75m = 199) 82.9%
Lt. Col. Hezekiah L. Andrews (k)
Maj. John Milton Hancock (w-c)
Capt. Van Brown

IVERSON'S BRIGADE
[1,380] (182k, 399w, 322m = 903) 65.4%
Brig. Gen. Alfred Iverson

5th North Carolina
[473] (64k, 125w, 100m = 289) 61.1%
Capt. Speight Brock West (w)
Capt. Benjamin Robinson (w)

12th North Carolina
[219] (12k, 60w, 7m = 79) 36.1%
Lt. Col. William Smith Davis

20th North Carolina
[372] (41k, 94w, 118m = 253) 68.0%
Lt. Col. Nelson Slough (w)
Maj. John Stanley Brooks (w)
Capt. Lewis T. Hicks

23rd North Carolina
[316] (65k, 120w, 97m = 282) 89.2%
Col. Daniel Harvey Christie (mw)
Maj. Charles Christopher Blacknall (w-c)
Capt. Abner D. Peace (w)
Capt. William H. Johnston (w)
Capt. Vines E. Turner

DOLES' BRIGADE
[1,319] (46k, 106w, 67m = 219) 16.6%
Brig. Gen. George Doles

4th Georgia
[341] (12k, 26w, 15m = 53) 15.5%
Lt. Col. David Read Evans Winn (k)
Maj. William Henry Willis

12th Georgia
[327] (12k, 28w, 13m = 53) 16.2%
Col. Edward Willis

21st Georgia
[287] (4k, 11w, 23m = 38) 13.2%
Col. John Thomas Mercer

44th Georgia
[364] (18k, 41w, 16m = 75) 20.6%
Col. Samuel Prophet Lumpkin (mw-c)
Maj. William Hubbard Peebles

RAMSEUR'S BRIGADE
[1,023] (39k, 149w, 97m = 285) 27.9%
Brig. Gen. Stephen Dodson Ramseur

2nd North Carolina
[243] (9k, 37w, 31m = 77) 31.7%
Maj. Daniel Washington Hurtt (w)
Capt. James Turner Scales

4th North Carolina
[196] (10k, 29w, 30m = 69) 35.2%
Col. Bryan Grimes

14th North Carolina
[308] (9k, 42w, 13m = 64) 20.8%
Col. Risden Tyler Bennett (w)
Maj. Joseph Harrison Lambeth

30th North Carolina
[276] (11k, 41w, 23m = 75) 27.2%
Col. Francis Marion Parker (w)
Maj. William Walter Sillers

O'NEAL'S BRIGADE
[1,685] (83k, 375w, 220+m = 678+) 40.2+%
Col. Edward Asbury O'Neal

3rd Alabama
[350] (17k, 74w, ?m = 91+) 26.0+%
Col. Cullen Andrews Battle

5th Alabama
[317] (26k, 116w, 67m = 209) 65.9%
Col. Josephus Marion Hall

6th Alabama
[382] (15k, 62w, 88m = 165) 43.2%
Col. James Newell Lightfoot (w)
Capt. Milledge L. Bowie

12th Alabama
[317] (17k, 66w, ?m = 83+) 26.2+%
Col. Samuel Bonneau Pickens

26th Alabama
[319] (8k, 57w, 65m = 130) 40.8%
Lt. Col. John Chapman Goodgame

ARTILLERY BATTALION (RODES' DIVISION)
[376] (11k, 22w, 4m = 37) 9.8%
Lt. Col. Thomas Henry Carter

**Reese's Battery, Jeff Davis (Alabama) Artillery
(Four 3-inch Ordnance Rifles)**
[79] (No losses reported)
Capt. William J. Reese

**Carter's Battery, King William (Virginia) Artillery
(Two Napoleons, Two 10-pounder Parrotts)**
[103] (5k, 3w, 2m = 10) 9.7%
Capt. William P. Carter

**Page's Battery, Louisa "Morris" (Virginia)
Artillery (Four Napoleons)**
[114] (5k, 18w = 23) 20.2%
Capt. Richard C. M. Page (w)
Lt. Samuel H. Pendleton

**Fry's Battery, Richmond "Orange" (Virginia)
Artillery (Two 3-inch Ordnance Rifles,
Two 10-pounder Parrotts)**
[80] (1k, 1w, 2m = 4) 5.0%
Capt. Charles W. Fry

JOHNSON'S DIVISION
[6,329] (389k, 1,079w, 467+m = 1,935+) 30.6+%
Maj. Gen. Edward Johnson

STEUART'S BRIGADE
[2,116] (149k, 385w, 235m = 769) 36.3%
Brig. Gen. George Hume Steuart

1st Maryland Battalion
[400] (56k, 118w, 15m = 189) 47.3%
Lt. Col. James Rawlings Herbert (w)
Maj. William Worthington Goldsborough (w-c)
Capt. James Parran Crane

1st North Carolina
[377] (14k, 40w, 97m = 151) 40.1%
Lt. Col. Hamilton Allen Brown

3rd North Carolina
[548] (48k, 140w, 30m = 218) 39.8%
Maj. William Murdock Parsley

10th Virginia
[276] (8k, 17w, 52m = 77) 27.9%
Col. Edward Tiffin Harrison Warren

23rd Virginia
[251] (3k, 15w, 18m = 36) 14.3%
Lt. Col. Simeon Taylor Walton

37th Virginia
[264] (20k, 55w, 23m = 98) 37.1%
Maj. Henry Clinton Wood

NICHOLLS' BRIGADE
[1,101] (66k, 229w, 19m+ = 314+) 28.5+%
Col. Jesse Milton Williams

1st Louisiana
[172] (11k, 28w, ?m = 39+) 22.7+%
Col. Michael Nolan (k)
Capt. Edward D. Willett

2nd Louisiana
[236] (15k, 47w, ?m = 62+) 26.3+%
Lt. Col. Ross Edwin Burke (w-c)
Maj. Michael A. Grogan

10th Louisiana
[226] (22k, 69w, 19m = 110) 48.7%
Maj. Thomas N. Powell

14th Louisiana
[281] (15k, 50w, ?m = 65+) 23.1+%
Lt. Col. David Zable

15th Louisiana
[186] (3k, 35w, ?m = 38+) 20.4+%
Maj. Andrew Brady

STONEWALL BRIGADE
[1,319] (65k, 183w, 100m = 348) 26.4%
Brig. Gen. James Walker

2nd Virginia
[333] (3k, 12w, 10m = 25) 7.5%
Col. John Quincy Adams Nadenbousch

4th Virginia
[257] (18k, 63w, 56m = 137) 53.3%
Maj. William Terry

5th Virginia
[345] (14k, 43w, 11m = 68) 19.7%
Col. John Henry Stover Funk

27th Virginia
[148] (11k, 29w, 8m = 48) 32.4%
Lt. Col. Daniel McElheran Shriver

33rd Virginia
[236] (19k, 36w, 15m = 70) 29.7%
Capt. Jacob Burner Golladay

JONES' BRIGADE
[1,446] (88k, 253w, 113m = 454) 31.4%
Brig. Gen. John Marshall Jones (w)
Lt. Col. Robert Henry Dungan

21st Virginia
[183] (8k, 32w, 10m = 50) 27.3%
Capt. William Perkins Moseley

25th Virginia
[280] (9k, 54w, 7m = 70) 25.0%
Col. John Carlton Higginbotham (w)
Lt. Col. John Armistead Robinson

42nd Virginia
[252] (16k, 47w, 26m = 89) 35.3%
Col. Robert Woodson Withers (w)
Capt. Samuel H. Saunders

44th Virginia
[227] (19k, 16w, 24m = 59) 26.0%
Maj. Norvell Cobb (w)
Capt. Thomas R. Buckner

48th Virginia
[252] (20k, 38w, 29m = 87) 34.5%
Lt. Col. Robert Henry Dungan
Maj. Oscar White

50th Virginia
[252] (16k, 66w, 17m = 99) 39.3%
Lt. Col. Logan Henry Neil Salyer

ARTILLERY BATTALION (JOHNSON'S DIVISION)
[347] (21k, 29w = 50) 14.4%
Maj. Joseph White Latimer (mw)
Capt. Charles I. Raine

Dement's Battery, 1st Maryland Battery (Four Napoleons)
[90] (1k, 4w = 5) 5.6%
Capt. William F. Dement

Carpenter's Battery, Alleghany Rough (Virginia) Artillery (Two Napoleons, Two 3-inch Ordnance Rifles)
[91] (10k, 14w = 24) 26.4%
Capt. John C. Carpenter

Brown's Battery, 4th Maryland Light (Chesapeake) Artillery (Four 10-pounder Parrotts)
[76] (8k, 9w = 17) 22.4%
Capt. William D. Brown (mw)
Lt. Walter S. Chew

Raine's Battery, Lynchburg (Virginia) "Lee" Battery (One 3-inch Ordnance Rifle, One 10-pounder Parrott, Two 20-pounder Parrotts)
[90] (2k, 2w = 4) 4.4%
Capt. Charles I. Raine
Lt. William M. Hardwicke

ARTILLERY RESERVE (EWELL'S CORPS)
[626] (3k, 25w, 5m = 33) 5.3%
Col. John Thompson Brown, Chief of Artillery

DANCE'S ARTILLERY BATTALION, 1ST VIRGINIA ARTILLERY
[358] (3k, 24w, 5m = 32) 8.9%
Capt. Willis Jefferson Dance

Watson's Battery, 2nd Richmond (Virginia) Howitzers (Four 10-pounder Parrotts)
[64] (2k, 1w = 3) 4.7%
Capt. David Watson

Smith's Battery, 3rd Richmond (Virginia) Howitzers (Four 3-inch Ordnance Rifles)
[62] (1k, 1w, 2m = 4) 6.5%
Capt. Benjamin H. Smith, Jr.

Cunningham's Battery, Powhatan (Virginia) Artillery (Four 3-inch Ordnance Rifles)
[78] (No losses reported) 0.0%
Lt. John M. Cunningham

Graham's Battery, 1st Rockbridge (Virginia) Artillery (Four 20-pounder Parrotts)
[85] (0k, 20w = 20) 23.5%
Capt. Archibald Graham

Griffin's (Hupp's) Salem (Virginia) Flying Artillery (Two Napoleons, Two 3-inch Ordnance Rifles)
[69] (0k, 2w, 3m = 5) 7.2%
Lt. Charles B. Griffin

NELSON'S BATTALION
[268] (0k, 1w = 1) 0.4%
Lt. Col. William Nelson

Amherst (Virginia) Artillery (Three Napoleons, One 3-inch Ordnance Rifle)
[105] (No losses reported) 0.0%
Capt. Thomas J. Kirkpatrick

Fluvanna (Virginia) Artillery (Three Napoleons, One 3-inch Ordnance Rifle)
[90] (0k, 1w = 1) 1.1%
Capt. John L. Massie

Georgia Battery (Two 3-inch Ordnance Rifles, One 10-pounder Parrott)
[73] (No losses reported) 0.0%
Capt. John Milledge, Jr.

HILL'S CORPS
[21,774] (1,715k, 4,587w, 1,980m = 8,282) 38.0%
Lt. Gen. Ambrose Powell Hill

ANDERSON'S DIVISION
[7,070] (381k, 1,112w, 523m+ = 2,016+) 28.5+%
Maj. Gen. Richard Heron Anderson

WILCOX'S BRIGADE
[1,721] (78k, 375w, 156m+ = 609+) 35.4+%
Brig. Gen. Cadmus Marcellus Wilcox

8th Alabama
[477] (40k, 146w, 80m = 266) 55.8%
Lt. Col. Hilary Abner Herbert

9th Alabama
[306] (8k, 32w, 76m = 116) 37.9%
Col. Joseph Horace King (w)
Capt. John N. Chisholm (w-c)
Capt. Gaines C. Smith (w-c)
Capt. M. G. May (w)

10th Alabama
[311] (15k, 89w, ?m = 104+) 33.4+%
Col. William Henry Forney (w-c)
Lt. Col. James Etter Shelley

11th Alabama
[311] (7k, 68w, ?m = 75+) 24.1+%
Col. John Caldwell Calhoun Sanders (w)
Lt. Col. George Edward Tayloe

14th Alabama
[316] (8k, 40w, ?m = 48+) 15.2+%
Col. Lucius Pinckard (w-c)
Lt. Col. James Andrew Broome

WRIGHT'S BRIGADE
[1,379] (184k, 343w, 169m = 696) 50.5%
Brig. Gen. Ambrose Rans Wright
(final command of brigade)
Col. William Gibson (w-c)

3rd Georgia
[411] (49k, 139w, 31m = 219) 53.3%
Col. Edward J. Walker

22nd Georgia
[400] (41k, 70w, 60m = 171) 42.8%
Col. Joseph Wasden (k)
Capt. Benjamin C. McCurry

48th Georgia
[395] (70k, 97w, 57m = 224) 56.7%
Col. William Gibson (w-c)
Capt. Matthew Robert Hall

2nd Georgia Battalion
[173] (24k, 37w, 21m = 82) 47.4%
Maj. George W. Ross (mw-c)
Capt. Charles Jackson Moffett

MAHONE'S BRIGADE
[1,538] (21k, 51w, 30m = 102) 6.6%
Brig. Gen. William Mahone

6th Virginia
[288] (0k, 4w, 7m = 11) 3.8%
Col. George Thomas Rogers

12th Virginia
[348] (3k, 11w, 8m = 22) 6.3%
Col. David Addison Weisiger

16th Virginia
[270] (2k, 15w, 5m = 22) 8.1%
Col. Joseph Hutchinson Ham

41st Virginia
[276] (11k, 11w = 22) 8.0%
Col. William Allen Parham

61st Virginia
[356] (5k, 10w, 10m = 25) 7.0%
Col. Virginius Despeaux Groner

PERRY'S BRIGADE
[739] (80k, 228w, 147m = 455) 61.6%
Col. David Lang

2nd Florida
[242] (24k, 71w, est. 49m = est. 144) est. 59.5%
Maj. Walter Raleigh Moore (w-c)
Capt. William Duncan Ballantine (w-c)
Capt. C. Seton Fleming

5th Florida
[321] (39k, 77w, est. 70m = est. 186) est. 57.9%
Capt. Richmond N. Gardner (w)
Capt. John S. Cochran (mw)
Capt. Council Allen Bryan
Capt. John W. Holleyman

8th Florida
[176] (17k, 80w, est. 28m = est. 125) est. 71.0%
Lt. Col. William Baya

POSEY'S BRIGADE
[1,318] (15k, 80w, 17m = 112) 8.5%
Brig. Gen. Carnot Posey

12th Mississippi
[305] (1k, 11w, 1m = 13) 4.3%
Col. William Henry Taylor

16th Mississippi
[385] (3k, 16w, 7m = 26) 6.8%
Col. Samuel E. Baker

19th Mississippi
[372] (5k, 26w, 3m = 34) 9.1%
Col. Nathaniel Harrison Harris

48th Mississippi
[256] (6k, 27w, 6m = 39) 15.2%
Col. Joseph McAfee Jayne

11TH GEORGIA "SUMTER FLYING ARTILLERY" ARTILLERY BATTALION (ANDERSON'S DIVISION)
[375] (3k, 35w, 4m = 42) 11.2%
Maj. John Lane

Company A (One 12-pounder Howitzer, One Napoleon, One 3-inch Navy Parrott Rifle, Three 10-pounder Parrotts)
[130] (1k, 11w, 1m = 13) 10.0%
Capt. Hugh Madison Ross

Company B (Four 12-pounder Howitzers, Two Napoleons)
[124] (2k, 6w, 1m = 9) 7.3%
Capt. George M. Patterson

Company C (Three 3-inch Navy Parrott Rifles, Two 10-pounder Parrotts)
[121] (0k, 18w, 2m = 20) 16.5%
Capt. John T. Wingfield (w)

HETH'S DIVISION
[7,423] (827k, 2,023w, 919m = 3,769) 50.8%
Maj. Gen. Henry Heth (w)
Brig. Gen. James Johnston Pettigrew (w)

PETTIGREW'S BRIGADE
[2,576] (410k, 977w, 229m = 1,616) 62.7%
Brig. Gen. James Johnston Pettigrew (w)
Col. James Keith Marshall (k)
Maj. John Thomas Jones (w)

11th North Carolina
[617] (108k, 200w, 58m = 366) 59.3%
Col. Collett Leventhorpe (w-c)
Maj. Egbert A. Ross (k)
Capt. Francis Wilder Bird

26th North Carolina
[839] (172k, 443w, 72m = 687) 81.9%
Col. Henry King Burgwyn, Jr. (k)
Lt. Col. John Randolph Lane (w)
Maj. John Thomas Jones (w)
Capt. Henry Clay Albright

47th North Carolina
[567] (53k, 159w, 5m = 217) 38.3%
Col. George Henry Faribault (w)
Lt. Col. John Azariah Graves (mw-c)
Maj. Archibald Davis Crudup (w-c)
Capt. William Crocker Lankford

52nd North Carolina
[553] (77k, 175w, 94m = 346) 62.6%
Col. James Keith Marshall (k)
Lt. Col. Marcus A. Parks (w-c)
Maj. John Quincy Adams Richardson (mw-c)
Capt. Nathaniel A. Foster

BROCKENBROUGH'S BRIGADE
[968] (41k, 106w, 77m = 224) 23.1%
Col. John Mercer Brockenbrough

40th Virginia
[254] (10k, 37w, 18m = 65) 25.6%
Capt. Thomas Edwin Betts (w-c)
Capt. Robert Beale Davis

47th Virginia
[209] (12k, 22w, 30m = 64) 30.6%
Col. Robert Murphy Mayo
Lt. Col. John Warner Lyell

55th Virginia
[268] (13k, 32w, 19m = 64) 23.9%
Col. William Steptoe Christian

22nd Virginia Battalion
[237] (6k, 15w, 10m = 31) 13.1%
Maj. John Samuel Bowles

ARCHER'S BRIGADE
[1,193] (69k, 218w, 396m = 683) 57.3%
Brig. Gen. James Jay Archer (c)
Col. Birkett Davenport Fry (w-c)
Lt. Col. Samuel George Shepard

5th Alabama Battalion
[135] (3k, 30w, 15m = 48) 35.6%
Maj. Albert Sebastian Van De Graaff

13th Alabama
[308] (11k, 46w, 157m = 214) 69.5%
Col. Birkett Davenport Fry (w-c)
Capt. Charles Edward Chambers (w-c)
Capt. Walter J. Taylor

1st Tennessee (Provisional Army)
[281] (16k, 67w, 95m = 178) 63.3%
Lt. Col. Newton Jefferson George (c)
Maj. Felix Grundy Buchanan (w)
(final command of regiment)
Capt. Jacob B. Turney (w-c)

7th Tennessee
[249] (24k, 38w, 54m = 116) 46.6%
Col. John Amenas Fite (c)
Lt. Col. Samuel George Shepard

14th Tennessee
[220] (15k, 37w, 75m = 127) 57.7%
Lt. Col. James W. Lockert (w-c)
Capt. Bruce L. Phillips

DAVIS' BRIGADE
[2,299] (307k, 717w, 200m = 1,224) 53.2%
Brig. Gen. Joseph Robert Davis

2nd Mississippi
[492] (56k, 176w = 232) 47.2%
Col. John Marshall Stone (w)
(final command of regiment)
Maj. John Alan Blair (c)
Lt. Col. David Word Humphries (k)
(led regiment on July 3)

11th Mississippi
[592] (102k, 168w, 42m = 312) 52.7%
Col. Francis M. Green (w)
Maj. Reuben Oscar Reynolds (w)
Lt. Daniel Featherston (k)
Lt. Robert A. McDowell

42nd Mississippi
[575] (75k, 190w = 265) 46.1%
Col. Hugh Reid Miller (mw-c)
Lt. Col. Hillery Moseley (w)
Maj. William A. Feeney (w)
Capt. Andrew McCampbell Nelson

55th North Carolina
[640] (74k, 183w, 158m = 415) 64.8%
Col. John Kerr Connally (w-c)
Lt. Col. Maurice Thompson Smith (mw)
Maj. Alfred Horatio Belo (w)
Capt. George A. Gilreath (k)
Capt. E. Fletcher Satterfield

ARTILLERY BATTALION (HETH'S DIVISION)
[387] (0k, 5w, 17m = 22) 5.7%
Lt. Col. John Jameson Garnett

Maurin's Battery, Donaldsville (Louisiana) Artillery (Two 3-inch Ordnance Rifles, One 10-pounder Parrott)
[114] (0k, 2w, 4m = 6) 5.3%
Capt. Victor Maurin

Moore's Battery, Huger (Virginia) Artillery (Two Napoleons, One 3-inch Ordnance Rifle, One 10-pounder Parrott)
[77] (Losses unknown)
Capt. Joseph D. Moore

Lewis' Battery, Pittsylvania (Virginia) Artillery (Two Napoleons, Two 3-inch Ordnance Rifles)
[90] (Losses unknown)
Capt. John W. Lewis

Grandy's Battery, Norfolk (Virginia) Light Artillery Blues (Two 3-inch Ordnance Rifles, Two 12-pounder Howitzers)
[106] (0k, 1w, 1m = 2) 1.9%
Capt. Charles R. Grandy

PENDER'S DIVISION

[6,567] (490k, 1,402w, 526m = 2,418) 36.8%
Maj. Gen. Willian Dorsey Pender (mw)
Brig. Gen. James Henry Lane (final command of division)
Maj. Gen. Isaac Ridgeway Trimble (w-c)

PERRIN'S BRIGADE

[1,878] (102k, 529w, 16m = 647) 34.5%
Col. Abner Perrin

1st South Carolina (Provisional Army)
[328] (19k, 94w, 2m = 115) 35.1%
Maj. Comillus Wycliffe McCreary

1st South Carolina Rifles
[366] (2k, 5w = 7) 1.9%
Capt. William M. Hadden

12th South Carolina
[366] (20k, 105w, 4m = 129) 35.2%
Col. John Lucas Miller

13th South Carolina
[390] (35k, 105w, 4m = 144) 36.9%
Lt. Col. Benjamin Thomas Brockman

14th South Carolina
[428] (26k, 220w, 6m = 252) 58.9%
Lt. Col. Joseph Newton Brown (w)
Maj. Edward Croft (w)
Capt. James Boatwright

LANE'S BRIGADE

[1,730] (178k, 376w, 228m = 782) 45.2%
Brig. Gen. James Henry Lane

7th North Carolina
[291] (32k, 66w, 61m = 159) 54.6%
Maj. John McLeod Turner (w-c)
Capt. James Gilmer Harris

18th North Carolina
[346] (16k, 38w, 34m = 88) 25.4%
Col. John Decatur Barry

28th North Carolina
[346] (65k, 135w, 37m = 237) 68.5%
Col. Samuel D. Lowe (w)
Lt. Col. William Henry Asbury Speer (w)

33rd North Carolina
[368] (30k, 54w, 38m = 122) 33.2%
Maj. Joseph Hubbard Saunders (w-c)
Lt. Wesley L. Battle (mw)

37th North Carolina
[379] (35k, 83w, 58m = 176) 46.4%
Col. William Morgan Barbour

THOMAS' BRIGADE

[1,244] (34k, 127w, 103m = 264) 21.2%
Brig. Gen. Edward Lloyd Thomas

14th Georgia
[305] (6k, 27w, 11m = 44) 14.4%
Col. Robert Warren Folsom

35th Georgia
[305] (11k, 37w, 42m = 90) 29.5%
Col. Bolling Hall Holt

45th Georgia
[305] (5k, 32w, 8m = 45) 14.8%
Col. Thomas Jefferson Simmons

49th Georgia
[329] (12k, 31w, 42m = 85) 25.8%
Col. Samuel Thomas Player

SCALES' BRIGADE

[1,347] (175k, 356w, 171m = 702) 52.1%
Brig. Gen. Alfred Moore Scales (w)
Lt. Col. George Tomline Gordon (w)
Col. William Lee Joshua Lowrance

13th North Carolina
[232] (55k, 98w, 26m = 179) 77.2%
Col. Joseph Henry Hyman (w)
Lt. Col. Henry A. Rogers

16th North Carolina
[321] (24k, 61w, 38m = 123) 38.3%
Capt. Leroy W. Stowe
Capt. Abel S. Cloud

22nd North Carolina
[267] (37k, 79w, 50m = 166) 62.2%
Col. James Conner

34th North Carolina
[311] (19k, 55w, 30m = 104) 33.4%
Col. William Lee Joshua Lowrance
Lt. Col. George Tomline Gordon (w)
Lt. Alexander A. Cathey (w-c)
Lt. Burwell T. Cotton

38th North Carolina
[216] (40k, 63w, 27m = 130) 60.2%
Col. William James Hoke (w)
Lt. Col. John Ashford (w)
Capt. William L. Thornburg (w)
Lt. John M. Robinson

ARTILLERY BATTALION (PENDER'S DIVISION)
[368] (1k, 14w, 8m = 23) 6.3%
Maj. William Thomas Poague

**Wyatt's Battery, Albemarle (Virginia) Artillery
(Two 3-inch Ordnance Rifles, One 10-pounder
Parrott, One 12-pounder Howitzer)**
[94] (0k, 12w, 1m = 13) 13.8%
Capt. James W. Wyatt

**Graham's Battery, Charlotte (North Carolina)
Artillery (Two Napoleons,
Two 12-pounder Howitzers)**
[125] (0k, 5m = 5) 4.0%
Capt. Joseph Graham

**Ward's Battery, Madison (Mississippi) Light Artillery
(Three Napoleons, One 12-pounder Howitzer)**
[91] (Unknown losses)
Capt. George Ward

**Brooke's Battery, Warrington (Virginia) Battery
(Two Napoleons, Two 12-pounder Howitzers)**
[58] (1k, 2w, 2m = 5) 8.6%
Capt. James V. Brooke

ARTILLERY RESERVE (HILL'S CORPS)
[714] (17k, 50w, 12m = 79) 11.1%
Col. Reuben Lindsay Walker

McIntosh's Battalion
[348] (8k, 13w, 9m = 30) 8.6%
Maj. David Gregg McIntosh

**Rice's Battery, Danville (Virginia) Artillery
(Four Napoleons)**
[114] (0k, 1w, 1m = 2) 1.8%
Capt. R. Sidney Rice

**Hurt's Battery, Hardaway (Alabama) Artillery
(Two 3-inch Ordnance Rifles, Two Whitworth Rifles)**
[71] (0k, 4w, 4m = 8) 11.3%
Capt. William B. Hurt

**Wallace's Battery, 2nd Rockbridge (Virginia)
Artillery (Four 3-inch Ordnance Rifles)**
[67] (3k, 7w = 10) 14.9%
Lt. Samuel Wallace

**Johnson's Battery, Richmond (Virginia) Battery
(Two Napoleons, Two 3-inch Ordnance Rifles)**
[96] (5k, 1w, 4m = 10) 10.4%
Capt. Marmaduke Johnson

Pegram's Battalion
[366] (9k, 37w, 3m = 49) 13.4%
Maj. William Ransom Johnson Pegram

**Crenshaw's Battery, Richmond (Virginia) Battery
(Two Napoleons, Two 12-pounder Howitzers)**
[76] (1k, 14w = 15) 19.7%
Capt. William Graves Crenshaw

**Marye's Battery, Fredericksburg (Virginia) Artillery
(Two Napoleons, Two 10-pounder Parrotts)**
[71] (2k = 2) 2.8%
Capt. Edward Avenmore Marye

**Brander's Battery, "Letcher" Richmond (Virginia)
Artillery (Two Napoleons, Two 10-pounder Parrotts)**
[65] (3k, 11w, 3m = 17) 26.2%
Capt. Thomas A. Brander

**Zimmerman's Battery, Pee Dee (South Carolina)
Artillery (Four 3-inch Ordnance Rifles)**
[65] (2k, 7w = 9) 13.8%
Lt. William Edward Zimmerman

**McGraw's Battery, "Purcell" (Virginia) Artillery
(Four Napoleons)**
[89] (1k, 5w = 6) 6.7%
Capt. Joseph McGraw

CAVALRY DIVISION
[7,823] (66k, 172w, 140m = 378+) 4.8%+
Maj. Gen. James Ewell Brown Stuart

STAFF

Adjutant General
Maj. Henry Brainerd McClellan

Inspector General
Maj. Andrew Reid Venable

Chief Engineer
Capt. William Willis Blackford
Lt. Francis Smith Robertson, Asst.

Chief Signal Officer
Capt. Richard Edgar Frayser

Provost Marshal
Lt. Garland Mitchell Ryals

Aides-de-Camp
Lt. Chiswell Dabney
Lt. Theodore Stanford Garnett
Lt. Walter Quarrier Hullihen
Lt. William "Henry" Hagan
Lt. Richard Byrd Kennon

Quartermaster
Maj. Norman Richard Fitzhugh
Capt. James Marshall Hangar, Asst.

Chief Surgeon
Talcott Eliason

Chief of Ordnance
Capt. John Esten Cooke

Chief Commissary
Maj. William J. Johnson

Orderlies
Acting Sgt. Samuel A. Nelson
(4th Virginia Cavalry, Company B)
Pvt. Edward Dorsey Cole
(15th Virginia Cavalry, Company H)
Pvt. Francis Henry Deane
(4th Virginia Cavalry, Company E)
Pvt. Augustine Henry Ellis
(13th Virginia Cavalry, Company H)
Pvt. Robert William Goode
(1st Virginia Cavalry, Company G)
Pvt. William Preston Jones
(9th Virginia Cavalry, Company E)
Pvt. William T. Thompson
(13th Virginia Cavalry, Company G)
Pvt. Benjamin Franklin Weller
(1st Virginia Cavalry, Company E)
Pvt. George N. Woodbridge
(4th Virginia Cavalry, Company E)

HAMPTON'S BRIGADE
[1,746] (21k, 53w, 37m = 111) 6.4%
Fought at Hunterstown, July 2 (see page 139)
and East Cavalry Field, July 3 (see page 148)
Brig. Gen. Wade Hampton (w)
Col. Laurence Simmons Baker

FITZ LEE'S BRIGADE
[1,908] (10k, 24w, 67m = 101) 5.3%
Fought at East Cavalry Field, July 3 (see page 148)
Brig. Gen. Fitzhugh Lee

WILLIAM HENRY FITZHUGH LEE'S BRIGADE
[1,169] (5k, 31w, 20m = 56) 4.8%
Fought at East Cavalry Field, July 3 (see page 148)
Col. John Randolph Chambliss, Jr.
(final command of brigade)
Col. James Lucius Davis

JENKINS' BRIGADE
[1,175] (7k, 7w, 9m = 23) 2.0%
Fought at East Cavalry Field, July 3 (see page 148)
Brig. Gen. Albert Gallatin Jenkins (w)
Col. Milton James Ferguson
(detailed to guard prisoners in the town on July 3)
Lt. Col. Vincent Addison Witcher

JONES' BRIGADE
[1,307] (12k, 42w, 6m = 60) 4.6%
Fought at Fairfield, PA, July 3 (see page 145);
(35th Battalion Virginia Cavalry
detached to Ewell's Corps)
Brig. Gen. William Edmonson Jones

IMBODEN'S NORTHWESTERN BRIGADE
[2,241] (No losses reported) 0%
Not on battlefield; engaged during retreat
(see page 175)
Brig. Gen. John Daniel Imboden

ROBERTSON'S BRIGADE
[962] (No losses reported) 0%
Not on battlefield; engaged during retreat
(see page 188)
Brig. Gen. Beverly Holcombe Robertson

STUART HORSE ARTILLERY
[518] (1k, 20w, 1m = 22) 4.3%
Maj. Robert Franklin Beckham

The losses suffered at Gettysburg devastated both armies. Nearly one-quarter of Meade's Army of the Potomac entered the books as casualties (killed, wounded, captured, or missing). A deeper examination reveals that Meade lost 3,100 commissioned officers, or nearly one-half of his entire officer corps. Of his seven corps commanders, one had been killed (Reynolds) and two others wounded (Sickles and Hancock).

Comparatively speaking, Robert E. Lee's losses were heavier and more costly because they could not be as easily replaced. Nearly one-third of his army had been killed, wounded, captured, or missing. Because slightly wounded soldiers were often not reported, and because many casualty and battle reports are missing, Lee's losses were almost certainly significantly higher than officially reported. Of his approximately 6,900 officers, more than 4,700 had been killed, wounded, or taken prisoner. By the end of the day on July 3, about one-half of his battered regiments were in the hands of officers below the rank of colonel.

Lee's wagon trains, including miles of wagons filled with wounded, left the area around Gettysburg early on the morning of July 4 for the long and agonizing journey back to Virginia. Southern infantry began a slow withdrawal in their wake. The Gettysburg Campaign, however, was far from over. In fact, it was simply entering a new and often overlooked phase. On July 5, Federal cavalry and infantry moved out in pursuit, shadowing and attacking whenever possible the rearguard elements of the Confederate army. Two dozen skirmishes and several significant combats would break out in Pennsylvania and Maryland before Lee put the Potomac River between his men and the Yankees.

THE BATTLE OF GETTYSBURG
ESTIMATES OF DAILY CASUALTIES

Several early attempts were undertaken to calculate daily casualties during the main battle. Publications such as Frederick Phisterer's landmark six volume *New York in the War of the Rebellion, 1861 to 1865* (Albany, NY: 1912), includes a table of estimated Federal casualties for each of the three days. John M. Vanderslice, in his *Gettysburg: Then and Now* (New York, NY: 1899), also made a reasonable attempt to list casualties suffered by both sides on portions of the battlefield over the three days of combat. Some participants and scores of historians and other writers have done their best to include such breakdowns in their primary and secondary works on Gettysburg.

These four tables provide ranges of the total number of casualties (killed, wounded, and captured/missing) suffered by each army on each day. Although many of the calculations are based on educated guesswork, they are grounded in years of archival research, interpolation, and the consensus of participants and scholars of the battle who have attempted to compile such statistics. Please keep in mind that many of the wounded listed here were also among the captured, with many more wounded Confederates being captured during the retreat from the battlefield from July 4-14.

Scholars and students of the battle have often tried to calculate the number of casualties suffered by each side during the three individual days of the main battle (July 1-3, 1863).

Unfortunately, detailed records that would make this possible were not kept then or later. As a result, constructing such tabulations is difficult and open to interpretation. In some cases it is fairly easy to calculate losses, but in other cases, very problematic. For example, if a particular unit (say a regiment or a brigade) did most of its fighting on one of the three days, it can be reasonably assumed that all or very nearly all of its reported battle casualties were suffered on that day. Some units participated in fighting on two or even all three days, which makes breaking out the losses much more difficult. In addition, many soldiers on both sides were wounded more than once during the battle. Some Confederates, for example, were only slightly wounded on July 1 or 2 and went on to

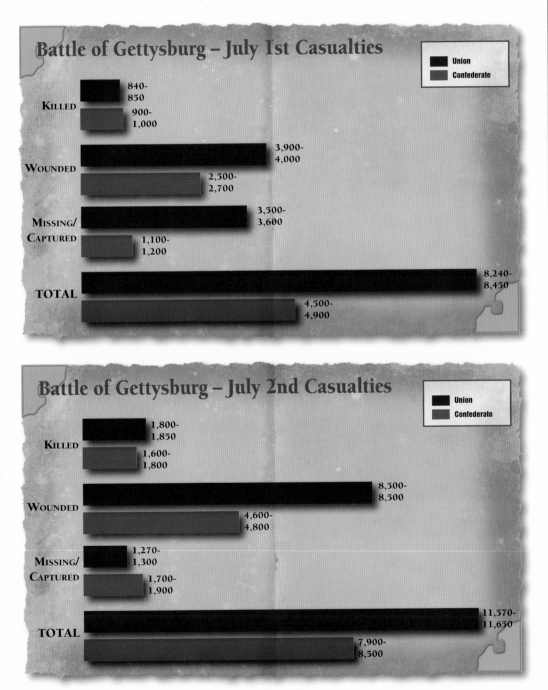

participate in Pickett's Charge or the fighting at Culp's Hill on July 3, and were killed, wounded, or captured during their last action. How should they be reported? How were they reported then? Additionally, a significant number of Southern troops captured on July 1 gained their freedom later that day when the Federals were routed west and north of the town. Few or none of these men were listed among the captured.

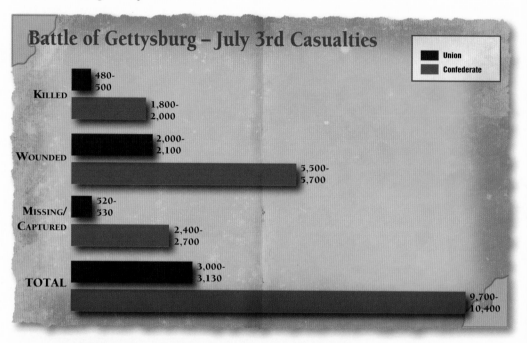

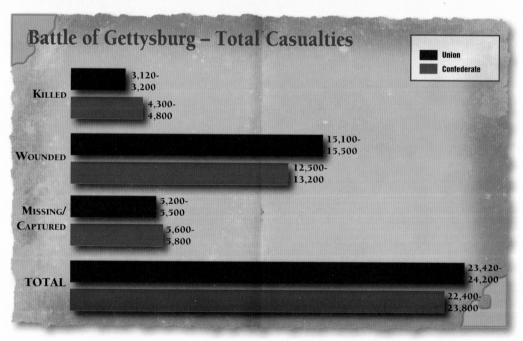

THE BATTLE OF HUNTERSTOWN, PA.

JULY 2, 1863

When word arrived during the early morning hours of July 2 for J.E.B. Stuart and his cavalry to make for Gettysburg, brigade commander **BRIG. GEN. WADE HAMPTON** saddled up his troopers at their camp near Dillsburg, Pennsylvania. His men still had charge of 125 cumbersome wagons seized several days earlier at Rockville, Maryland. Hampton's long column reached Hunterstown early that afternoon, passed through the town square under the suspicious gazes of the townsfolk, and continued along a road leading to the York Pike and then to the Confederate lines north of Gettysburg.

Brig. Gen. Wade Hampton
Image courtesy of Library of Congress

Hampton's rearguard, about forty troopers from Company C of Cobb's Legion under Col. Pierce M. B. Young, was riding out of the square when Federal cavalry was spotted on the road behind them to their east. The Yankees, Company A of the 18th Pennsylvania Cavalry, also numbered about forty men. The Pennsylvanians had been part of the cavalry riding at the rear of **BRIG. GEN. JUDSON KILPATRICK**'s column on June 30 at Hanover when they were attacked by Stuart's cavalry. Captain Llewellyn Estes of Kilpatrick's staff led these Pennsylvanians, who on this day formed the advance guard of Kilpatrick's division. Earlier that morning, Kilpatrick received orders to ride from north of Hanover to the Federal right flank at Gettysburg. That directive put him on a collision course with Hampton's column.

Brig. Gen. Judson Kilpatrick
Image courtesy of Libary of Congress

Estes formed his men in a line and charged Young's Southern troopers with sabers drawn. Hand-to-hand combat raged for a short time, but Young knew he had to break free and notify Hampton that Federal cavalry was on his heels. The Southerners galloped away to warn Hampton, and Estes did the same to notify Kilpatrick of the presence of Rebel cavalry at Hunterstown.

After reconnoitering to the west, Kilpatrick formed a battle line on a ridge just southwest of Hunterstown to face Hampton's position farther south. Young was in the road with his detail between the two lines, as if to defy the Federals to attack him a second time.

Brigadier General George A. Custer personally led Company A of his 6th Michigan Cavalry in a mounted charge against Young — Custer's first such charge as a brigadier general.

Custer's horse was shot during the charge and he was trapped beneath the dead animal. He may well have been killed had he not been saved, literally, in the nick of time by one of his orderlies. The Wolverines of Company A suffered heavy casualties when they were surrounded by Young's troopers, the Phillips' Legion and the 2nd South Carolina Cavalry. After Custer barely escaped with his life, the Confederates countercharged Kilpatrick's position. Federal artillery fire

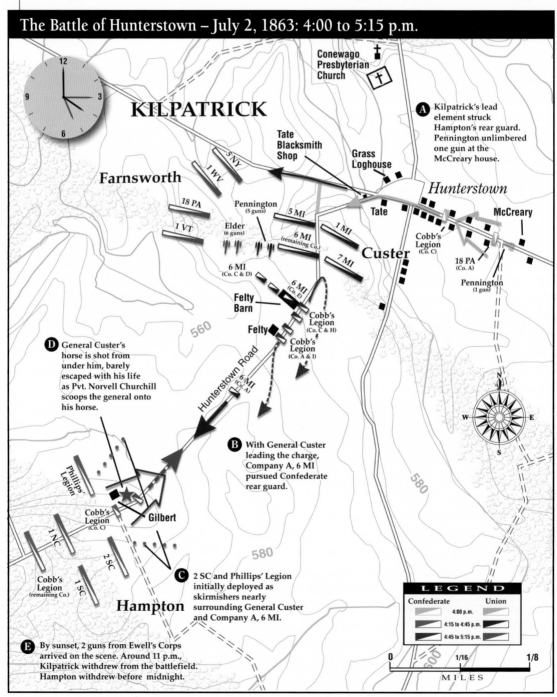

The Battle of Hunterstown – July 2, 1863: 4:00 to 5:15 p.m.

from Lt. Alexander C. M. Pennington's battery, coupled with the fire of dismounted Michigan troopers, eventually drove them back. When Hampton received artillery support from two guns of Capt. Charles A. Greene's Battery of Ewell's infantry corps, an artillery duel broke out that lasted well after dark, with Pennington getting the better of the exchange.

The fight at Hunterstown was the final — and wholly unexpected — confrontation with Yankees before all of Stuart's cavalry reached Gettysburg. The engagement prevented Kilpatrick's cavalry from reaching deeper into the Confederate left flank.

FEDERAL

ARMY OF THE POTOMAC
CAVALRY CORPS

THIRD CAVALRY DIVISION
[4,134] (1k, 3mw, 27w, 1w-c, 2c, 9m = 43) 1.0%
Brig. Gen. Hugh Judson Kilpatrick

HEADQUARTERS GUARDS AND ORDERLIES

1st Ohio Cavalry, Company A
[40] (No losses reported) 0.0%
Capt. Noah Jones

1st Ohio Cavalry, Company C
[37] (No losses reported) 0.0%

FIRST BRIGADE
[1,924] (0k, 2w, 1m = 3) 0.2%
Brig. Gen. Elon John Farnsworth

5th New York Cavalry
[420] (0k, 1m = 1) 0.2%
Maj. John Hammond

18th Pennsylvania Cavalry
[509] (0k, 1w = 1) 0.2%
Lt. Col. William Penn Brinton

1st Vermont Cavalry
[600] (0k, 1w = 1) 0.2%
Lt. Col. Addison Webster Preston

1st West Virginia Cavalry
[395] (No losses reported) 0.0%
Col. Nathaniel Pendleton Richmond

ARTILLERY
4th United States Horse Artillery, Battery E (Four 3-inch Ordnance Rifles)
[61] (No losses reported) 0.0%
Lt. Samuel Sherer Elder

SECOND BRIGADE
[1,955] (1k, 3mw, 25w, 1w-c, 2c, 8m = 40) 2.0%
Brig. Gen. George Armstrong Custer

1st Michigan Cavalry
[427] (0k, 1mw = 1) 0.2%
Col. Charles Henry Town

5th Michigan Cavalry
[645] (No losses reported) 0.0%
Col. Russell Alexander Alger

6th Michigan Cavalry
[501] (1k, 2mw, 25w, 1w-c, 2c, 3m = 34) 6.8%
Col. George Gray

7th Michigan Cavalry
[382] (0k, 5m = 5) 1.3%
Col. William D'Alton Mann

ARTILLERY
2nd United States Horse Artillery, Battery M (Six 3-inch Ordnance Rifles)
[117] (No losses reported) 0.0%
Lt. Alexander Cummings McWhorter Pennington, Jr.

CONFEDERATE

ARMY OF NORTHERN VIRGINIA
CAVALRY DIVISION
[1,778] (10k, 20w, 7m = 37) 2.1%

HAMPTON'S BRIGADE
[1,778] (7k, 2mw, 5w, 7m = 21) 1.2%
Brig. Gen. Wade Hampton

1st North Carolina Cavalry
[407] (No losses reported) 0.0%
Col. Laurence Simmons Baker

1st South Carolina Cavalry
[339] (No losses reported) 0.0%
Lt. Col. John David Twiggs (?)
(Col. John Logan Black, wounded at Upperville,
later stated that Maj. William Walker commanded
the regiment at this time.)

2nd South Carolina Cavalry
[186] (No losses reported) 0.0%
Maj. Thomas Jefferson Lipscomb

Cobb's (Georgia) Legion Cavalry
[330] (2k, 2mw, 1w-c = 5) 1.5%
Col. Pierce Manning Butler Young

Jeff Davis (Mississippi) Legion Cavalry
[246] (Losses unknown)
Lt. Col. Joseph Frederick Waring

Phillips' (Georgia) Legion Cavalry
[238] (Losses unknown)
Lt. Col. William Wofford Rich

ATTACHED ARTILLERY

Green's Battery, Louisiana Guard Artillery
(One Section of Two 10-pounder Parrotts)
[32] (1k, 15w = 16) 50.0%
Capt. Charles A. Green
(Attached to Ewell's Second Corps, but sent
to Hunterstown at Hampton's request, and
remained with Hampton's Brigade through July 3.)

Kilpatrick withdrew his forces after dark and was ordered to ride to Two Taverns behind the Federal lines. The Union commander reported higher losses than the records indicate, but the difference may be because a number of slightly wounded troopers quickly returned to the saddle. Hampton, meanwhile, left a small force at Hunterstown to watch the area and also withdrew. The South Carolinian completed his mission by delivering the captured Federal wagons to Confederate lines at Gettysburg. When Robert E. Lee earlier learned from Stuart that he had captured and shepherded with him the enormous train of wagons, the general is said to have replied, "They are an impediment to me now." The wagons would soon see a very different service when they were impressed to carry Confederate wounded from Gettysburg back to the Confederacy following the main battle.

THE SKIRMISH AT BRINKERHOFF'S RIDGE, PA.

JULY 2, 1863

J.E.B. Stuart and two of his brigades under Col. John R. Chambliss and Brig. Gen. Fitzhugh Lee rode all night and through the morning of July 2 from Carlisle south to Gettysburg. Stuart's third brigade under Brig. Gen. Wade Hampton, who maintained possession of the Federal wagons captured at Rockville, guided his command in the same direction from near Dillsburg. Stuart's troopers arrived that afternoon on the left flank of Robert E. Lee's army while Hampton's brigade moved through the small village of Hunterstown about four miles northeast of Gettysburg.

Brig. Gen. James Walker
Image courtesy of Library of Congress

Stuart rode ahead of his column and arrived in Gettysburg shortly after noon to seek out Lee at his headquarters on Seminary Ridge west of Gettysburg. According to several accounts, the meeting was a rocky one for both commanders and especially for Stuart. Once it ended the cavalryman rode back to the left flank to prepare for the arrival of his troopers. Later that afternoon, skirmishing broke out along the Hanover Road on the Confederate left. The Stonewall Brigade, about 1,300 Confederate infantry led by **BRIG. GEN. JAMES WALKER** (part of Ewell's Second Corps), had moved out of its line facing the Federal position atop Culp's Hill to face a potential new threat: Yankee cavalry reported to the east along the Hanover Road.

Brig. Gen. David M. Gregg
Image courtesy of Library of Congress

The enemy riders belonged to **BRIG. GEN. DAVID M. GREGG**'s Federal cavalry division, which was fronting the Union army's right flank. Gregg was moving his men north in pursuit of the Rebels and had arrived on the battlefield from Hanover just past noon on July 2. Only part of Gregg's command was available — fewer than 1,000 troopers. But that was enough to concern Walker about the safety of the unanchored Confederate left flank. About 6:00 p.m., Walker marched his Virginians from their position on the flank to the Henry Brinkerhoff farm near a ridge intersecting the Hanover Road. When Gregg's dismounted skirmish line of the 10th New York Cavalry approached the ridge, Walker ordered the 2nd Virginia to deploy and meet them.

The Virginians were advancing when a spectator with a special interest in the developing fight arrived on the field. J.E.B. Stuart, accompanied by some of his staff, watched as the intensity of the skirmishing increased. Both sides fought stubbornly for a prominent stone wall along the ridge near Brinkerhoff's farm, a waist-high wall that would afford protection to the side that could seize and hold it. Gregg's troopers were supported by two guns of the 3rd Pennsylvania Heavy Artillery, while Walker had no artillery to respond. Possession of the wall see-sawed back and forth as fighting raged on nearby Culp's Hill until about 8:00 p.m., when Walker, confident he held back any Union threat to the flank, drew his men off. Casualties were light, but the 2nd Virginia and Gregg's troopers had fought stubbornly for the wall, which was left in Federal hands when the Virginians retreated to the west.

FEDERAL

ARMY OF THE POTOMAC
CAVALRY CORPS

SECOND CAVALRY DIVISION
[988] (2k, 5w, 3m = 10) 1.0%
Brig. Gen. David McMurtrie Gregg

FIRST BRIGADE
[600] (0k, 1w =1) 0.2%
Col. John Baillie McIntosh

Purnell (Maryland) Legion, Company A
[66] (No losses reported) 0.0%
Capt. Robert E. Duvall

1st New Jersey Cavalry (9 Companies)
[199] (No losses reported) 0.0%
Maj. Myron Holley Beaumont

3rd Pennsylvania Cavalry
[335] (0k, 1w = 1) 0.3%
Lt. Col. Edward S. Jones

THIRD BRIGADE
Col. John Irvin Gregg

10th New York Cavalry
[333] (2k, 4w, 3m = 9) 2.7%
Maj. Matthew Henry Avery

ATTACHED ARTILLERY
**3rd Pennsylvania Heavy Artillery, Battery H
(One Section) (Two 3-inch Ordnance Rifles)**
[55] (No losses reported) 0.0%
Capt. William D. Rank

CONFEDERATE

ARMY OF NORTHERN VIRGINIA
EWELL'S CORPS

JOHNSON'S DIVISION

STONEWALL BRIGADE

2nd Virginia
[333] (0k, 3w = 3) 0.9%
Col. John Quincy Adams Nadenbousch

The small and seemingly indecisive skirmish on Brinkerhoff's Ridge played a much more significant role in the battle of Gettysburg than many people appreciate. J.E.B. Stuart watched the skirmishing for less than an hour, but the engagement likely figured into his plans for offensive operations on the following day, July 3. Stuart enjoyed a good view of the terrain behind the Federal right flank and recognized that it was rather flat and open with intermittent ridges and woodlots. In other words, it was ideal for mounted cavalry operations.

More important was the effect the small skirmish had on the fighting for Culp's Hill later that same evening (July 2). Walker, who had no idea whether the enemy cavalry was screening a larger infantry flanking effort, pulled his entire brigade out of line without orders to do so to confront Gregg's troopers. That decision removed 1,300 veteran Southern infantrymen from the forthcoming attack against Culp's Hill. As the fighting demonstrated, the Federals barely held onto the summit of Culp's Hill in the desperate fight that evening because Meade had stripped that sector to reinforce other parts of his line farther south. If the Stonewall Brigade had been part of the attacking force that evening, the battle for Culp's Hill may well have turned out differently.

THE BATTLE OF FAIRFIELD, PA.

JULY 3, 1863

About the same time as Pickett's Charge and the fighting on East Cavalry Field was taking place on the afternoon of July 3, another battle between opposing cavalry forces erupted well away from the main battlefield at the small village of Fairfield, Pennsylvania, directly behind the Army of Northern Virginia seven miles southwest of Gettysburg. The road through Fairfield, which divided into several routes through passes in the South Mountain range, was a critical line of retreat for Robert E. Lee's army. Fairfield and the surrounding area witnessed the passage of tens of thousands of troops from both armies before, during, and after several sharp conflicts beginning on July 4.

About 400 troopers under fifty-two year-old **MAJ. SAMUEL H. STARR** of the 6th United States Cavalry, a regiment of Regulars in Brig. Gen. Wesley Merritt's brigade (Brig. Gen. John Buford's division), left camp near Emmitsburg, Maryland,

Maj. Samuel H. Starr
Image courtesy of Library of Congress

on the morning of July 3 on its way to Fairfield. Merritt had information that Confederates were there with a long train of captured Pennsylvania booty, and he intended to capture it by sending Starr and his men in pursuit.

Starr's column arrived in Fairfield in the early afternoon, not long before Pickett's Charge began on the main battlefield to the northeast. Starr sent a flanking detail under Capt. George C. Cram to the north to watch his left flank and proceeded through the town. Locals told his advance guard under Lt. Christian Balder that Confederates and a large number of wagons were on the road leading to Ortanna. Balder pursued them, found the Confederates in force farther north, and informed Major Starr.

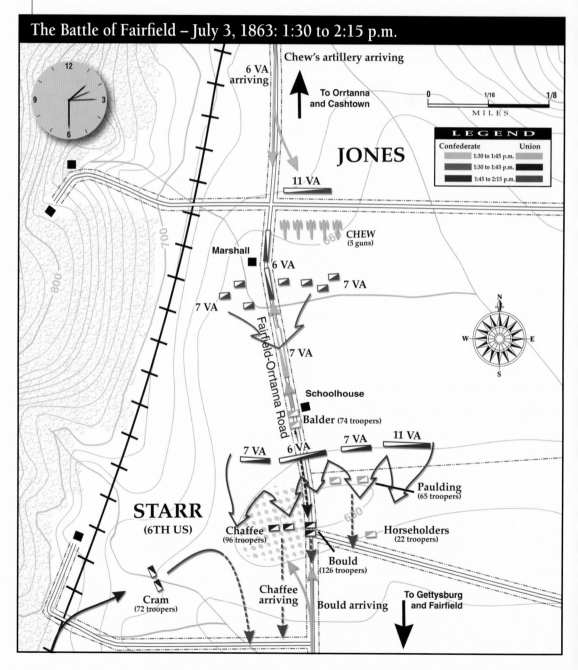

The Battle of Fairfield – July 3, 1863: 1:30 to 2:15 p.m.

Brig. Gen. William E. Jones
Image courtesy of Library of Congress

Starr led his men to a ridge across the road opposite the Confederates and set up a line of battle. **BRIG. GEN. WILLIAM E. JONES,** whose cavalry brigade was protecting the wagon train, dispatched his 7th Virginia Cavalry in a mounted charge against Starr. The Virginians were easily repulsed. Starr was heavily outnumbered, but for reasons that remain unclear, led a mounted countercharge of his own. Within minutes his command was surrounded by the 6th Virginia Cavalry and the reformed troopers of the 7th Virginia. The flanking detail Starr had earlier dispatched under Capt. Cram attempted to come to Starr's aid, but Cram's men were also engulfed. Of the 424 men Starr carried into battle, more than two dozen were killed or wounded and more than half of his regiment was captured. As a result, the 6th United States Cavalry enjoys the unenviable distinction of having suffered one of the highest casualty rates of any unit on either side during the Battle of Gettysburg.

FEDERAL

ARMY OF THE POTOMAC
CAVALRY CORPS

FIRST CAVALRY DIVISION
REGULAR BRIGADE
6th United States Cavalry
[424] (6k, 28w, 208m = 242) 57.1%
Maj. Samuel Henry Starr (w-c)
Capt. George Clarence Cram (c)
Capt. Ira Claflin (final command of regiment)
Lt. Louis Henry Carpenter
Lt. Nicholas Nolan

CONFEDERATE

ARMY OF NORTHERN VIRGINIA
CAVALRY DIVISION
[1,400] (12k, 40w, 6m = 58) 4.1%

JONES' BRIGADE
[1,307] (12k, 40w, 6m = 58) 4.4%
Brig. Gen. William Edmonson Jones

6th Virginia Cavalry
[552] (4k, 19w, 5m = 28) 5.1%
Maj. Cabell Edward Flournoy

7th Virginia Cavalry
[378] (8k, 21w, 1m = 30) 7.9%
Lt. Col. Thomas A. Marshall, Jr.

11th Virginia Cavalry
(On the field but held in reserve)
[377] (No losses reported) 0.0%
Col. Lunsford Lindsay Lomax

ATTACHED ARTILLERY
Chew's Battery (Virginia), Ashby Horse Artillery
(One 3-inch Ordnance Rifle, One 12-pounder Howitzer,
Three unknown attached from another unit)
[93] (No losses reported) 0.0%
Capt. Roger Preston Chew

Major Starr was badly wounded in the Fairfield fighting and captured along with most of his officer corps. Those of the 6th United States not captured, killed, or wounded fled back toward Fairfield and most of them eventually made their way into Federal lines. The regiment's Gettysburg campaign saga against the Virginia troopers of Jones' Brigade, however, was not yet at an end. Just a few days later on July 7, the 6th United States would meet the same adversary during the retreat from Gettysburg, with results nearly as devastating.

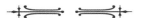

THE FIGHT AT
EAST CAVALRY FIELD, PA.

JULY 3, 1863

Overshadowed by Pickett's Charge is the swirling cavalry combat that took place on East Cavalry Field about the same time on July 3. Although not the largest, it is the most well-known of the many cavalry fights during the entire campaign.

During the early evening of July 2, Confederate cavalry commander **MAJ. GEN. J.E.B. STUART** watched the Brinkerhoff Ridge skirmishing on the Rebel left flank between the Stonewall Brigade (Ewell's Second Corps) and Federal cavalry from **BRIG. GEN. DAVID M. GREGG**'s division. Stuart seems to have recognized the favorable ground for cavalry operations behind the enemy lines, and determined the next day to draw Gregg into a fight.

Maj. Gen. J.E.B. Stuart
Image courtesy of Library of Congress

Early on the morning of July 3, Stuart moved out from his camp near the Confederate left with approximately 6,000 troopers. Riding along the York Pike and then north of the John Rummel farm, Stuart arrived at a rise of ground called Cress Ridge about two miles opposite the intersection of the Hanover and Low Dutch roads, the latter being the position he expected Gregg to be holding. Gregg received word of Stuart's approach and decided to do whatever it took to protect that flank. When Brig. Gen. George A. Custer and his brigade of cavalry from Judson Kilpatrick's division arrived from Two Taverns on their way to the opposite flank, Gregg asked Custer to remain with him to augment his force. Defying his own orders to continue onward, Custer agreed to stay.

Brig. Gen. David M. Gregg
Image courtesy of Library of Congress

Stuart brought forward one gun of Capt. Thomas E. Jackson's Battery and ordered a few shots fired in Gregg's direction. He hoped the rounds would elicit a response from Gregg and reveal the Federals' position. When one of Custer's batteries under Lt. Alexander C. M. Pennington responded, the fight for the Rummel Farm began. Roughly speaking, the cavalry combat got underway about the same time that the artillery barrage preceding Pickett's Charge opened several miles to the southwest.

Dismounted Confederate cavalry advanced toward the Rummel Farm and engaged Gregg's dismounted troopers in a sharp firefight around the farm buildings. The Federals held their ground, but before long nearly 300 men of the 1st Virginia Cavalry galloped at them. Gregg ordered Custer's 7th Michigan Cavalry to countercharge, and they moved out with Custer in the lead. The Yankees were soon outnumbered and driven back when more mounted Confederates were poured into the growing fight. Stuart concluded that a larger attack might force the Federals from the field completely and give him access behind General Meade's right flank at the Hanover Road. Within a short time more than 1,000 gray troopers were galloping toward enemy lines.

While Federal artillery hammered at the approaching Southern horsemen, Custer lined up his men and led them north to meet the Rebels, shouting, "Come on, you Wolverines!" The two forces collided at full speed south of Rummel's buildings like a shock wave, sending men and horses reeling end-over-end. Hand-to-hand fighting swirled over the field and cavalrymen from Gregg's 3rd Pennsylvania fired into Stuart's left flank from a hidden position in a swale. Unable to break Custer, the Confederates slowly withdrew north, leaving behind a field strewn with dead and wounded on both sides. One of the most famous casualties was Wade Hampton, who suffered saber cuts to the head and a shrapnel wound in his hip.

Stuart's planned assault on the Federal right flank was over. His repulse mirrored that suffered by Confederate infantry attacking the center of the main Federal line of battle along Cemetery Ridge known to history as Pickett's Charge.

FEDERAL

ARMY OF THE POTOMAC

CAVALRY CORPS
[3,936] (33k, 166w, 82m = 281) 7.1%

SECOND CAVALRY DIVISION
[1,904] (1k, 28w, 4m = 33) 1.7%
Brig. Gen. David McMurtrie Gregg

First Brigade
[874] (0k, 18w, 4m = 22) 2.5%
Col. John Baillie McIntosh

1st Maryland Cavalry (11 Companies)
[285] (0k, 2w, 1m = 3) 1.1%
Lt. Col. James Monroe Deems

Purnell (Maryland) Legion, Company A
[66] (No losses reported) 0.0%
Capt. Robert E. Duvall

1st New Jersey Cavalry (9 Companies)
[199] (0k, 9w = 9) 4.5%
Maj. Myron Holley Beaumont

3rd Pennsylvania Cavalry
[324] (0k, 7w, 3m = 10) 3.1%
Lt. Col. Edward S. Jones

THIRD BRIGADE
[988] (1k, 8w = 9) 0.9%
(On the field but not engaged except for
one section of attached artillery)
Col. John Irvin Gregg

1st Maine Cavalry
[315] (1k, 4w = 5) 1.6%
Lt. Col. Charles H. Smith

10th New York Cavalry
[324] (No losses reported) 0.0%
(An estimated 5 were wounded on the evening of
July 3 from shell fire after battle had ended.)
Maj. Matthew Henry Avery

16th Pennsylvania Cavalry
[349] (0k, 4w = 4) 1.1%
Lt. Col. John K. Robinson

ATTACHED ARTILLERY
**1st United States Horse Artillery, Batteries E and G
(Four 12-pounder Napoleons)**
[42] (0k, 2w = 2) 4.8%
Capt. Alanson Merwin Randol
(Only one section engaged, commanded
by Lt. James Chester)

THIRD CAVALRY DIVISION
[2,032] (32k, 138w, 78m = 248) 12.2%

SECOND BRIGADE
[1,915] (32k, 137w, 78m = 247) 12.9%
Brig. Gen. George Armstrong Custer

1st Michigan Cavalry
[426] (10k, 43w, 20m = 73) 17.1%
Col. Charles Henry Town

5th Michigan Cavalry
[645] (8k, 30w, 18m = 56) 8.7%
Col. Russell Alexander Alger

6th Michigan Cavalry
[467] (1k, 26w, 1m = 28) 6.0%
Col. George Gray

7th Michigan Cavalry
[377] (13k, 38w, 39m = 90) 23.9%
Col. William D'Alton Mann

ATTACHED ARTILLERY
**2nd United States Horse Artillery, Battery M
(Six 3-inch Ordnance Rifles)**
[117] (0k, 1w = 1) 0.9%
Lt. Alexander Cummings McWhorter Pennington, Jr.

CONFEDERATE

ARMY OF NORTHERN VIRGINIA
CAVALRY DIVISION
[6,109] (38k, 113w, 2c, 112m = 265) 4.3%
Maj. Gen. James Ewell Brown Stuart

HAMPTON'S BRIGADE
[1,740] (15k, 48w, 2c, 31m = 96) 5.5%
Brig. Gen. Wade Hampton (w)
Col. Laurence Simmons Baker

1st North Carolina Cavalry
[407] (2k, 17w, 25m = 44) 10.8%
Col. Laurence Simmons Baker
Lt. Col. James Byron Gordon

1st South Carolina Cavalry (detachment)
[339] (1k, 9w, 4m = 14) 4.1%
Lt. Col. John David Twiggs (?)
(Col. John Logan Black, wounded at Upperville,
later stated that Maj. William Walker commanded
the regiment at this time)

2nd South Carolina Cavalry
[186] (2k, 5w = 7) 3.8%
Maj. Thomas Jefferson Lipscomb

Cobb's (Georgia) Legion
[325] (3k, 2c, 1m = 6) 1.8%
Col. Pierce Manning Butler Young

Jeff Davis (Mississippi) Legion
[245] (4k, 10w, 1m = 15) 6.1%
Lt. Col. Joseph Frederick Waring (w)

Phillips' (Georgia) Legion
[238] (3k, 7w = 10) 4.2%
Lt. Col. William Wofford Rich

FITZHUGH LEE'S BRIGADE
[1,682] (10k, 22w, 52m = 84) 5.0%
Brig. Gen. Fitzhugh Lee

1st Virginia Cavalry
[359] (6k, 7w, 10m = 23) 6.4%
Col. James Henry Drake

2nd Virginia Cavalry
[448] (3k, 6w, 10m = 19) 4.2%
Col. Thomas Taylor Munford

3rd Virginia Cavalry
[247] (1k, 8w = 9) 3.6%
Col. Thomas Howerton Owen

4th Virginia Cavalry
[628] (0k, 1w, 32m = 33) 5.3%
Col. Williams Carter Wickham

5th Virginia Cavalry
(Not engaged, on picket duty)
Col. Thomas Lafayette Rosser

WILLIAM HENRY FITZHUGH LEE'S BRIGADE
[1,314] (5k, 31w, 20m = 56) 4.3%
Col. John Randolph Chambliss, Jr.

2nd North Carolina Cavalry
[161] (1k, 2w, 6m = 9) 5.6%
Capt. William A. Graham, Jr. (w)
Lt. Joseph Baker

9th Virginia Cavalry
[558] (2k, 9w, 7m = 18) 3.2%
Col. Richard Lee Turberville Beale

10th Virginia Cavalry (10 Companies)
[265] (1k, 9w, 2m = 12) 4.5%
Col. James Lucius Davis

13th Virginia Cavalry
[330] (1k, 11w, 5m = 17) 5.2%
Capt. Benjamin Franklin Winfield

JENKINS' BRIGADE
[1,089] (7k, 6w, 9m = 22+) 2.0+%
Lt. Col. Vincent Addison Witcher

14th Virginia Cavalry
[267] (4k, 2w = 6) 2.2%
Maj. Benjamin Franklin Eakle

16th Virginia Cavalry
[260] (2k, 2w, 3m = 7) 2.7%
Maj. James Henry Nounnan

17th Virginia Cavalry
[265] (0k, 2w, 6m = 8) 3.0%
Col. William Henderson French

34th Battalion Virginia Cavalry
[172] (Unknown losses)
Lt. Col. Vincent Addison Witcher

36th Battalion Virginia Cavalry
[125] (1k = 1) 0.8%
Capt. Cornelius Timothy Smith

STUART HORSE ARTILLERY
[264] (0k, 6w = 6) 2.3%
Maj. Robert Franklin Beckham

Breathed's (Virginia) Battery, 1st Stuart Horse Artillery (Four 3-inch Ordnance Rifles)
[105] (0k, 1w = 1) 1.0%
Capt. James Williams Breathed

McGregor's (Virginia) Battery, 2nd Stuart Horse Artillery (One Blakely Rifle, One unknown)
[52] (No losses reported) 0.0%
Capt. William Morrell McGregor

Jackson's (Virginia) Battery, Charlottesville Horse Artillery (Two 3-inch Ordnance Rifles, Two 12-pounder Howitzers)
[107] (0k, 5w = 5) 4.7%
Capt. Thomas Edwin Jackson

ATTACHED ARTILLERY

Green's Battery, Louisiana Guard Artillery (One Section) (Two 10-pounder Parrotts)
[20] (1k = 1) 5.0%
Capt. Charles A. Green
(Attached to Ewell's Second Corps, but remained with Cavalry Division this day after serving with Hampton's Brigade at Hunterstown on July 2.)

The casualties suffered by both sides were remarkably similar, but Custer's audacious countercharge, supported by a part of Gregg's troops and well-placed shots by the Federal artillery, held Stuart to a standstill. Contrary to the belief of some readers, Stuart's attack was not coordinated with Pickett's Charge. However, if the two assaults had been successful, Stuart may well have been able to create havoc behind the Federal right flank along two possible arteries of retreat for Meade's army: the Hanover Road and the Baltimore Pike.

Following the battle on East Cavalry Field, Stuart withdrew his forces back to the Confederate left flank. Although exhausted after their long ride north to Pennsylvania and the heavy fighting they had already waged, the tasks facing Stuart's cavalrymen were just beginning. That evening, Lee decided to retreat from Gettysburg. It fell to Stuart and his veteran troopers to guide the Army of Northern Virginia to the Potomac River and protect it along the way.

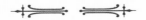

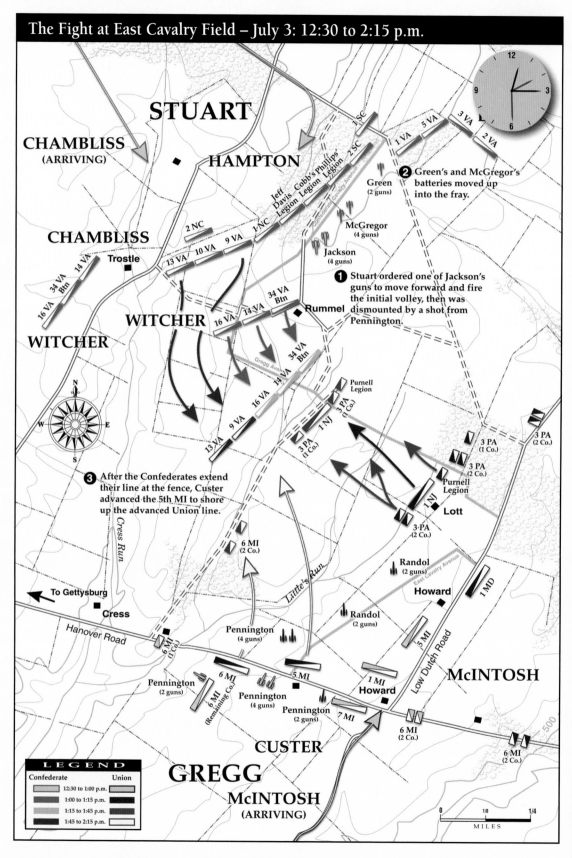

The Fight at East Cavalry Field – July 3: 12:30 to 2:15 p.m.

STUART

CHAMBLISS
(ARRIVING)

HAMPTON

1 SC

5 VA

3 VA

2 VA

1 VA

CHAMBLISS

Trostle

2 NC

13 VA   10 VA   9 VA

Jeff Davis Legion

Cobb's Legion

Phillips' Legion

2 SC

1 NC

Green
(2 guns)

2 Green's and McGregor's batteries moved up into the fray.

McGregor
(4 guns)

34 VA Btn

16 VA

WITCHER

WITCHER

16 VA   14 VA   34 VA Btn

Jackson
(4 guns)

Rummel

1 Stuart ordered one of Jackson's guns to move forward and fire the initial volley, then was dismounted by a shot from Pennington.

16 VA   14 VA   34 VA Btn

13 VA   9 VA

Purnell Legion

3 PA
(1 Co.)

3 PA
(1 Co.)   1 NJ

3 PA
(1 Co.)

3 PA
(2 Co.)

3 PA
(1 Co.)

3 PA
(2 Co.)

Purnell Legion

1 NJ

Lott

3 PA
(2 Co.)

3 After the Confederates extend their line at the fence, Custer advanced the 5th MI to shore up the advanced Union line.

6 MI
(2 Co.)

To Gettysburg

Cress

Hanover Road

6 MI
(1 Co.)

Pennington
(4 guns)

Pennington
(2 guns)

6 MI
(Remaining Co.)

6 MI

Pennington
(4 guns)

5 MI

Pennington
(2 guns)

7 MI

Randol
(2 guns)

Howard

Randol
(2 guns)

5 MI

1 MI

Howard

6 MI
(2 Co.)

1 MD

McINTOSH

500

CUSTER

GREGG

McINTOSH
(ARRIVING)

6 MI
(2 Co.)

LEGEND

Confederate   Union

12:30 to 1:00 p.m.
1:00 to 1:15 p.m.
1:15 to 1:45 p.m.
1:45 to 2:15 p.m.

N
W   E
S

Cress Run

Little's Run

Gregg Avenue

Confederate Cavalry Avenue

East Cavalry Avenue

Low Dutch Road

0   1/8   1/4
MILES

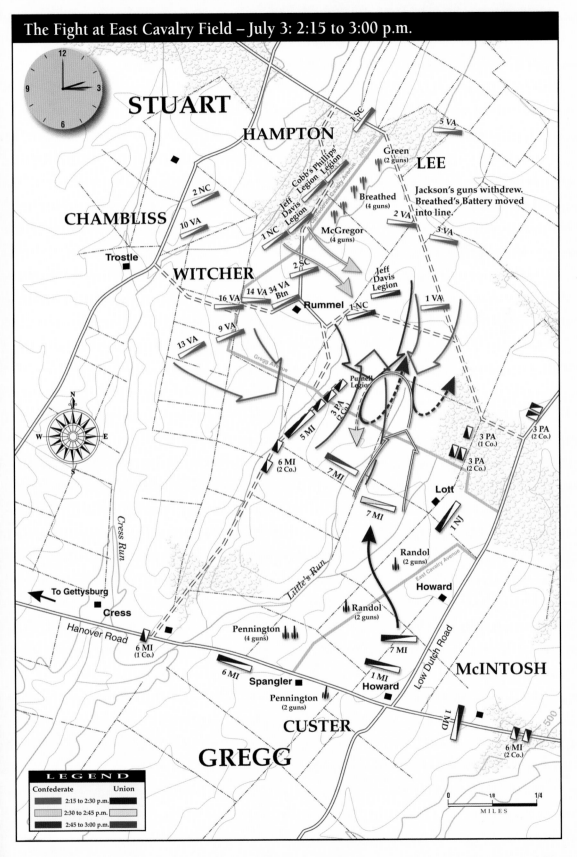

The Fight at East Cavalry Field – July 3: 2:15 to 3:00 p.m.

STUART

HAMPTON

CHAMBLISS

LEE

1 SC

5 VA

2 NC

Green
(2 guns)

Cobb's Phillips'
Legion Legion

Jeff
Davis
Legion

1 NC

Breathed
(4 guns)

Jackson's guns withdrew.
Breathed's Battery moved
into line.

10 VA

McGregor
(4 guns)

2 VA

3 VA

Trostle

WITCHER

16 VA

14 VA 34 VA
Btn

2 SC

Jeff
Davis
Legion

1 VA

Rummel

1 NC

13 VA

9 VA

Gregg Avenue

Purnell
Legion

3 PA
(2 Co.)

5 MI

3 PA

3 PA
(2 Co.)

3 PA
(1 Co.)

3 PA
(2 Co.)

6 MI
(2 Co.)

7 MI

Lott

N

7 MI

1 NJ

W   E

Randol
(2 guns)

S

Cress Run

Randol
(2 guns)

Howard

To Gettysburg

Pennington
(4 guns)

Cress

7 MI

Hanover Road

6 MI
(1 Co.)

6 MI

Spangler

1 MI

Pennington
(2 guns)

Howard

East Cavalry Avenue

Low Dutch Road

McINTOSH

1 MD

CUSTER

500

GREGG

6 MI
(2 Co.)

LEGEND

Confederate	Union
2:15 to 2:30 p.m.	
2:30 to 2:45 p.m.	
2:45 to 3:00 p.m.	

0   1/8   1/4

MILES

153

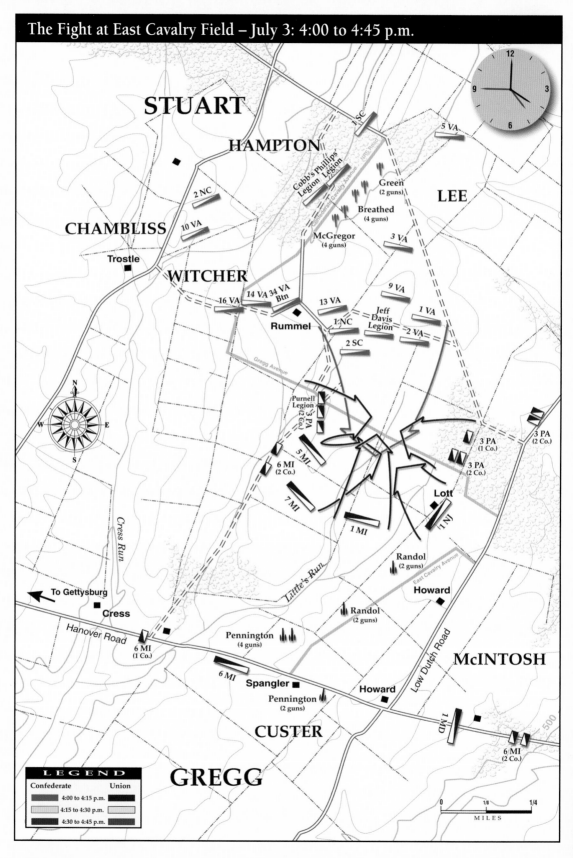

The Fight at East Cavalry Field – July 3: 4:00 to 4:45 p.m.

KILPATRICK PURSUES THE CONFEDERATES

THE BATTLE OF MONTEREY PASS, PA.

JULY 4-5, 1863

Robert E. Lee selected two major lines of retreat from Gettysburg. The long wagon train holding thousands of his wounded — said to be eleven miles long — was sent west along the road to Cashtown, where it would proceed over South Mountain and then south to the Potomac River crossing at Williamsport, Maryland. Most of the army and supply wagons took the road southwest to Fairfield, over South Mountain via the Fairfield and Monterey gaps, and then south to the river crossings at Williamsport and Falling Waters, Maryland.

The wagon train of the wounded, escorted and protected by Brig. Gen. John D. Imboden's Northwestern Brigade of cavalry and mounted infantry, began departing the battlefield on the afternoon of July 4. Earlier that morning, survivors from Maj. Gen. George Pickett's division,

Brig. Gen. William Jones
Image courtesy of Library of Congress

who had been guarding Federals captured during the battle, started marching on the Fairfield Road. The corps supply wagons (also carrying some wounded) of Lt. Gen. Richard S. Ewell's Second Corps marched behind Pickett's men.

When no further Confederate attacks materialized on July 4, Federal army commander Maj. Gen. George G. Meade dispatched cavalry to see what the Southerners were up to and, if possible, to interdict their lines of possible retreat. Colonel John Gregg's brigade of the Second Division rode north toward Cashtown via Hunterstown,

Brig. Gen. Judson Kilpatrick
Image courtesy of Library of Congress

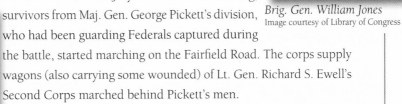

but the rest rode south. Colonel Pennock Huey's brigade, which had spent the battle in the area of Emmitsburg, Maryland, joined **BRIG. GEN. JUDSON KILPATRICK**'s division for a planned move on the South Mountain gaps above Fairfield to attack a wagon train spotted by Union signalmen.

Kilpatrick's column approached Monterey Pass late in the evening under a torrential rainstorm. When a local civilian informed Kilpatrick that a large Confederate wagon train was rolling through the pass, the Union general sent the 1st Vermont Cavalry under Lt. Col. Addison W. Preston along a road to the south to attempt a flanking movement. The rest of the Federals advanced with Brig. Gen. George A. Custer's Michigan brigade in the lead. Without any advance warning, a lone cannon from Capt. William A. Tanner's Southern battery fired from a rise in the road ahead. The shell knocked down several of Custer's troopers and stopped the Federals in their tracks. A few dozen troopers from Capt. George M. Emack's company of the 1st Maryland Cavalry Battalion supporting Tanner's gun crew charged Custer's men in the dark and sent the surprised Federals

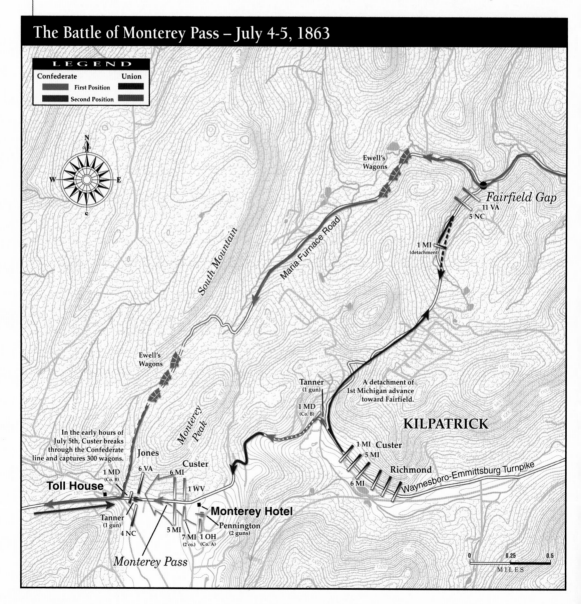

The Battle of Monterey Pass – July 4-5, 1863

retreating. Kilpatrick sent forward dismounted Michiganders, who could barely see anything in the dark and driving rain. A volley from Emack's troopers fooled the Federals into thinking they were facing a much larger force.

When Confederate **BRIG. GEN. WILLIAM E. JONES** heard the fighting, he galloped toward the combat and found Emack's and Tanner's men waging a determined delaying action in front of the pass. Jones sent troopers from his cavalry brigade forward to engage Kilpatrick, who mounted a counterattack of his own. The rain and darkness, however, made effective fighting all but impossible.

By 3:00 a.m. on July 5, Kilpatrick's troops had pushed the Confederates nearly back to the pass itself, where they finally captured Tanner's lone artillery piece before launching a charge toward Ewell's wagons. Lieutenant Alexander C. M. Pennington's Federal battery supported the effort and hammered the train with shells. The mounted Federals captured hundreds of Confederate infantry around Ewell's wagons, including wounded soldiers, slaves, various support personnel, and cavalrymen. Prisoners were corralled all along the pass while Custer's men went to work and burned many of the 250 captured wagons.

FEDERAL

ARMY OF THE POTOMAC
CAVALRY CORPS

THIRD CAVALRY DIVISION
[4,546] (7k, 1mw, 11w, 27m = 46) 1.0%
Brig. Gen. Hugh Judson Kilpatrick

HEADQUARTERS GUARDS AND ORDERLIES

1st Ohio Cavalry, Company A
[40] (1k est., 2w = 3) 7.5%
Capt. Noah Jones

1st Ohio Cavalry, Company C
[37] (1k est., 1w = 2) 5.4%
Capt. Samuel N. Stanford

FIRST BRIGADE
[1,292] (2k, 2w, 5m = 9) 0.7%
Col. Nathaniel Pendleton Richmond

5th New York Cavalry
[414] (0k, 4m = 4) 1.0%
Maj. John Hammond

18th Pennsylvania Cavalry
[495] (0k, 1m = 1) 0.2%
Lt. Col. William P. Brinton

1st West Virginia Cavalry
[383] (2k, 2w = 4) 1.0%
Maj. Charles E. Capehart
(1st Vermont Cavalry sent to Leitersburg)

ATTACHED ARTILLERY
**4th United States Horse Artillery,
Battery E (Four 3-inch Ordnance Rifles)**
[60] (No losses reported) 0.0%
Lt. Samuel Sherer Elder

SECOND BRIGADE
[1,673] (3k, 1mw, 6w, 22m = 32) 1.9%
Brig. Gen. George Armstrong Custer

1st Michigan Cavalry
[355] (3k, 1mw, 1w, 22m = 27) 7.6%
Col. Charles Henry Town

5th Michigan Cavalry
[590] (No losses reported) 0.0%
Col. Russell Alexander Alger

6th Michigan Cavalry
[443] (0k, 5w = 5) 1.1%
Col. George Gray

7th Michigan Cavalry
[285] (No losses reported) 0.0%
Col. William D'Alton Mann

ATTACHED ARTILLERY

**2nd United States Horse Artillery, Battery M
(Two sections of Four 3-inch Ordnance Rifles)**
[77] (No losses reported) 0.0%
(One section of two ordnance rifles sent
to Leitersburg with 1st Vermont Cavalry.)
Lt. Alexander Cummings McWhorter Pennington, Jr.

SECOND CAVALRY DIVISION
[1,367] (No losses reported) 0.0%

SECOND BRIGADE (ATTACHED)
[1,225] (No losses reported) 0.0%
Col. Pennock Huey

2nd New York Cavalry
[220] (No losses reported) 0.0%
Lt. Col. Otto Harhaus

4th New York Cavalry
[245] (No losses reported) 0.0%
Lt. Col. Augustus Pruyn

6th Ohio Cavalry (10 Companies)
[420] (No losses reported) 0.0%
Maj. William Stedman

8th Pennsylvania Cavalry
[340] (No losses reported) 0.0%
Capt. William A. Corrie

ATTACHED ARTILLERY

**3rd United States Horse Artillery,
Battery C (Six 3-inch Ordnance Rifles)**
[142] (No losses reported) 0.0%
Lt. William Duncan Fuller

CONFEDERATE

ARMY OF NORTHERN VIRGINIA
[unknown] (1k+, 6w+, 1,341c+ = 1,348+)

CAVALRY DIVISION
[1,087+ est.] (1k+, 6w+, 241c+ = 248+) 22.8%+

JONES' BRIGADE
[550 est.] (0k, 2c = 2) 0.4% est.
Brig. Gen. William Edmonson Jones

6th Virginia Cavalry
[300 est.] (0k, 1c = 1) 0.3% est.
Maj. Cabell Edward Flournoy

11th Virginia Cavalry
[250 est.] (0k, 1c = 1) 0.4% est.
Col. Lunsford Lindsay Lomax

ROBERTSON'S BRIGADE

4th North Carolina Cavalry (detachment)
[150 est.] (0k, 90c = 90) 60.0% est.
Col. Dennis Dozier Ferebee

FITZ LEE'S BRIGADE
[322] (1k, 6w, 148c = 155) 48.1%

1st Maryland Cavalry Battalion
[161] (0k, 3w, 74c = 77) 47.8%

Company B
[40] (1k, 1w, 25c = 27) 67.5%
Capt. George Malcolm Emack (w)

Company C
[36] (0k, 11c = 11) 30.6%

Company D
[50] (0k, 2w, 35c = 37) 74.0%
Capt. Warner G. Welsh

Company E
[35] (0k, 3c = 3) 8.6%

**10th Virginia Cavalry
(Unknown company/squadron)**
[Unknown] (Unknown losses)

OTHERS
[Unknown] (1,100c est.)
Infantry and wounded primarily of Maj. Gen. Robert
E. Rodes' Division of Lt. Gen. Richard Ewell's Corps;
teamsters, slaves, free Blacks and logistical personnel

ATTACHED ARTILLERY
[65] (0k, 1c = 1) 1.5%
**Tanner's Battery, Richmond "Courtney" Artillery
(One Napoleon)**
[20] (0k, 1c = 1) 5.0%
Capt. William Tanner
**Chew's Battery, Ashby Horse Artillery
(One unknown)**
[45] (No losses reported) 0.0%
Capt. Roger Preston Chew

In addition to capturing the wagons, Kilpatrick's and Huey's troopers also netted nearly 1,400 Confederates and support personnel. During the early morning hours of July 5, Kilpatrick set up his headquarters at the impressive Monterey house near the pass, and after securing his prisoners determined to continue riding south to Maryland in an effort to get ahead of the Confederates and block their retreat.

When the sun rose on the main battlefield the morning of July 5, skirmish fire broke out because General Lee had left a covering force behind to mask the retreat of his army. Federal army commander George G. Meade was still not sure whether Lee was making a full-scale withdrawal from the field.

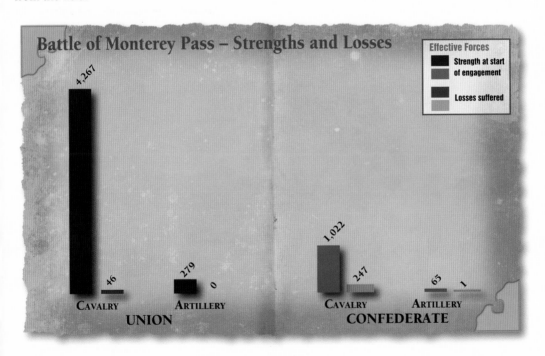

THE SKIRMISH AT LEITERSBURG, MD.

JULY 5, 1863

Before the fighting broke out at Monterey Pass on the night of July 4, Judson Kilpatrick dispatched the 1st Vermont Cavalry on a flanking movement against the Confederate wagon train rolling through the mountain gap. Guided by a local civilian, **LT. COL. ADDISON W. PRESTON** led his Vermonters through the dark and rainy night to Smithsburg, Maryland. When no enemy was found there, Preston continued on to Leitersburg. The Union cavalry approached the hamlet just before sunrise on July 5. Bolts of lightning illuminated what Preston and his troopers sought: the other column of wagons belonging to Richard Ewell's Second Corps, a two-mile long reserve train making its way over the mountain along a rocky road. The Vermonters drew their pistols, spurred their horses, and set off in pursuit of the rolling stock.

Lt. Col. Addison W. Preston
Image courtesy of J.D. Petruzzi

Preston's regiment cut through the small Rebel rearguard and struck at the train itself with pistols blazing and swords slashing. Most of the wagons were filled with Confederate wounded. The Vermonters shot several drivers, but most of the teamsters surrendered as soon as they figured out what was taking place. After the long column of wagons was brought to a halt, Preston's men removed the wounded and torched the carriages.

FEDERAL

ARMY OF THE POTOMAC

CAVALRY CORPS

THIRD CAVALRY DIVISION

FIRST BRIGADE
[574] (No losses reported) 0.0%

1st Vermont Cavalry
[535] (No losses reported) 0.0%
Lt. Col. Addison Webster Preston

2nd United States Horse Artillery, Battery M
(One section of Two 3-inch Ordnance Rifles)
[39] (No losses reported) 0.0%

CONFEDERATE

ARMY OF NORTHERN VIRGINIA
EWELL'S CORPS

[Unknown] (0k, ?w, 100c est. = 100+)
(Ewell's Second Corps Reserve Wagon Train and teamsters;
slaves, free Blacks and wounded soldiers.)

The Vermonters gathered up their prisoners, who consisted mainly of the wagon teams and wounded that could be safely moved, about 100 in all, and set off to rejoin the rest of Kilpatrick's troops making for Smithsburg. Although the small skirmish at Leitersburg did not have an impact on the campaign, it made life that much more miserable for the Southern wounded.

THE SKIRMISH AT SMITHSBURG, MD.

JULY 5, 1863

Early on the morning of July 5, Confederate cavalry leader **MAJ. GEN. J.E.B. STUART** guided a portion of his cavalry division (those units not detailed to escort and protect the army along its two main lines of retreat) away from the Gettysburg battlefield south to Emmitsburg, Maryland. Following a short skirmish there, the Confederates captured several dozen Federals as well as a cache of much-needed medical supplies.

It was there that Stuart learned about the combat raging in the Monterey Pass that night and the loss of many of Richard Ewell's wagons at Leitersburg. The ominous news meant that Federal cavalry was on or near the roads Stuart wanted to take to rejoin General Lee's retreating infantry. After consulting a map of the area, Stuart saddled up his men and rode in the direction of Creagerstown and the direct road to Frederick, Maryland.

Maj. Gen. J.E.B. Stuart
Image courtesy of Library of Congress

Brig. Gen. Judson Kilpatrick
Image courtesy of Library of Congress

Stuart was unaware that after **BRIG. GEN. JUDSON KILPATRICK** cut his way through Monterey Pass, the Yankee general and his troopers had ridden as far as Smithsburg and the hills commanding the route Stuart and his cavalrymen were now taking. Kilpatrick's pickets spotted Stuart's column near Raven Rock Pass east of Smithsburg and exchanged shots with the Southern horsemen before riding back to inform Kilpatrick that the enemy was approaching. Kilpatrick deployed his own brigades and that of Col. Pennock Huey and his artillery on rising pieces of ground surrounding Smithsburg.

When Stuart's troopers poured through Raven Rock Pass about 5:00 p.m., Kilpatrick's artillery opened fire. The combat on the west side of South Mountain facing Smithsburg also involved mounted and dismounted skirmishers from both sides trading shots in an effort to feel out the other and find an advantage to pursue. Stuart brought up Capt. Wiley H. Griffin's battery to counter Kilpatrick's guns, and some of the Confederate shells fell into the town.

When some of the Confederate cavalry withdrew about dusk, Kilpatrick believed he had forced Stuart back into the mountain pass. Kilpatrick withdrew his command through Smithsburg and rode south approximately sixteen miles to Boonsborough, Maryland. Once the Federals were gone, however, Stuart moved his men into Smithsburg and took control of the town. He immediately dispatched a courier to find General Lee and report on their operations and enemy movements.

FEDERAL

ARMY OF THE POTOMAC
CAVALRY CORPS

THIRD CAVALRY DIVISION
[4,545] (0k, 5w, 3m = 8) 0.2%
Brig. Gen. Hugh Judson Kilpatrick

HEADQUARTERS GUARDS AND ORDERLIES

1st Ohio Cavalry, Company A
[37] (No losses reported) 0.0%
Capt. Noah Jones

1st Ohio Cavalry, Company C
[35] (No losses reported) 0.0%
Capt. Samuel N. Stanford

FIRST BRIGADE
(Present on field but not engaged)
[1,288] (0k, 5w, 3m = 8) 0.6%
Col. Nathaniel Pendleton Richmond

5th New York Cavalry
[414] (No losses reported) 0.0%
Maj. John Hammond

18th Pennsylvania Cavalry
[495] (0k, 5w, 3m = 8) 1.6%
Lt. Col. William P. Brinton

1st West Virginia Cavalry
[379] (No losses reported) 0.0%
Maj. Charles E. Capehart

SECOND BRIGADE
[1,641] (No losses reported) 0.0%
(Present on field but not engaged;
supported Pennington's battery)
Brig. Gen. George Armstrong Custer

1st Michigan Cavalry
[328] (No losses reported) 0.0%
Col. Charles Henry Town

6th Michigan Cavalry
[438] (No losses reported) 0.0%
Col. George Gray

5th Michigan Cavalry
[590] (No losses reported) 0.0%
Col. Russell Alexander Alger

7th Michigan Cavalry
[285] (No losses reported) 0.0%
Col. William D'Alton Mann

SECOND CAVALRY DIVISION
[1,544] (No losses reported) 0.0%

SECOND BRIGADE
[1,225] (No losses reported) 0.0%
(Only skirmishers of brigade engaged)
Col. Pennock Huey

2nd New York Cavalry
[220] (No losses reported) 0.0%
Lt. Col. Otto Harhaus

4th New York Cavalry
[245] (No losses reported) 0.0%
Lt. Col. Augustus Pruyn

6th Ohio Cavalry
[420] (No losses reported) 0.0%
Maj. William Stedman

8th Pennsylvania Cavalry
[340] (No losses reported) 0.0%
Capt. William A. Corrie

ATTACHED ARTILLERY
[319] (No losses reported) 0.0%

2nd United States Horse Artillery, Battery M
(Two sections of Four 3-inch Ordnance Rifles)
(On the field but not engaged)
[117] (No losses reported) 0.0%
Lt. Alexander Cummings McWhorter Pennington, Jr.

4th United States Horse Artillery, Battery E
(Four 3-inch Ordnance Rifles)
[60] (No losses reported) 0.0%
Lt. Samuel Sherer Elder

3rd United States Horse Artillery, Battery C
(Six 3-inch Ordnance Rifles)
[142] (No losses reported) 0.0%
Lt. William Duncan Fuller

CONFEDERATE

ARMY OF NORTHERN VIRGINIA

CAVALRY DIVISION
[2,865] (1k, 3w = 4) 0.1%
Maj. Gen. James Ewell Brown Stuart

WILLIAM HENRY FITZHUGH LEE'S BRIGADE
[1,258] (No losses reported) 0.0%
Col. John Randolph Chambliss, Jr.

2nd North Carolina Cavalry
[152] (No losses reported) 0.0%
Lt. Joseph Baker

9th Virginia Cavalry
[540] (No losses reported) 0.0%
Col. Richard Lee Turberville Beale

10th Virginia Cavalry
[253] (No losses reported) 0.0%
Col. James Lucius Davis

13th Virginia Cavalry
[313] (No losses reported) 0.0%
Capt. Benjamin Franklin Winfield

JENKINS' BRIGADE
[1,063] (1k, 3w = 4) 0.4%
Col. Milton James Ferguson

14th Virginia Cavalry
[261] (1k, 3w = 4) 1.5%
Maj. Benjamin Franklin Eakle

16th Virginia Cavalry
[253] (No losses reported) 0.0%
Maj. James Henry Nounnan

17th Virginia Cavalry
[257] (No losses reported) 0.0%
Col. William Henderson French

34th Battalion Virginia Cavalry
[168] (No losses reported) 0.0%
Lt. Col. Vincent Addison Witcher

36th Battalion Virginia Cavalry
[124] (No losses reported) 0.0%
Capt. Cornelius Timothy Smith

JONES' BRIGADE

7th Virginia Cavalry (attached)
[348] (No losses reported) 0.0%
Lt. Col. Thomas A. Marshall, Jr.

ATTACHED ARTILLERY
[196] (No losses reported) 0.0%

**Breathed's (Virginia) Battery, 1st Stuart Horse
Artillery (Four 3-inch Ordnance Rifles)**
[91] (No losses reported) 0.0%
Capt. James Williams Breathed

**Griffin's (Maryland) Battery, 2nd Baltimore
Battery (Four 10-pounder Parrotts)**
[105] (No losses reported) 0.0%
Capt. Wiley Hunter Griffin

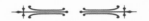

Kilpatrick's decision to break off the engagement was a mistake, because his withdrawal left the critical area between the South Mountain range and Hagerstown under Southern control and thus available for the Confederates to use during their retreat. Similarly, Kilpatrick had also vacated Monterey Pass, which left that vital artery open for use. Kilpatrick reached Boonsborough, Maryland, just before midnight and went into camp. A short time later, Brig. Gen. John Buford arrived with his division and the two cavalry commanders discussed strategies for the next day.

FEDERAL INFANTRY BEGINS THE PURSUIT

THE SKIRMISH AT GRANITE HILL, PA.

JULY 5, 1863

On the Gettysburg battlefield, many soldiers of the Federal Army of the Potomac spent the morning of July 5 tending to wounded, burying the dead, and keeping an eye on the Confederate positions to their west and north. Reports from Union signal stations reached army commander Maj. Gen. George G. Meade that large columns of Confederates were marching west toward Fairfield and Cashtown. Additional reports arrived of Judson Kilpatrick's fight at Monterey Pass and of long Confederate wagon trains heading west and south through the mountains. As a result, Meade dispatched additional cavalry under Brig. Gen. David M. Gregg toward Cashtown to ascertain whether the Southern army was in fact retreating (see narrative at the end of this engagement for more details) and whether Gen. Robert E. Lee intended to make another stand along South Mountain.

Brig. Gen. John B. Gordon
Image courtesy of Library of Congress

Infantry would also play a role in the pursuit and gathering of information. **MAJOR GENERAL JOHN SEDGWICK**'s 6th Corps, which had seen very little action during the main battle, was available for immediate use. About mid-morning, Meade ordered Sedgwick to move across the battlefield to the Fairfield Road, which was behind Confederate lines. Under a steady rain Sedgwick led his men across the field where Pickett's Charge had taken place, crossed Seminary Ridge, and reached the Fairfield Road about noon. With Brig. Gen.

Maj. Gen. John Sedgwick
Image courtesy of Library of Congress

1863

| THE CAMPAIGN BEGINS JUNE 3 | THE BATTLE OF GETTYSBURG JULY 1-3 | GRANITE HILL & FAIRFIELD JULY 5-6 | LEE'S ARMY CROSSES THE POTOMAC RIVER JULY 14 |

Alfred T. A. Torbert's New Jersey brigade in the lead, the corps reached a rise in the road in time to see a Confederate wagon train winding its way toward Fairfield and the mountain passes beyond.

With skirmishers leading his column, Sedgwick pushed his men ahead to a prominent rise in the road in an area today called Granite Hill. The Union advance was now a little more than two miles east of Fairfield. Once there, the Jersey men shook out a battle line on both sides of the road. The Confederate wagon train belonged to Maj. Gen. Jubal Early's division of Richard Ewell's Second Corps. Lieutenant Colonel Elijah V. White's 35th Battalion Virginia Cavalry and Capt. Charles A. Greene's battery were tasked with protecting the rear of the train. When White notified Early about the approaching enemy, the division commander ordered Greene to fire at the Yankees to discourage an aggressive pursuit and ordered the wagons to quicken their pace.

When the Southern artillery opened on his advance, Sedgwick ordered up Capt. George W. Adams' Battery G of the 1st Rhode Island Light Artillery. Sedgwick's skirmishers advanced under the thunder of a gunnery duel to trade shots with White's troopers. White's rearguard was soon reinforced by the 26th and 31st Georgia from **BRIG. GEN. JOHN B. GORDON**'s Brigade. When the Federals stepped within 100 yards the Georgians charged, and Sedgwick's men scampered for the safety of Granite Hill. Except for killing some horses in the artillery batteries, neither side suffered any casualties (although some soldiers may have been slightly wounded on both sides).

FEDERAL

ARMY OF THE POTOMAC
VI ARMY CORPS
[1,445] (No losses reported) 0.0%
Maj. Gen. John Sedgwick

FIRST DIVISION
[1,445] (No losses reported) 0.0%
Brig. Gen. Horatio Gouverneur Wright

FIRST BRIGADE
(Skirmishers of the brigade were
the only infantry engaged)
[1,319] (No losses reported) 0.0%
Brig. Gen. Alfred Thomas Archimedes Torbert

1st New Jersey
[265] (No losses reported) 0.0%
Lt. Col. William Henry, Jr.

2nd New Jersey
[351] (No losses reported) 0.0%
Lt. Col. Charles Wiebecke

3rd New Jersey
[293] (No losses reported) 0.0%
Col. Henry W. Brown

15th New Jersey
[410] (No losses reported) 0.0%
Col. William H. Penrose

ATTACHED ARTILLERY
1st Rhode Island Light Artillery, Battery G (Six 10-pounder Parrotts)
[126] (No losses reported) 0.0%
Capt. George W. Adams

CONFEDERATE

ARMY OF NORTHERN VIRGINIA
EWELL'S CORPS
EARLY'S DIVISION
[748] (No losses reported) 0.0%

GORDON'S BRIGADE
[470] (No losses reported) 0.0%
Brig. Gen. John Brown Gordon

26th Georgia
[283] (No losses reported) 0.0%
Col. Edmund Nathan Atkinson

31st Georgia
[187] (No losses reported) 0.0%
Col. Clement Anselm Evans

ATTACHED CAVALRY

35th Battalion Virginia Cavalry
[225] (No losses reported) 0.0%
Lt. Col. Elijah Viers White

ATTACHED ARTILLERY

Green's Battery, Louisiana Guard Artillery
(Two 3-inch Ordnance Rifles,
Two 10-pounder Parrotts)
[53] (No losses reported) 0.0%
Capt. Charles A. Green

Even though Sedgwick had his entire 6th Corps of about 14,000 soldiers available along the Fairfield Road to trail Jubal Early's retreating wagons, White's and Gordon's thin but stubborn defense held the Federals in place. As a result, the Confederate wagons continued moving through the hills above Fairfield. Sedgwick slowly and cautiously continued his pursuit all the way to Fairfield, but he did not fully engage the Southerners until the following day. Why Sedgwick did not act more aggressively is difficult to understand.

Also on July 5, as noted earlier, General Meade dispatched most of Brig. Gen. David M. Gregg's Second Cavalry Division west along the Chambersburg Pike to determine Confederate activity in that direction. Within a short time Gregg's troopers also ran into a long retreating wagon train full of Confederate wounded. After clashing with the Southern rearguard east of Caledonia (in the area of Thaddeus Stevens' Iron Works), Gregg's troopers rounded up some 2,000 Confederate stragglers (units unknown) and another 3,000 wounded. Additional pursuit by the 4th Pennsylvania Cavalry, also part of Gregg's division, bagged yet another 500 prisoners. Heavily laden with wagons, prisoners, and enemy wounded, Gregg called off the pursuit and spent the rest of the night at Caledonia.

The next day on July 6, Gregg's troopers continued pursuing the retreating enemy as far as Greencastle, Pennsylvania, where they rounded up several hundred more Confederate stragglers and wounded. Believing that his division was inadequate to deal with what Lee might be able to concentrate against him, however, Gregg fell back to the area around Chambersburg and would not ride into Maryland until July 8. The troopers then camped at the base of South Mountain at Middletown, Maryland, on July 9 and rejoined the rest of the Federal Cavalry Corps near Boonsborough on July 11.

THE SKIRMISH AT FAIRFIELD, PA.

JULY 6, 1863

Before daybreak on July 6, Maj. Gen. John Sedgwick sent orders to **COL. EMORY UPTON** to advance the 121st New York from its camp along the Fairfield Road toward the Fairfield Pass cutting through the South Mountain range to feel out the enemy position. Accompanied by a squadron of cavalry, Upton's New Yorkers moved out around 9:00 a.m. and discovered Confederate defenses blocking the pass. The two sides traded shots for nearly an hour until the Southerners retreated up the mountain. Upton reported the engagement to Sedgwick who, in a reprise of the previous evening's events, decided against an aggressive pursuit. Although neither side reported any losses, it is likely a few men on both sides were wounded.

Col. Emory Upton
Image courtesy of Library of Congress

FEDERAL

ARMY OF THE POTOMAC
VI ARMY CORPS
HEADQUARTERS AND PROVOST GUARD

1st New Jersey Cavalry, Company L	**1st Pennsylvania Cavalry, Company H**
[32] (No losses reported) 0.0%	[41] (No losses reported) 0.0%
Capt. William H. Hick	*Capt. William S. Craft (Command of the squadron)*

FIRST DIVISION
SECOND BRIGADE

121st New York
[427] (No losses reported) 0.0%
Col. Emory Upton

CONFEDERATE

Unknown rear guard
[Unknown] (Losses unknown)

By July 6 — two days after Lee's Confederate army began withdrawing from around Gettysburg — General Meade had still not launched a full-scale pursuit against the retreating and defeated Rebels. Sedgwick reported the engagements at Fairfield, but Meade feared the dangers of fighting for, and within, the mountain passes and refused to launch a full offensive at them. Later that day, Meade withdrew most of Sedgwick's 6th Corps from Fairfield and set into motion his plans for a flanking maneuver against the retreating Southerners on the other side of the mountains. Meade ordered the 1st, 3rd, and 6th Corps to march for Middletown, Maryland, via the Catoctin Mountain while the 5th and 11th Corps moved to Middletown by way of Emmitsburg, Maryland, and the 2nd and 12th Corps to the same location via Frederick, Maryland. Meade hoped that by splitting the army into three wings (which is how it had marched from Virginia to Pennsylvania), he could make good marching time and put his troops into a position to attack the Confederates between South Mountain and the Potomac River.

Federal cavalry divisions under Judson Kilpatrick and John Buford were still on the move on July 6, making their way toward the critical junctions in Maryland at Hagerstown and Williamsport. Unknown to the cavalry leaders, the Confederates were already garrisoning both places to protect the river crossings.

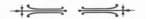

STUART SHIELDS THE CONFEDERATES

THE FIRST BATTLE OF HAGERSTOWN, MD.

JULY 6, 1863

Once the July 5 engagement ended at Smithsburg, Maryland, Confederate cavalry commander **MAJ. GEN. J.E.B. STUART** had no clue where **BRIG. GEN. JUDSON KILPATRICK**'s Federal cavalry had gone. Stuart was well aware, however, that the land between South Mountain and the important town of Hagerstown, Maryland, had to remain clear and open for the Southern retreat to the Potomac River. Hagerstown commanded the roads leading to the crossings at Williamsport and Falling Waters (the latter about four miles downriver from Williamsport). To defend Hagerstown, Stuart led four of his brigades there on the morning of July 6.

Maj. Gen. J.E.B. Stuart
Image courtesy of Library of Congress

By midday, miles of Confederate wagons and thousands of Lee's infantry were passing through Hagerstown west toward the Potomac River. Kilpatrick learned about the enemy wagons at Hagerstown while he and his troopers were in camp at Boonsborough. John Buford, meanwhile, learned that Confederates were marching to and crossing at Williamsport. With this key news in hand, Kilpatrick mounted his division and headed for Hagerstown while Buford's troopers saddled up and rode for Williamsport.

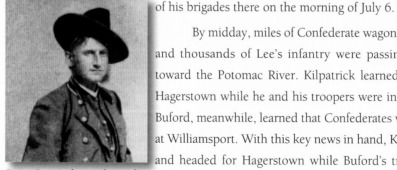

Brig. Gen. Judson Kilpatrick
Image courtesy of Library of Congress

| THE CAMPAIGN BEGINS JUNE 3 | THE BATTLE OF GETTYSBURG JULY 1-3 | FIRST HAGERSTOWN JULY 6 | LEE'S ARMY CROSSES THE POTOMAC RIVER JULY 14 |

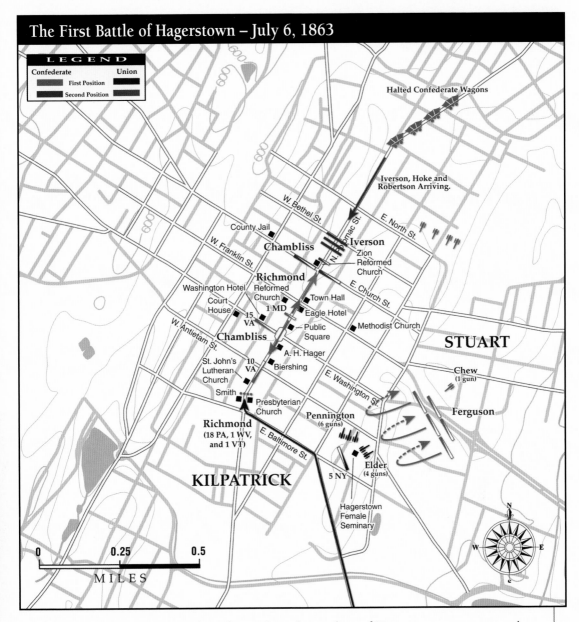

The First Battle of Hagerstown – July 6, 1863

LEGEND

Confederate — Union

First Position

Second Position

Halted Confederate Wagons

Iverson, Hoke and Robertson Arriving.

W. Bethel St.

County Jail

E. North St.

W. Franklin St.

Chambliss

Iverson

Zion Reformed Church

Richmond

Washington Hotel / Reformed Church

Court House

1 MD

15 VA

E. Church St.

Town Hall

Eagle Hotel

Public Square

Methodist Church

STUART

W. Antietam St.

Chambliss

A. H. Hager

St. John's Lutheran Church

10 VA

Biershing

E. Washington St.

Chew (1 gun)

Smith

Presbyterian Church

Ferguson

Richmond (18 PA, 1 WV, and 1 VT)

E. Baltimore St.

Pennington (6 guns)

Elder (4 guns)

KILPATRICK

5 NY

Hagerstown Female Seminary

0   0.25   0.5

MILES

N
W   E
S

Kilpatrick's initial advance from the south on the outskirts of Hagerstown was unopposed, but once his advance guard approached the court house it found the streets barricaded. A firefight erupted with pickets of Col. J. Lucius Davis' 10th Virginia Cavalry, which was soon reinforced by Capt. Frank Bond's Company of the 1st Maryland Cavalry Battalion (CSA).

Kilpatrick readied his men for a full-scale assault and deployed them on the roads leading to Boonsborough and Williamsport. Two more Virginia cavalry regiments rode up to support their comrades. A Federal charge drove the Confederates to the center of town and eventually all the way to the town square. Waiting there, however, were three batteries of Stuart's horse artillery, whose gunners pounded Kilpatrick's men. Kilpatrick hurriedly called up his own artillery and, from their perch on high ground south of town, watched as an artillery duel ensued. While the guns dueled the opposing cavalry charged and countercharged in the streets below.

The rumble of the urban combat reached the ears of Maj. Gen. Jubal A. Early, who was retreating westward with his division of infantry. Recognizing the importance of holding Hagerstown, Early turned his brigades around and marched back toward the raging fight. The addition of Early's men essentially balanced the two warring sides. A determined push through the streets by Confederate cavalry and Brig. Gen. Alfred Iverson's depleted brigade of infantry finally drove Kilpatrick's troopers back. In contrast to the handling of his men at Gettysburg, Iverson's steady handling of his command at Hagerstown helped turned the tide against the Federals.

Unable to hold the town Kilpatrick withdrew south, hotly pursued by Confederate infantry and cavalry under J.E.B. Stuart's personal direction. While directing the pursuit Stuart could hear the sound of artillery booming less than ten miles to the southwest at Williamsport, where Buford and his Federal cavalry division was making his presence known. Kilpatrick heard the same fighting and decided to join Buford there.

FEDERAL

ARMY OF THE POTOMAC
CAVALRY CORPS
[4,978] (21k, 60w, 220m = 301+) 6.0%+

THIRD CAVALRY DIVISION
[3,713] (21k, 59w, 220m = 300+) 8.1%+
Brig. Gen. Hugh Judson Kilpatrick

HEADQUARTERS GUARDS AND ORDERLIES

1st Ohio Cavalry, Company A
[37] (No losses reported) 0.0%
Capt. Noah Jones

1st Ohio Cavalry, Company C
[35] (No losses reported) 0.0%
Capt. Samuel N. Stanford

FIRST BRIGADE
[1,823] (20k, 45w, 219m = 284) 15.6%
Col. Nathaniel Pendleton Richmond

5th New York Cavalry
[414] (5k, 6w, 79m = 90) 21.8%
Maj. John Hammond

18th Pennsylvania Cavalry
[495] (8k, 19w, 71m = 98) 19.8%
Lt. Col. William P. Brinton

1st Vermont Cavalry
[535] (5k, 16w, 55m = 76) 14.2%
Lt. Col. Addison Webster Preston

1st West Virginia Cavalry
[379] (2k, 4w, 14m = 20) 5.3%
Maj. Charles E. Capehart

ATTACHED ARTILLERY

4th United States Horse Artillery, Battery E (Four 3-inch Ordnance Rifles)
[60] (1k, 2w = 3) 5.0%
Lt. Samuel Sherer Elder

SECOND BRIGADE
[1,641] (1k, 8w, 1m = 9+) 0.5%+
Brig. Gen. George Armstrong Custer

1st Michigan Cavalry
[328] (Losses unknown)
Col. Charles Henry Town

5th Michigan Cavalry
[590] (Losses unknown)
Col. Russell Alexander Alger

6th Michigan Cavalry
[438] (Losses unknown)
Col. George Gray

7th Michigan Cavalry
[285] (0k, 1m = 1) 0.4%
Col. William D'Alton Mann

ATTACHED ARTILLERY
**2nd United States Horse Artillery,
Battery M (Six 3-inch Ordnance Rifles)**
[117] (0k, 4w = 4) 3.4%
Lt. Alexander Cummings McWhorter Pennington, Jr.

SECOND CAVALRY DIVISION
[1,265] (?k, 1w+, ?m = 1+) 0.08%+

SECOND BRIGADE (ATTACHED)
[1,225] (?k, 1w+, ?m = 1+) 0.1%+
Col. Pennock Huey

2nd New York Cavalry
[220] (Unknown losses)
Lt. Col. Otto Harhaus

4th New York Cavalry
[245] (Unknown losses)
Lt. Col. Augustus Pruyn

6th Ohio Cavalry (10 Companies)
[420] (0k, 1w = 1) 0.2%
Maj. William Stedman

8th Pennsylvania Cavalry
[340] (Unknown losses)
Capt. William A. Corrie

ATTACHED ARTILLERY
**3rd United States Horse Artillery,
Battery C (One section of 3-inch Ordnance Rifles)**
[40] (No losses reported) 0.0%
Lt. Henry C. Meinell

CONFEDERATE

ARMY OF NORTHERN VIRGINIA
[4,610 Total Forces] (11k+, 1mw, 50w+, 1w-c, 38m+ = 101+) 2.2%+

CAVALRY DIVISION
[3,982] (2k+, 1mw, 25w+, 1w-c, 38m+ = 67+) 1.7%+
Maj. Gen. James Ewell Brown Stuart

WILLIAM HENRY FITZHUGH LEE'S BRIGADE
[1,190] (2k+, 14w+, 34m+ = 50+) 4.2%+
Col. John Randolph Chambliss, Jr.

2nd North Carolina Cavalry
[140] (Unknown losses)
Lt. Joseph Baker

9th Virginia Cavalry
[510] (2k, 14w, 6m = 22) 4.3%
Col. Richard Lee Turberville Beale

10th Virginia Cavalry
[240] (Unknown losses)
Col. James Lucius Davis (w-c)
Lt. Col. Robert Alexander Caskie

13th Virginia Cavalry
[300] (?k, ?w, 28m = 28+) 9.3%+
Capt. Benjamin Franklin Winfield

JENKINS' BRIGADE
[994] (?k, 1w+ = 1+) 0.1%+
Col. Milton James Ferguson

14th Virginia Cavalry
[245] (Unknown losses)
Maj. Benjamin Franklin Eakle

16th Virginia Cavalry
[240] (Unknown losses)
Maj. James Henry Nounnan

17th Virginia Cavalry
[242] (Unknown losses)
Col. William Henderson French

34th Battalion Virginia Cavalry
[152] (Unknown losses)
Lt. Col. Vincent Addison Witcher

36th Battalion Virginia Cavalry
[115] (?k, 1w+ = 1+) 0.9%+
Capt. Cornelius Timothy Smith

ROBERTSON'S BRIGADE
[845] (Unknown losses)
Brig. Gen. Beverly Holcombe Robertson

4th North Carolina Cavalry
[395] (Unknown losses)
Col. Dennis Dozier Ferebee

5th North Carolina Cavalry
[450] (Unknown losses)
Lt. Col. Stephen B. Evans

JONES' BRIGADE
[705] (?k, 9w+, 4m+ = 13+) 1.8%+
Brig. Gen. William Edmonson Jones

7th Virginia Cavalry
[340] (Unknown losses)
Lt. Col. Thomas A. Marshall, Jr.

11th Virginia Cavalry
[365] (0k, 9w, 4m = 13) 3.6%
Col. Lunsford Lindsay Lomax

(DETACHED UNIT)
1st Maryland Cavalry Battalion, Company A
[47] (0k, 1w, 1w-c = 2) 4.3%
Capt. Frank Augustus Bond (w-c)

ATTACHED ARTILLERY
[201] (0k, 1mw = 1) 0.5%

**Breathed's Battery, 1st Stuart (Virginia)
Horse Artillery (Four 3-inch Ordnance Rifles)**
[104] (No losses reported) 0.0%
Capt. James Williams Breathed

**McGregor's Battery, 2nd Stuart (Virginia)
Horse Artillery (One Blakely, One unknown)**
[52] (No losses reported) 0.0%
Capt. William Morrell McGregor

**Chew's Battery, Ashby (Virginia) Horse Artillery
(One 3-inch Ordnance Rifle)**
[45] (0k, 1mw = 1) 2.2%
Capt. Roger Preston Chew

EWELL'S CORPS
[628] (9k est., 25w est., ?m = 34+) 5.4%+

EARLY'S DIVISION

HOKE'S BRIGADE

54th North Carolina (Four Companies)
[168] (6k est., 19w est. = 25 est.) 14.9% est.
Lt. Col. Anderson Ellis

RODES' DIVISION

IVERSON'S BRIGADE
[460] (3k, 6w, ?m = 9+) 2.0%+
Brig. Gen. Alfred Iverson

5th North Carolina
[180] (Unknown losses)
Capt. Benjamin Robinson

12th North Carolina
[135] (Unknown losses)
Lt. Col. William Smith Davis

20th North Carolina
[115] (Unknown losses)
Capt. Lewis T. Hicks

23rd North Carolina
[30] (Unknown losses)
Capt. Vines E. Turner

Casualty reports for the Hagerstown battle are incomplete, especially on the Confederate side. They are even less plentiful for the remaining days of the retreat. According to our best estimate, both sides lost about the same number of men (in excess of 300 killed, wounded, and captured for each side).

While Kilpatrick battled at Hagerstown, Buford's division advanced on the river crossing town of Williamsport, Maryland. Although they would outnumber their adversaries, the Federals would find themselves up against one of the most stubborn defensive efforts of the entire Gettysburg retreat.

IMBODEN SAVES CONFEDERATE WOUNDED

THE BATTLE OF WILLIAMSPORT, MD.

JULY 6, 1863

Because four major roads converged on the river town of Williamsport, it was essential to the Confederate retreat. On the morning of July 6, **BRIG. GEN. JOHN D. IMBODEN**, who was in charge of the immense wagon train of Confederate wounded, learned that **BRIG. GENS. JOHN BUFORD** and Judson Kilpatrick were closing in on Hagerstown and Williamsport. Knowing he was sorely under-strength, Imboden set about organizing a defense. The former artillery officer gathered up several batteries of guns and deployed them on high ground surrounding the town, and armed as many of the walking wounded as possible.

Confederate artillery fired on Buford's cavalry as it advanced near the College of St. James six miles east of Williamsport. Lieutenant John H. Calef's Federal battery deployed and dueled with the Southern guns while the blue troopers probed Confederate infantry defending the approaches to Williamsport across a three-mile front. After two hours of fitful but often intense fighting, Buford drove the defenders back. When the Federals reached the outskirts of Williamsport, however, Imboden's artillery opened on them. By this time Brig. Gen. William E. Jones and his staff had arrived. Jones also gathered teamsters and wagoneers and sent them with muskets to the front. Jones ordered Imboden to hold on as best he could and then rode off to enlist as much cavalry as could be found to join the defense.

Brig. Gen. John D. Imboden
Image courtesy of Library of Congress

Brig. Gen. John Buford
Image courtesy of Library of Congress

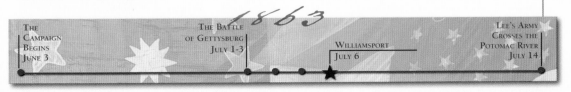

1863

| THE CAMPAIGN BEGINS JUNE 3 | THE BATTLE OF GETTYSBURG JULY 1-3 | WILLIAMSPORT JULY 6 | LEE'S ARMY CROSSES THE POTOMAC RIVER JULY 14 |

Buford, meanwhile, deployed his division for a full-scale attack on Williamsport. He set Col. William Gamble's brigade on the left, Brig. Gen. Wesley Merritt's brigade of Regulars in the center, and Col. Thomas C. Devin's brigade on the right. Buford's artillery batteries were skillfully deployed to deal with Imboden's cannons. Gamble's dismounted troopers advanced and gained ground against Imboden's right while Merritt's cavalry attacked straight in from the east. Imboden's armed wounded, teamsters, and artillerists were mounting a masterful defense, but in the face of determined pressure they were now in danger of breaking.

The fighting looked like it could end only one way when Imboden received welcome news: Brig. Gen. Fitzhugh Lee, whose cavalry brigade had been protecting the rear of the Confederate wagon train of wounded, was on his way to Williamsport. Lee's arrival would add more than 1,500 veteran defenders. What none of the Confederates realized, however, was that Brig. Gen. Judson

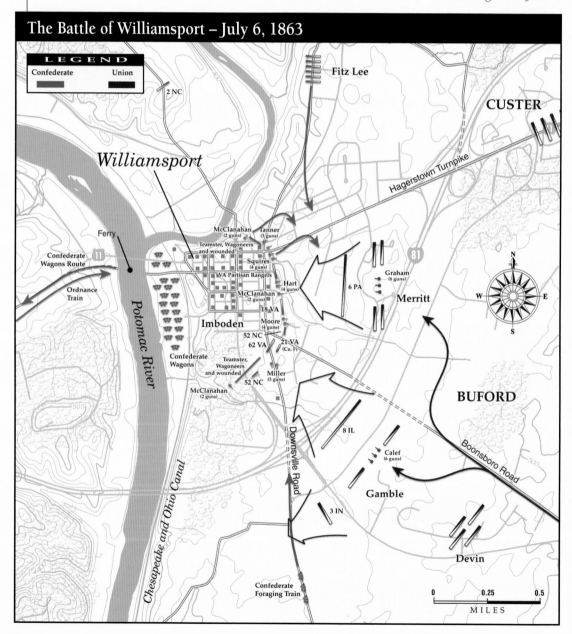

The Battle of Williamsport – July 6, 1863

Kilpatrick, who had just been repulsed at Hagerstown, was also on his way to Williamsport with more than 4,000 Federal cavalry.

Kilpatrick reached Williamsport first. He deployed some of Brig. Gen. George A. Custer's troopers as dismounted skirmishers, but well-placed shots from Confederate artillery held them in check. To Imboden's great relief, Fitz Lee arrived with his Virginia cavalrymen, organized his brigade as fast as possible, and attacked Kilpatrick's troops and Buford's right flank. By this time darkness was approaching and Kilpatrick decided to withdraw. The cavalryman had been repulsed twice that day, first at Hagerstown and again at Williamsport. The frustrated John Buford likewise withdrew with Col. Devin's brigade covering the movement.

FEDERAL

ARMY OF THE POTOMAC
CAVALRY CORPS
[8,616] (1k+, 3mw+, 5w+ = 172+ est.) 2.0%+

FIRST CAVALRY DIVISION
[3,983] (72 total est.) 1.8%
Brig. Gen. John Buford

FIRST BRIGADE
[1,435] (1k, 3mw, 1w = 5) 0.3%
Col. William Gamble

8th Illinois Cavalry
[450] (1k, 3mw, 1w = 5) 1.1%
Maj. John Lourie Beveridge

12th Illinois Cavalry (4 Companies)
[205] (Unknown losses)

3rd Indiana Cavalry (6 Companies)
[260] (Unknown losses)
Col. George Henry Chapman
(Capt. George Washington Shears had subordinate command of the 12th Illinois)

8th New York Cavalry
[520] (Unknown losses)
Lt. Col. William Markell

SECOND BRIGADE
[1,005] (Unknown losses)
(In reserve, covered division's withdrawal after the battle)
Col. Thomas Casimer Devin

6th New York Cavalry
[165] (Unknown losses)
Maj. William Elliott Beardsley

9th New York Cavalry
[345] (Unknown losses)
Col. William Sackett

17th Pennsylvania Cavalry
[445] (Unknown losses)
Col. Josiah Holcomb Kellogg

3rd West Virginia Cavalry (2 Companies)
[50] (Unknown losses)
Capt. Seymour Beach Conger

RESERVE BRIGADE
[1,360] (Unknown losses)
Brig. Gen. Wesley Merritt

6th Pennsylvania Cavalry
[220] (Unknown losses)
Maj. James H. Haseltine

1st United States Cavalry
[330] (Unknown losses)
Capt. Richard Stanton C. Lord

2nd United States Cavalry
[380] (Unknown losses)
Capt. Theophilus Francis Rodenbough

5th United States Cavalry
[290] (Unknown losses)
Capt. Julius Wilmot Mason

6th United States Cavalry
[140 est.] (Unknown losses)
Capt. Ira Claflin

ATTACHED ARTILLERY
[183] (Unknown losses)

**1st United States Horse Artillery,
Battery K (Six 3-inch Ordnance Rifles)**
[113] (Unknown losses)
Capt. William Montrose Graham, Jr.

**2nd United States Horse Artillery,
Battery A (Six 3-inch Ordnance Rifles)**
[70] (No losses reported) 0.0%
Lt. John Haskell Calef

THIRD CAVALRY DIVISION
[4,633] (0k, 4w = 4+) 0.09%+
(Joined battle after it was opened by the First Division)
Brig. Gen. Hugh Judson Kilpatrick

HEADQUARTERS GUARDS AND ORDERLIES

1st Ohio Cavalry, Company A
[37] (No losses reported) 0.0%
Capt. Noah Jones

1st Ohio Cavalry, Company C
[35] (No losses reported) 0.0%
Capt. Samuel N. Stanford

FIRST BRIGADE
[1,520] (Unknown losses)
(In reserve, covered division's
withdrawal after the battle)
Col. Nathaniel Pendleton Richmond

5th New York Cavalry
[325] (Unknown losses)
Maj. John Hammond

18th Pennsylvania Cavalry
[395] (No losses reported) 0.0%
Lt. Col. William P. Brinton

1st Vermont Cavalry
[450] (Unknown losses)
Lt. Col. Addison Webster Preston

1st West Virginia Cavalry
[350] (Unknown losses)
Col. Charles Capehart

ATTACHED ARTILLERY

**4th United States Horse Artillery,
Battery E (Four 3-inch Ordnance Rifles)**
[57] (Unknown losses)
Lt. Samuel Sherer Elder

SECOND BRIGADE
[1,625] (Unknown losses)
Brig. Gen. George Armstrong Custer

1st Michigan Cavalry
[325] (Unknown losses)
Col. Charles Henry Town

5th Michigan Cavalry
[585] (Unknown losses)
Col. Russell Alexander Alger

6th Michigan Cavalry
[435] (Unknown losses)
Col. George Gray

7th Michigan Cavalry
[280] (Unknown losses)
Col. William D'Alton Mann

ATTACHED ARTILLERY

**2nd United States Horse Artillery,
Battery M (Six 3-inch Ordnance Rifles)**
[114] (0k, 4w = 4) 3.5%
Lt. Alexander Cummings McWhorter Pennington, Jr.

SECOND CAVALRY DIVISION
[1,245] (100+ est.) 8.0%+

SECOND BRIGADE (ATTACHED)
[1,205] (100 total est.) 8.3% est.
Col. Pennock Huey

2nd New York Cavalry
[215] (Unknown losses)
Lt. Col. Otto Harhaus

4th New York Cavalry
[240] (Unknown losses)
Lt. Col. Augustus Pruyn

6th Ohio Cavalry (10 Companies)
[415] (Unknown losses)
Maj. William Stedman

8th Pennsylvania Cavalry
[335] (Unknown losses)
Capt. William A. Corrie

ATTACHED ARTILLERY

**3rd United States Horse Artillery,
Battery C (One section of 3-inch Ordnance Rifles)**
[40] (No losses reported) 0.0%
Lt. Henry C. Meinell

CONFEDERATE

ARMY OF NORTHERN VIRGINIA
[7,310 Total Forces] (14k+, 117w+, 1c+, 46m+ = 178+) 2.4%+

CAVALRY DIVISION
[5,607] (7k+, 70w+, 1c+, 26m+ = 104+) 1.9%+

Imboden's Northwestern Brigade
[2,045] (5k+, 54w+ = 59+) 2.9%+
Brig. Gen. John Daniel Imboden

18th Virginia Cavalry
[890] (Unknown losses)
Col. George William Imboden

62nd Virginia Mounted Infantry
[1,070] (5k, 54w = 59) 5.5%
Col. George Hugh Smith

Virginia Partisan Rangers
[85] (Unknown losses)
Capt. John Hanson McNeill

Fitz Lee's Brigade
[1,835] (?k, 2w+, 20m+ = 22+) 1.2%+
Brig. Gen. Fitzhugh Lee

1st Virginia Cavalry
[320] (0k, 6m = 6) 1.9%
Col. James Henry Drake

2nd Virginia Cavalry
[415] (0k, 2w, 14m = 16) 3.9%
Col. Thomas Taylor Munford

3rd Virginia Cavalry
[220] (Unknown losses)
Col. Thomas Howerton Owen

4th Virginia Cavalry
[580] (Unknown losses)
Col. Williams Carter Wickham

5th Virginia Cavalry
[140] (Unknown losses)
Col. Thomas Lafayette Rosser

1st Maryland Cavalry Battalion
[160] (Unknown losses)
Maj. Ridgely Brown
(Maj. Harry Ward Gilmor turned command
of the assembled forces of wounded,
teamsters, etc. over to Brown.)

Attached Artillery
Chew's Battery, Ashby Horse Artillery
(One 3-inch Ordnance Rifle,
One 12-pounder Howitzer)
[93] (No losses reported) 0.0%
Capt. Roger Preston Chew

William Henry Fitzhugh Lee's Brigade
[1,530] (2k+, 14w+, 6m+ = 22+) 1.4%+
Lt. Col. John Randolph Chambliss, Jr.

2nd North Carolina Cavalry
[130] (Unknown losses)
Lt. Joseph Baker

9th Virginia Cavalry
[480] (2k, 14w, 6m = 22) 4.6%
Col. Richard Lee Turberville Beale

10th Virginia Cavalry
[230] (Unknown losses)
Col. James Lucius Davis

13th Virginia Cavalry
[260] (Unknown losses)
Capt. Benjamin Franklin Winfield

5th North Carolina Cavalry (temporarily attached)
[430] (Unknown losses)
Lt. Col. Stephen B. Evans

Attached Artillery
Breathed's Battery, 1st Stuart (Virginia) Horse
Artillery (Four 3-inch Ordnance Rifles)
[104] (0k, 1c = 1) 1.0%
Capt. James Williams Breathed

WILLIAMSPORT DEFENSES
[1,703 Total Forces] (7k+, 47w+, 20m = 74+) 4.4%+

ARTILLERY
[663] (?k, 21w+ = 21+) 3.2%+

**McClanahan's Battery, Staunton (Virginia)
Horse Artillery (Six unknown)**
[142] (Unknown losses)
Capt. John H. McClanahan

**Tanner's Battery, Richmond (Virginia) "Courtney"
Artillery (Three 3-inch Ordnance Rifles)**
[65] (Unknown losses)
Capt. William A. Tanner

**Moore's Battery, Norfolk (Virginia)
Battery (Two Napoleons, One 3-inch
Ordnance Rifle, One 10-pounder Parrott)**
[75] (0k, 4w = 4) 5.3%
Capt. Joseph D. Moore

**Hart's Battery, Washington (South Carolina)
Horse Artillery (Three Blakely Rifles)**
[106] (Unknown losses)
Capt. James Franklin Hart

Washington (Louisiana) Artillery Battalion
[275] (0k, 17w = 17) 6.2%
Maj. Benjamin F. Eshelman

1st Company (One Napoleon)
[65] (Unknown losses)
Capt. Charles W. Squires

**2nd Company (Two Napoleons,
One 12-pounder Howitzer)**
[65] (Unknown losses)
Capt. John B. Richardson

3rd Company (Three Napoleons)
[75] (Unknown losses)
Capt. Merritt B. Miller

**4th Company (Two Napoleons,
One 12-pounder Howitzer)**
[70] (Unknown losses)
Lt. Harry A. Battles

OTHER UNITS

Quartermasters and teamsters of various commands
[180] (5k, 9w, 20m = 34) 18.9%
Maj. Harry Ward Gilmor (w-c – escaped)

Walking wounded able to fight
[700 est.] (Unknown losses)

EWELL'S CORPS

EARLY'S DIVISION

HOKE'S BRIGADE

54th North Carolina (4 Companies)
[160 est.] (2k, 17w = 19) 11.9% est.
Lt. Col. Anderson Ellis

The failure of Buford and Kilpatrick to break the motley Confederate defensive effort at Williamsport left the town and the river crossing open for the use of Lee's army. The successful defense of Williamsport by outnumbered wounded, teamsters, and cavalry, particularly during the initial fighting directed by General Imboden, was nothing short of impressive. Everyone involved realized the importance of holding or seizing Williamsport. As a result, when it became obvious the Federals were retreating, the Confederate rank and file cheered their commanders. Dead and wounded were strewn in and around Williamsport and along the road leading to Hagerstown. Very few records of casualties for the Williamsport combat exist, but interpolation of the few available accounts indicates that each side suffered approximately 250 to 300 from all causes.

Although Imboden, W. H. F. Lee, and the embattled Confederates had saved Williamsport, the issue now turned to whether the defensive effort had been in vain. The heavy rains that continued on July 6 swelled the Potomac River further, making any attempts to cross both slow and perilous. Many men in Lee's army marching hard for the crossings from the Pennsylvania line through Maryland feared that the rising water would trap them before they could escape to the safety of the opposite bank.

STUART HOLDS FEDERAL CAVALRY AT BAY

THE SKIRMISH AT FUNKSTOWN, MD.

JULY 7, 1863

While the rest of Brig. Gen. William E. Jones' cavalry brigade was embroiled in the fighting at Williamsport on July 6, all but one Company of **LT. COL. THOMAS A. MARSHALL**'s 7th Virginia Cavalry was on picket duty near Funkstown, Maryland. (Company C was picketing the road to Williamsport.) While most of Brig. Gen. John Buford's Federal cavalry division rested from another skirmish with Confederate infantry near the College of St. James on the morning of July 7, the 6th U.S. Cavalry of his Reserve Brigade conducted a reconnaissance mission along the National Road north toward Funkstown. The 6th U.S. Cavalry had heavy losses fighting Jones' Brigade on July 3 at Fairfield, Pennsylvania, about the same time Pickett's Charge was raging on the Gettysburg battlefield. Before their near-annihilation, however, the Federal Regulars had broken a mounted charge by the 7th Virginia Cavalry. Now, the Federals were riding toward Funkstown and a replay of the Fairfield collision — only this time the Virginians were about to get a healthy measure of revenge.

As the 6th U.S. troopers neared Funkstown, the Virginians ambushed them and fired into the hapless advance guard of the Regulars. Lieutenant Colonel Marshall called up most of the rest of his regiment to set spurs and charge into the surprised Federals. Outnumbered more than three to one, the 6th U.S. troopers were quickly surrounded. Several Federals were captured during the melee, and barely half the regiment was able to escape. Those troopers of the 6th U.S. Cavalry who did manage to escape rallied and attempted a countercharge. The Virginians killed several and wounded others including 6th U.S. Cavalry commander **CAPT. IRA CLAFLIN**, and the fighting ended when the few dozen Federal survivors galloped back down the National Road out of harm's way. Those wounded who could be moved were stripped of their horses and weapons and marched to the rear.

THE CAMPAIGN BEGINS JUNE 3 — THE BATTLE OF GETTYSBURG JULY 1-3 — 1863 — FUNKSTOWN, BOONSBOROUGH, & SECOND HAGERSTOWN JULY 7-12 — LEE'S ARMY CROSSES THE POTOMAC RIVER JULY 14

FEDERAL

ARMY OF THE POTOMAC
CAVALRY CORPS

REGULAR BRIGADE
6th U.S. Cavalry
[est. 130] (10k, 15w, 66c = 91) est. 70.0%
Capt. Ira Claflin (w)
Lt. Louis Henry Carpenter

CONFEDERATE

ARMY OF NORTHERN VIRGINIA
CAVALRY DIVISION

JONES' BRIGADE
7th Virginia Cavalry (11 Companies)
[485] (0k, 2w, 9m = 11) 2.3%
Lt. Col. Thomas A. Marshall, Jr.

The short skirmish's only real impact was to rebuild the reputation of the 7th Virginia Cavalry following its dismal Fairfield performance. It also closed the bitter campaign chapter that witnessed the thorough pummeling of the 6th U.S. Cavalry. Within four days, the Regulars lost 80% of their numbers. By the evening of July 7, barely a few dozen 6th U.S. cavalrymen were available to gather around a campfire to console each other. Referring to the Funkstown brawl, General Jones boasted in his official report, "the day at Fairfield is nobly and fully avenged."

The continuing heavy rains raised the water level of the Potomac River, making it impossible for the main Confederate army to cross once it reached the wide waterway. The inclement weather and terrible road conditions also bogged down the Union army's pursuit. Federal army commander Maj. Gen. George G. Meade still intended to catch and defeat Robert E. Lee's retreating army somewhere north of the Potomac, but whether he could get enough of his army into a position to strike before the Confederates escaped remained an open question.

THE SKIRMISH AT BEAVER CREEK BRIDGE AND BOONSBOROUGH, MD.

JULY 8, 1863

For the first time since the Battle of Gettysburg ended, the skies cleared about daybreak on July 8. With the sun came the ability to dry clothes and gear. As one of **BRIG. GEN. JOHN BUFORD**'s Yankee cavalrymen noted, until that morning his feet had "been wet for two weeks."

The respite from the rain was a welcomed one, but there was little rest between the running fights that punctuated the entire retreat. The old town of Boonsborough (Boonsboro today), Maryland where the Federal cavalry divisions of Buford and Kilpatrick bivouacked after the July 6 battles for Hagerstown and Williamsport, commanded the approaches to South Mountain. Confederate cavalry commander **MAJ. GEN. J.E.B. STUART** knew he had to take and hold Boonsborough in order to allow Lee's army to continue its retreat to the

Maj. Gen. J.E.B. Stuart
Image courtesy of Library of Congress

Potomac. That morning, Stuart moved nearly his entire cavalry division from near Williamsport and Funkstown to Boonsborough along the National Road.

Buford's division was camped north of Boonsborough, and Stuart drove straight at the enemy troopers across Beaver Creek around four miles north of town. Brigadier General William E. Jones' Brigade led the way. His Virginians pushed Buford's pickets back about 10:00 a.m. while Capt. William M. McGregor's Battery unlimbered on a high hill overlooking the approach to town. Because the ground was soggy from the recent rains, both Stuart and Buford had no choice but to dismount their men and send them forward in more traditional lines of battle. The two sides fought like infantry for more than an hour when Kilpatrick's division arrived to reinforce Buford. Stuart had sent Albert Jenkins' Brigade (commanded by Col. Milton J. Ferguson) to the right to flank Buford, so Kilpatrick advanced to meet the new threat.

Brig. Gen. John Buford
Image courtesy of Library of Congress

By mid-afternoon the Federals were running low on ammunition and slowly retired south toward Boonsborough. Stuart called off his advance about 7:00 p.m. after the nearly-all day fight when Federal infantry from the 6th and 11th Corps marched through the mountain gaps and began deploying to face the Southern cavalry. Stuart's bold effort had purchased an additional day for Lee's army to continue moving east to the Potomac by blunting any planned attack by Buford or Kilpatrick before it could even get started.

FEDERAL

ARMY OF THE POTOMAC
CAVALRY CORPS
[7,287] (5k+, 33w+, 5m+ = 43+) 0.6%+

FIRST CAVALRY DIVISION
[3,828] (3k+, 24w+ = 27+) 0.7%+
Brig. Gen. John Buford

FIRST BRIGADE
[1,405] (3k+, 22w+ = 25+) 1.8%+
Col. William Gamble

8th Illinois Cavalry
[440] (3k, 22w = 25) 5.7%
Maj. John Lourie Beveridge

12th Illinois Cavalry (4 Companies)
[200] (Unknown losses)

3rd Indiana Cavalry (6 Companies)
[250] (Unknown losses)
Col. George Henry Chapman
(Capt. George Washington Shears had subordinate command of the 12th Illinois)

8th New York Cavalry
[515] (Unknown losses)
Lt. Col. William Markell

SECOND BRIGADE
[1,005] (?k, 1w+ = 1) 0.01%+
Col. Thomas Casimer Devin

6th New York Cavalry
[165] (?k, 1w+ = 1) 0.6%+
Maj. William Elliott Beardsley

9th New York Cavalry
[345] (Unknown losses)
Col. William Sackett

17th Pennsylvania Cavalry
[445] (No losses reported) 0.0%
Col. Josiah Holcomb Kellogg

3rd West Virginia Cavalry (2 Companies)
[50] (Unknown losses)
Capt. Seymour Beach Conger

RESERVE BRIGADE
[1,235] (Unknown losses)
Brig. Gen. Wesley Merritt

6th Pennsylvania Cavalry
[215] (Unknown losses)
Maj. James H. Haseltine

1st United States Cavalry
[325] (Unknown losses)
Capt. Richard Stanton C. Lord

2nd United States Cavalry
[375] (Unknown losses)
Capt. Theophilus Francis Rodenbough

5th United States Cavalry
[285] (Unknown losses)
Capt. Julius Wilmot Mason

6th United States Cavalry
[35] (Unknown losses)
Lt. Louis Henry Carpenter

ATTACHED ARTILLERY
[183] (?k, 1w = 1) 0.5%

1st United States Horse Artillery, Battery K
(Six 3-inch Ordnance Rifles)
[113] (Unknown losses)
Capt. William Montrose Graham, Jr.

2nd United States Horse Artillery, Battery A
(Six 3-inch Ordnance Rifles)
[70] (0k, 1w = 1) 1.4%
Lt. John Haskell Calef

THIRD CAVALRY DIVISION
[3,459] (2k, 9w, 5m = 16+) 0.5%+
Brig. Gen. Hugh Judson Kilpatrick

HEADQUARTERS GUARDS AND ORDERLIES

1st Ohio Cavalry, Company A
[37] (No losses reported) 0.0%
Capt. Noah Jones

1st Ohio Cavalry, Company C
[35] (No losses reported) 0.0%
Capt. Samuel N. Stanford

FIRST BRIGADE
[1,500] (2k, 8w, 5m = 15) 1.0%
Col. Nathaniel Pendleton Richmond

5th New York Cavalry
[320] (No losses reported) 0.0%
Maj. John Hammond

18th Pennsylvania Cavalry
[390] (No losses reported) 0.0%
Lt. Col. William P. Brinton

1st Vermont Cavalry
[440] (2k, 8w, 5m = 15) 3.4%
Lt. Col. Addison Webster Preston

1st West Virginia Cavalry
(Not engaged – supported Elder's battery)
[350] (No losses reported) 0.0%
Col. Charles Capehart

ATTACHED ARTILLERY

4th United States Horse Artillery,
Battery E (Four 3-inch Ordnance Rifles)
[57] (No losses reported) 0.0%
Lt. Samuel Sherer Elder

SECOND BRIGADE
[1,605] (0k, 1w =1) 0.1%
Brig. Gen. George Armstrong Custer

1st Michigan Cavalry
[320] (No losses reported) 0.0%
Col. Charles Henry Town

5th Michigan Cavalry
[580] (0k, 1w = 1) 0.2%
Col. Russell Alexander Alger (w)
Lt. Col. Ebenezer Gould

6th Michigan Cavalry
[430] (No losses reported) 0.0%
Col. George Gray

7th Michigan Cavalry
[275] (No losses reported) 0.0%
Col. William D'Alton Mann

ATTACHED ARTILLERY
[225] (No losses reported) 0.0%

2nd United States Horse Artillery,
Battery M (Six 3-inch Ordnance Rifles)
[110] (No losses reported) 0.0%
Lt. Alexander Cummings McWhorter Pennington, Jr.

3rd United States Horse Artillery,
Battery C (Six 3-inch Ordnance Rifles)
[115] (No losses reported) 0.0%
Lt. William Duncan Fuller

CONFEDERATE

ARMY OF NORTHERN VIRGINIA
CAVALRY DIVISION
[6,933] (26k+, 132w+, 13m = 171+) 2.5%+
Maj. Gen. James Ewell Brown Stuart

FITZHUGH LEE'S BRIGADE
[1,645] (10k+, 80w+ = 90+) 5.5%+
Brig. Gen. Fitzhugh Lee

1st Virginia Cavalry
[310] (9k, 79w = 88) 28.4%
Col. James Henry Drake

2nd Virginia Cavalry
[405] (Unknown losses)
Col. Thomas Taylor Munford

3rd Virginia Cavalry
[225] (No losses reported) 0.0%
Col. Thomas Howerton Owen

4th Virginia Cavalry
[570] (1k, 1w = 2) 0.4%
Col. Williams Carter Wickham

5th Virginia Cavalry
[135] (Unknown losses)
Col. Thomas Lafayette Rosser

JONES' BRIGADE
[1,175] (13k, 47w, 12m = 72) 6.1%
Brig. Gen. William Edmonson Jones

6th Virginia Cavalry
[480] (No losses reported) 0.0%
Maj. Cabell Edward Flournoy

7th Virginia Cavalry
[335] (13k, 41w, 12m = 66) 19.7%
Lt. Col. Thomas A. Marshall, Jr.

11th Virginia Cavalry
[360] (0k, 6w = 6) 1.7%
Col. Lunsford Lindsay Lomax

WILLIAM HENRY FITZHUGH LEE'S BRIGADE
[1,090] (Unknown losses)
Col. John Randolph Chambliss, Jr.

2nd North Carolina Cavalry
[130] (Unknown losses)
Lt. Joseph Baker

9th Virginia Cavalry
[475] (Unknown losses)
Col. Richard Lee Turberville Beale

10th Virginia Cavalry
[230] (Unknown losses)
Col. James Lucius Davis

13th Virginia Cavalry
[255] (Unknown losses)
Capt. Benjamin Franklin Winfield

HAMPTON'S BRIGADE
[1,620] (1k+, 1w+ = 2+) 0.1%+
Col. Laurence Simmons Baker

1st North Carolina Cavalry
[360] (Unknown losses)
Lt. Col. James Byron Gordon

1st South Carolina Cavalry
[320] (Unknown losses)
Lt. Col. John David Twiggs

2nd South Carolina Cavalry
[175] (Unknown losses)
Maj. Thomas Jefferson Lipscomb

Cobb's (Georgia) Legion
[315] (Unknown losses)
Col. Pierce Manning Butler Young

Jeff Davis (Mississippi) Legion
[225] (1k, 1w = 2) 0.9%
Lt. Col. Joseph Frederick Waring

Phillips' (Georgia) Legion
[225] (Unknown losses)
Lt. Col. William Wofford Rich

JENKIN'S BRIGADE
[975] (2k+, 4w+, 1m+ = 7+) 0.7%+
Col. Milton James Ferguson

14th Virginia Cavalry
[240] (Unknown losses)
Maj. Benjamin Franklin Eakle

16th Virginia Cavalry
[235] (Unknown losses)
Maj. James Henry Nounnan

17th Virginia Cavalry
[240] (2k, 4w, 1m = 7) 2.9%
Col. William Henderson French

34th Battalion Virginia Cavalry
[150] (Unknown losses)
Lt. Col. Vincent Addison Witcher

36th Virginia Cavalry
[110] (Unknown losses)
Capt. Cornelius Timothy Smith

STUART HORSE ARTILLERY
[428] (Unknown losses)
Maj. Robert Franklin Beckham

Breathed's Battery, 1st Stuart (Virginia) Horse Artillery (Four 3-inch Ordnance Rifles)
[90] (Unknown losses)
Capt. James Williams Breathed

2nd Stuart (Virginia) Horse Artillery (One Blakely, One unknown)
[40] (Unknown losses)
Capt. William Morrell McGregor

Chew's Battery, Ashby (Virginia) Horse Artillery (One 3-inch Ordnance Rifle, One 12-pounder Howitzer)
[91] (Unknown losses)
Capt. Roger Preston Chew

Griffin's Battery, 2nd Baltimore (Maryland) Battery (Four 10-pounder Parrotts)
[105] (Unknown losses)
Capt. Wiley Hunter Griffin

Moorman's Battery, Lynchburg (Virginia) "Beauregard" Rifles (One Napoleon, One unknown)
[102] (Unknown losses)
Capt. Marcellus Newton Moorman

More than 14,000 cavalrymen participated at some level in the fighting at Boonsborough which was the largest engagement of cavalry since the July 3 fighting at East Cavalry Field near Gettysburg. It was nearly as large as the June 9 Battle of Brandy Station. Because Stuart's movement against Boonsborough was more of a feint to buy time for the retreat than an all-out attack, casualties were lower than they would otherwise have been. Stuart's losses are difficult to tabulate, but were almost certainly in excess of 200 killed and wounded. Federal losses were about the same.

Throughout the day, the remainder of Meade's army continued marching on the boggy roads toward its concentration point at Middletown, Maryland. Because of the poor conditions, the march was slow and difficult for most of his units, which only made a few miles by sundown. Meade now had information that Lee was entrenching his army on a line stretching from Hagerstown to Falling Waters, but none of the Federals had any idea about the strength of that defensive position. General-in-Chief Henry W. Halleck warned Meade from Washington to concentrate his army before launching an attack, and also promised reinforcements in the form of Pennsylvania volunteer militia. That night, Meade ordered all of his corps to continue marching west to further tighten the noose on the Army of Northern Virginia, which had a swelled river at its back that could not yet be crossed.

THE BATTLE OF
FUNKSTOWN, MD.

JULY 10, 1863

Throughout July 9, most of the Confederate army trudged through the area of Hagerstown, Maryland. Several sharp skirmishes broke as Federal cavalry picked and prodded against portions of the long Rebel columns of infantry and cavalry, and tested Gen. Robert E. Lee's developing entrenchments along Salisbury Ridge. All seven of Maj. Gen. George Meade's infantry corps were moving west to get into position opposite the Southern defensive line.

On the morning of July 10, **BRIG. GEN. JOHN BUFORD** cautiously moved his Federal cavalry division along the National Road from Boonsborough toward Funkstown to find and engage **MAJ. GEN. J.E.B STUART**'s cavalry. Stuart had set up a three-mile defensive line at Funkstown after withdrawing from his prodding feint

Maj. Gen. J.E.B. Stuart
Image courtesy of Library of Congress

attacks around Boonsborough on July 8. About 8:00 a.m., brigade commander Col. Thomas C. Devin dismounted his regiments and drove back Stuart's skirmishers while brigades under Brig. Gen. Wesley Merritt and Col. William Gamble extended Buford's line. All the while, artillery on both sides kept up a steady fire. The weight of three Federal brigades eventually cracked Stuart's line and the Confederates conducted a well-organized fighting withdrawal through Funkstown. Stuart, who knew he would need additional assistance, called for infantry support.

Lieutenant General James Longstreet heeded the call by sending the pair of brigades of George T. Anderson (commanded by Col. William W. White) and Paul Semmes (commanded by Col. Goode Bryan) from their camps along the Hagerstown Road to support Stuart's embattled cavalry. The Georgians arrived about noon and went into line on Stuart's center and left, where their stubborn defense brought Buford's men to a halt. Stuart was not the only one with infantry support, however. Brigadier General Albion P. Howe's Second

Brig. Gen. John Buford
Image courtesy of Library of Congress

Division of Maj. Gen. John Sedgwick's 6th Corps had trailed Buford to Funkstown, and Howe's Vermont regiments moved up to deploy in line of battle in front of the Confederate center while Buford's division shifted right. The clash of the Vermonters and Georgians was the first time infantry fought infantry since the Battle of Gettysburg.

By the time darkness arrived, the opposing sides had been fighting for nearly twelve hours and the Confederate cavalry and infantry had been driven through and out of Funkstown. Because it was too dark to maneuver safely, Buford decided against launching a pursuit and instead withdrew south toward Beaver Creek just north of Boonsborough. Although he had been driven back, Stuart's stout defense (aided by Georgia infantry) had once again delayed the Federal pursuit for another full day.

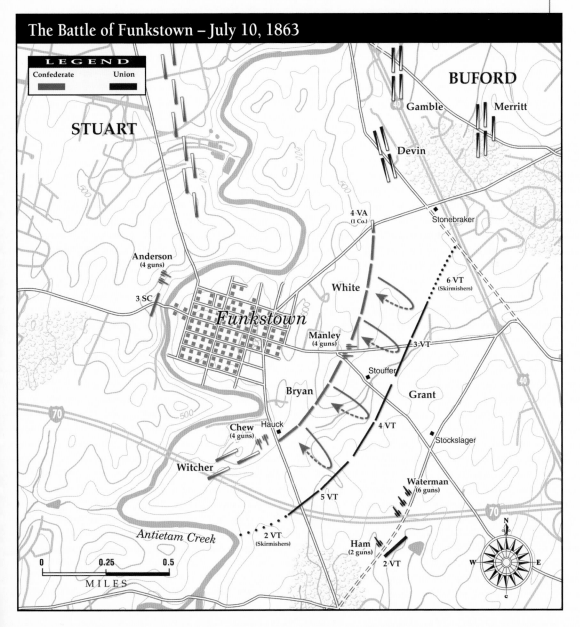

The Battle of Funkstown – July 10, 1863

FEDERAL

ARMY OF THE POTOMAC
CAVALRY CORPS
[5,854] (16k+, 90w+, ?m = 106+) 1.8%+

FIRST CAVALRY DIVISION
[3,784] (1k+, 31w+, ?m = 32+) 0.9%+
Brig. Gen. John Buford

FIRST BRIGADE
[1,390] (1k+, 30w+ = 31+) 2.2%+
Col. William Gamble

8th Illinois Cavalry
[435] (1k, 2w = 3) 0.7%
Maj. John Lourie Beveridge

12th Illinois Cavalry (4 Companies)
[195] (Unknown losses)

3rd Indiana Cavalry (6 Companies)
[250] (Unknown losses)
Col. George Henry Chapman
(Capt. George Washington Shears had
subordinate command of the 12th Illinois)

8th New York Cavalry
[510] (Unknown losses)
Lt. Col. William Markell (w)
Maj. William H. Benjamin

SECOND BRIGADE
[995] (Unknown losses)
Col. Thomas Casimer Devin

6th New York Cavalry
[160] (Unknown losses)
Maj. William Elliott Beardsley

9th New York Cavalry
[340] (Unknown losses)
Col. William Sackett

17th Pennsylvania Cavalry
[445] (Unknown losses)
Col. Josiah Holcomb Kellogg

3rd West Virginia Cavalry (2 Companies)
[50] (Unknown losses)
Capt. Seymour Beach Conger

RESERVE BRIGADE
[1,220] (Unknown losses)
Brig. Gen. Wesley Merritt

6th Pennsylvania Cavalry
[210] (Unknown losses)
Maj. James H. Halseltine

1st United States Cavalry
[325] (Unknown losses)
Capt. Richard Stanton C. Lord (w)
Capt. Samuel McKee

2nd United States Cavalry
[370] (Unknown losses)
Capt. Theophilus Francis Rodenbough

5th United States Cavalry
[280] (Unknown losses)
Capt. Julius Wilmot Mason

6th United States Cavalry
[35] (Unknown losses)
Lt. Louis Henry Carpenter

ATTACHED ARTILLERY
[179] (0k, 1w = 1) 0.6%

1st United States Horse Artillery, Battery K
(Six 3-inch Ordnance Rifles)
[110] (No losses reported) 0.0%
Capt. William Montrose Graham, Jr.

2nd United States Horse Artillery, Battery A
(Six 3-inch Ordnance Rifles)
[69] (0k, 1w = 1) 1.4%
Lt. John Haskell Calef

VI ARMY CORPS
[2,070] (15k+, 59w+ = 74+) 3.6%+

SECOND DIVISION

SECOND BRIGADE
[1,845] (15k, 59w = 74) 3.8%
Col. Lewis Addison Grant

2nd Vermont
[450] (?k, 1w = 1+) 0.2%+
Col. James Hicks Walbridge

3rd Vermont
[370] (Unknown losses)
Col. Thomas Orville Seaver

4th Vermont
[385] (?k, 2w+ = 2+) 0.5%+
Col. Charles B. Stoughton (w)
Lt. Col. George Perkins Foster

5th Vermont
[300] (Unknown losses)
Lt. Col. John R. Lewis

6th Vermont
[340] (3k+, 19w+ = 22+) 6.5%+
Col. Elisha L. Barney

ATTACHED ARTILLERY
[225] (Unknown losses)

3rd New York Independent Battery
(Six 10-pounder Parrotts)
[110] (Unknown losses)
Capt. William A. Harn

1st Rhode Island Light Artillery, Battery C
(One section) (Two 3-inch Ordnance Rifles)
[115] (Unknown losses)
Capt. Richard Waterman

CONFEDERATE

ARMY OF NORTHERN VIRGINIA
[9,753] (29k+, 1mw, 114w+, 1m+ = 275+) 2.8%+

CAVALRY DIVISION
[7,588] (1k+, 1mw, 9w+, ?m = 75+) 1.0%+
Maj. Gen. James Ewell Brown Stuart

FITZ LEE'S BRIGADE
[1,518] (Unknown losses)
Brig. Gen. Fitzhugh Lee

1st Virginia Cavalry
[220] (3k, 4w, 2m = 9) 4.1%
Col. James Henry Drake

2nd Virginia Cavalry
[375] (Unknown losses)
Col. Thomas Taylor Munford

3rd Virginia Cavalry
[225] (Unknown losses)
Col. Thomas Howerton Owen

4th Virginia Cavalry
[568] (Unknown losses)
Col. Williams Carter Wickham

5th Virginia Cavalry
[130] (Unknown losses)
Col. Thomas Lafayette Rosser

JONES' BRIGADE
[1,104] (Unknown losses)
Brig. Gen. William Edmonson Jones

6th Virginia Cavalry
[480] (No losses reported) 0.0%
Maj. Cabell Edward Flournoy

7th Virginia Cavalry
[270] (Unknown losses)
Lt. Col. Thomas A. Marshall, Jr.

11th Virginia Cavalry
[354] (No losses reported) 0.0%
Col. Lunsford Lindsay Lomax

WILLIAM HENRY FITZHUGH LEE'S BRIGADE
[1,070] (Unknown losses)
Col. John Randolph Chambliss, Jr.

2nd North Carolina Cavalry
[125] (Unknown losses)
Lt. Joseph Baker

9th Virginia Cavalry
[470] (Unknown losses)
Col. Richard Lee Turberville Beale

10th Virginia Cavalry
[225] (Unknown losses)
Col. James Lucius Davis

13th Virginia Cavalry
[250] (Unknown losses)
Capt. Benjamin Franklin Winfield

HAMPTON'S BRIGADE
[1,595] (1k+, 3w+ = 4+) 0.3%+
Col. Laurence Simmons Baker

1st North Carolina Cavalry
[355] (?k, 2w = 2+) 0.6%+
Lt. Col. James Byron Gordon

1st South Carolina Cavalry
[315] (Unknown losses)
Lt. Col. John David Twiggs

2nd South Carolina Cavalry
[175] (Unknown losses)
Maj. Thomas Jefferson Lipscomb

Cobb's (Georgia) Legion
[310] (Unknown losses)
Col. Pierce Manning Butler Young

Jeff Davis (Mississippi) Legion
[220] (1k, 1w = 2) 0.9%
Lt. Col. Joseph Frederick Waring

Phillips' (Georgia) Legion
[220] (Unknown losses)
Lt. Col. William Wofford Rich

JENKINS' BRIGADE
[938] (Unknown losses)
Col. Milton James Ferguson

14th Virginia Cavalry
[230] (Unknown losses)
Maj. Benjamin Franklin Eakle

16th Virginia Cavalry
[225] (Unknown losses)
Maj. James Henry Nounnan

17th Virginia Cavalry
[233] (Unknown losses)
Col. William Henderson French

34th Battalion Virginia Cavalry
[145] (Unknown losses)
Lt. Col. Vincent Addison Witcher

36th Virginia Cavalry
[105] (Unknown losses)
Capt. Cornelius Timothy Smith

ROBERTSON'S BRIGADE
[830] (?k, 1w+ = 1+) 0.1%+
Brig. Gen. Beverly Holcombe Robertson

4th North Carolina Cavalry
[390] (Unknown losses)
Col. Dennis Dozier Ferebee

5th North Carolina Cavalry
[440] (?k, 1w = 1+) 0.2%+
Lt. Col. Stephen B. Evans

STUART HORSE ARTILLERY
[546] (?k, 1mw, 5w+ = 6+) 1.1%+
Maj. Robert Franklin Beckham

**Breathed's Battery, 1st Stuart (Virginia)
Horse Artillery (Four 3-inch Ordnance Rifles)**
[103] (0k, 1w = 1) 1.0%
Capt. James Williams Breathed

**2nd Stuart (Virginia) Horse Artillery
(One Blakely Rifle, One unknown)**
[40] (Unknown losses)
Capt. William Morrell McGregor

**Chew's Battery, Ashby (Virginia) Horse
Artillery (One 3-inch Ordnance Rifle,
One 12-pounder Howitzer)**
[91] (Unknown losses)
Capt. Roger Preston Chew

**Hart's Battery, Washington (South Carolina)
Horse Artillery (Three Blakely Rifles)**
[105] (Unknown losses)
Capt. James Franklin Hart

**Griffin's Battery, 2nd Baltimore
(Maryland) Battery (Four 10-pounder Parrotts)**
[105] (Unknown losses)
Capt. Wiley Hunter Griffin

**Moorman's Battery, Lynchburg (Virginia)
"Beauregard" Rifles (One Napoleon,
One unknown)**
[102] (0k, 1mw, 4w = 5) 4.9%
Capt. Marcellus Newton Moorman

LONGSTREET'S CORPS
[2,165] (28k+, 105w+, 1m+ = 200+) 9.2%+

MCLAWS' DIVISION
[1,250] (2k+, 4w+, 1m+ = 7+) 0.6%+

SEMMES' BRIGADE
[940] (1k+, 4w+, 1m+ = 6+) 0.6%+
Col. Goode Bryan

10th Georgia
[202] (?k, 1w = 1+) 0.5%+
Col. John B. Weems

50th Georgia
[207] (Unknown losses)
Col. William Richard Manning

51st Georgia
[208] (1k, 2w+, 1m+ = 4+) 1.9%+
Col. Edward Ball

53rd Georgia
[323] (?k, 1w = 1+) 0.3%+
Col. James Phillip Simms

KERSHAW'S BRIGADE

3rd South Carolina
[310] (1k = 1) 0.3%
Col. James Drayton Nance

HOOD'S DIVISION

ANDERSON'S BRIGADE
[785] (26k, 101w, ?m = 127+) 16.2%+
Col. William Wilkinson White

8th Georgia
[143] (?k, 1w+ = 1+) 0.7%+
Col. John Reed Towers

9th Georgia
[151] (?k, 1w+ = 1+) 0.7%+
Capt. George Hillyer

11th Georgia
[108] (1k+, 8w+, ?m = 9+) 8.3%+
Maj. Henry Dickerson McDaniel (w)
Capt. William H. Mitchell (k)

59th Georgia
[383] (2k, 10w = 12) 3.1%
Capt. Mastin G. Bass

ATTACHED ARTILLERY

1st North Carolina Light Artillery, Battery A
(Two Napoleons, Two 3-inch Ordnance Rifles)
[130] (Unknown losses)
Capt. Basil Charles Manly

As is true for most of the engagements that took place during the hectic Gettysburg retreat, except for a few units the casualties for the fighting at Funkstown are impossible to precisely determine. In the reports that are available, the commanders simply lumped in the Funkstown losses with other engagements during the retreat or added them to the casualty lists for the entire campaign. In other words, they are often not broken out by conflict or even day. A careful assessment leads to the conclusion that Federal losses from all causes at Funkstown total 106+, and Confederate losses 275+.

The battle at Funkstown marked the first time Confederate cavalry faced both Federal troopers and infantry at the same time during the retreat. Without infantry support of his own, Stuart would not have been able to hold back the probing enemy. By the evening of July 10, three Federal corps were concentrating between Boonsborough and Funkstown, the scene of nearly constant fighting since July 6.

The Funkstown battle and additional intelligence indicated to Lee that Meade's Federals were enveloping his army, which was essentially trapped against the swollen Potomac River. Lee issued a circular to his troops, admonishing them that only their fortitude and endurance could hold off a Federal onslaught. The Southerners would need both strength and a healthy dose of good fortune if they were going to keep the Army of the Potomac at bay until they could cross the flooded river.

THE SECOND BATTLE OF HAGERSTOWN, MD.

JULY 12, 1863

From July 10–12, the individual corps of the Federal army took up positions along a long line stretching from near Hagerstown in the north through Boonsborough and Downville to the south. The line faced the north-south defensive position taken up by Lee's Army of Northern Virginia a mile or so to the west along prominent terrain known locally as Salisbury Ridge. During the Battle of Gettysburg, Federal cavalry destroyed the pontoon bridges Lee's army used to cross the Potomac River on its northward trek. Heavy rains had swollen the river, which crested on July 9 and thus prevented a quick passage back to the safety of the opposite bank. Only now was the water beginning to recede.

A number of small skirmishes broke out on July 11 as the two armies jockeyed for position and Federal units probed Lee's reinforced lines. The Confederates at Williamsport, meanwhile, worked overtime to rebuild a pontoon bridge across the surging but now slowly subsiding Potomac. By that evening, Lee's defensive line was heavily fortified, strongly manned by infantry, and bristling with artillery. Most of Meade's army, which had been reinforced with volunteer militia from Harrisburg, Pennsylvania, was in place hugging the enemy line. About dark, a Union signalman reported to Meade's headquarters that only about 6,000 Confederates held Hagerstown and the critical road network leading to Williamsport on Meade's right flank. The time seemed right to attack and capture it.

Brig. Gen. Judson Kilpatrick
Image courtesy of Library of Congress

Early on the morning of Sunday, July 12, Brig. Gen. George A. Custer's Michigan brigade led the advance of **BRIG. GEN. JUDSON KILPATRICK**'s Federal cavalry division into Hagerstown from the east. The cavalrymen captured many of the Confederate pickets holding the approach and scattered the rest. Custer's brigade then rode into town, followed by an infantry brigade from the Federal 11th Corps, and scattered the surprised Confederates in Hagerstown. Most of the supposed 6,000 Rebels expected there had left the previous evening, but the Federals corralled several hundred prisoners by the time they took possession of town. They also freed a few dozen of their Union comrades who had been captured during the July 6 Hagerstown fight and in other engagements during the retreat.

FEDERAL

ARMY OF THE POTOMAC
CAVALRY CORPS

FIRST CAVALRY DIVISION
[1,901] (0k, 4w = 4) 0.2%
Brig. Gen. Hugh Judson Kilpatrick

HEADQUARTERS GUARDS AND ORDERLIES

1st Ohio Cavalry, Company A
[37] (No losses reported) 0.0%
Capt. Noah Jones

1st Ohio Cavalry, Company C
[35] (No losses reported) 0.0%
Capt. Samuel N. Stanford

SECOND BRIGADE
[1,604] (0k, 4w = 4) 0.2%
Brig. Gen. George Armstrong Custer

7th Michigan Cavalry
[275] (No losses reported) 0.0%
Col. William D'Alton Mann

1st Michigan Cavalry
[320] (0k, 1w = 1) 0.3%
Col. Charles Henry Town

ATTACHED ARTILLERY
[225] (No losses reported) 0.0%

5th Michigan Cavalry
[579] (0k, 1w = 1) 0.2%
Lt. Col. Ebenezer Gould (w)
Maj. Crawley P. Dake

2nd United States Horse Artillery,
Battery M (Six 3-inch Ordnance Rifles)
[110] (No losses reported) 0.0%
Lt. Alexander Cummings McWhorter Pennington, Jr.

6th Michigan Cavalry
[430] (0k, 2w = 2) 0.5%
Col. George Gray

3rd United States Horse Artillery,
Battery C (Six 3-inch Ordnance Rifles)
[115] (No losses reported) 0.0%
Lt. William Duncan Fuller

CONFEDERATE

ARMY OF NORTHERN VIRGINIA
[Unknown] (est. 400-500 total)

CAVALRY DIVISION

WILLIAM HENRY FITZHUGH LEE'S BRIGADE

9th Virginia Cavalry
[470] (0k, 5w, ?m = 5+) 1.1%+
Col. Richard Lee Turberville Beale

EWELL'S CORPS

JOHNSON'S DIVISION

JONES' BRIGADE

25th Virginia Infantry
[210] (Unknown losses)
Lt. Col. John Armistead Robinson

OTHER UNITS
[Unknown] (400-500 total est.)
Units of various infantry, cavalry, and artillery commands

The fight for the possession of Hagerstown only lasted about one hour. Following behind Custer's successful charge through the town's streets, the balance of Kilpatrick's division and the 11th Corps infantry rounded up additional prisoners and secured the objective. Commander Maj. Gen. Oliver O. Howard of the 11th Corps arrived later and climbed a church steeple. From that vantage point he could see much of Lee's well-fortified defensive position to the southwest, heavily braced with artillery.

General Meade called a council of war that evening (July 12) with his corps commanders to discuss what to do next. He was determined to attack Lee the next day and argued as much, but more than half of his generals present (with votes permitted by Meade) voted against assuming the offensive. They argued that Lee's entrenched position was too strong to assail — the ridge was high ground, and was heavily protected with artillery that could devastatingly rake the ground over which any assault would proceed. Too, some emphasized, their own army had been seriously injured during the Gettysburg battle and exhausted by the subsequent pursuit. A disappointed Meade acceded to the wishes of his commanders and decided to put off the assault for another day. This would give his army all of July 13 to get comfortable with their new positions, conduct additional reconnaissance and probe enemy lines, and rest and refit. Those precious twenty-four hours, however, would trigger a major controversy that still reverberates to this day.

FEDERAL RECONNAISSANCE

THE SKIRMISHES AT PARIS, VA.

JULY 12, 1863

Throughout the Gettysburg Campaign, many engagements large and small erupted throughout northern Virginia, West Virginia, Maryland, and Pennsylvania that did not involve well-known elements of either army. Most of these minor fights garner but passing mention in the *Official Records* or other accounts left by participants. Unfortunately, writers since the war have all but completely ignored them. Some of these little-noted combats, however, involved interesting events important to the overall campaign and deserve to be remembered.

On July 10, while the Federal army was moving into position opposite the Confederate defensive line fronting Williamsport to Falling Waters, Federal army commander Maj. Gen. George G. Meade wanted to know the whereabouts of the head of the Southern retreat. That day, 28-year-old **COL. CHARLES RUSSELL LOWELL** was ordered to scout northern Virginia east of the Blue Ridge Mountains with his 2nd Massachusetts Cavalry. Lowell's regiment (a unit of the Defenses of Washington), which he had personally recruited that spring, had already conducted a number of scouting excursions in Virginia during the campaign but had not seen any combat yet.

The next day, July 11, Lowell and his men arrived in Aldie, Virginia, about 6:00 p.m., and on July 12 moved through Middleburg and Upperville — the scenes of deadly cavalry fighting the previous month. According to his scouts, the only troops in the area belonged to J.E.B. Stuart's cavalry: detachments from Brig. Gen. William E. Jones' Brigade at Snicker's Gap and Brig. Gen. Beverly H. Robertson's Brigade at Ashby's Gap.

When Lowell arrived at Paris, Virginia, at the eastern base of Ashby's Gap about noon, he discovered a squadron of Robertson's Confederate cavalry. Lowell's troopers charged, drove the Rebels into the gap (where the Southerners were joined by some of Jones' men as well as some of Col. John S. Mosby's scouts) and chased them for several miles. The Massachusetts cavalry captured a dozen enemy riders, but lost sixteen of their own as casualties.

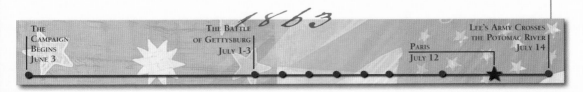

FEDERAL

DEFENSES OF WASHINGTON
CAVALRY DIVISION
[365] (2k, 1mw, 4w, 4c, 5m = 16) 4.4%

2nd Massachusetts Cavalry
[305] (2k, 1mw, 4w, 4c, = 11) 3.6%

Additional cavalry troops from the Defenses
[60] (0k, 5m = 5) 8.3%
Col. Charles Russell Lowell, Jr.

CONFEDERATE

ARMY OF NORTHERN VIRGINIA
CAVALRY DIVISION
[60+ est.] (0k, 12c = 12) 20.0%+

JONES' BRIGADE [Unknown] (0k, 1c = 1) **6th Virginia Cavalry (detachment)** [Unknown] (0k, 1c = 1) **12th Virginia Cavalry (detachment)** [Unknown] (No losses reported) 0.0%	ROBERTSON'S BRIGADE **4th North Carolina Cavalry (2 Companies)** [60 est.] (0k, 6c = 6) 10.0% est. *Capt. Lewis A. Johnson* **Various members of Col. John Singleton Mosby's** **43rd Battalion Virginia Cavalry** (1 captured), **Engineers** (2 captured), **and** **local citizens** (2 captured)

With his captives in tow, Lowell returned the next day via Leesburg, Virginia, where he snatched up three more Confederates. The Paris skirmish was the maiden engagement for both Lowell and his Massachusetts regiment. Once it ended, Lowell confidently reported back to Meade that there were no Confederates in force on the east side of the Blue Ridge Mountains. This intelligence answered two important questions for Meade: most of Lee's army was still north of the Potomac River, and he did not have enough men in place to protect the passes through the Blue Ridge range. Unfortunately for the Federals, these conditions were about to quickly change.

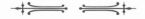

THE CONFEDERATES ESCAPE

THE SKIRMISH AT FALLING WATERS, MD.

JULY 14, 1863

By the afternoon of July 13, Robert E. Lee's engineers had completed a new pontoon bridge at Falling Waters. Luckily for the Confederates, the Potomac River had subsided enough to be safely crossed there and at the Williamsport ford a few miles farther north. Lee ordered the crossings to secretly and quietly begin after dark. Lieutenant General Richard S. Ewell's Second Corps and the rest of the wagons of wounded were to cross at Williamsport, while the corps of Lt. Gens. James Longstreet and A. P. Hill, together with most of the Confederate cavalry, would withdraw at Falling Waters.

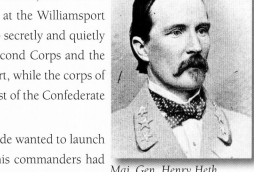

Maj. Gen. Henry Heth
Image courtesy of Library of Congress

Federal army commander Maj. Gen. George G. Meade wanted to launch an attack against Lee's defenses on July 13, but most of his commanders had voted against it during the July 12 war council. By the evening of July 13, Meade decided to attack early the following morning, and many of the frontline troops were ordered to sleep on their arms. About 7:00 a.m. on July 14, Federal skirmishers advanced westward toward the powerful defenses fronting Williamsport, only to discover that the Southern entrenchments had been abandoned during the night. Most of Lee's soldiers had already crossed the river.

Brig. Gen. John Buford
Image courtesy of Library of Congress

Federal cavalry divisions under **BRIG. GENS. JOHN BUFORD** and Judson Kilpatrick advanced toward Falling Waters early that morning and met and pushed back Southern rearguard skirmishers about a mile and a half from the river. The Rebels conducted a stubborn fighting withdrawal from ridge to ridge until they reached additional Confederates still holding the crossing. This rearguard was composed of about 4,000 Confederates from two depleted divisions from A. P. Hill's Third Corps, most of whom were already crossing the pontoon bridge.

Confederate division commander **MAJ. GEN. HENRY HETH** ordered Brig. Gen. James J. Pettigrew (who had been slightly wounded during Pickett's Charge on July 3) to organize his brigade to conduct a defense one mile from the river while the balance of the men crossed safely. At the same time, Federal cavalrymen from Brig. Gen. George A. Custer's brigade were busy forming a line of battle just a few hundred yards away.

Major Peter A. Weber of Custer's 6th Michigan Cavalry, whose regiment had spent most of the campaign fighting dismounted, wanted to launch a mounted saber charge against a small portion of Pettigrew's front. His squadron of Companies B and F set spurs and struck hard. Weber was shot through the head and killed during the swirling melee that followed, and General Pettigrew was shot in the stomach, a mortal wound that claimed his life three days later.

John Buford attempted a flanking assault against the Rebels, but the Michiganders' impetuous charge scattered Heth's men and Buford was unable to coordinate his attack before most of the enemy was across the pontoon bridge. Those Confederates still on the Maryland side of the river, however, were surrounded by Federal cavalry and as many as 1,500 were captured. Kilpatrick's and Buford's men also netted two artillery pieces and three battle flags, including one from the 55th Virginia, which had participated in Pickett's Charge. According to available reports, all of the 57 men from the 55th Virginia still on the wrong side of the river that day were captured.

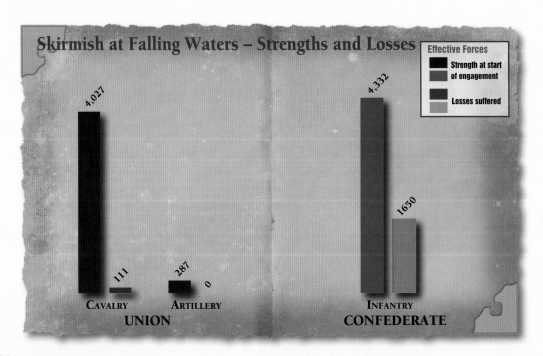

Skirmish at Falling Waters – Strengths and Losses

Effective Forces

Strength at start of engagement

Losses suffered

4,027

4,332

1650

111

287

0

CAVALRY   ARTILLERY

UNION

INFANTRY

CONFEDERATE

FEDERAL

ARMY OF THE POTOMAC
CAVALRY CORPS
[4,314] (29k, 42w, 40m = 111) 2.6%

FIRST CAVALRY DIVISION
[2,532] (0k, 6w = 6) 0.2%
Brig. Gen. John Buford

FIRST BRIGADE
[1,372] (0k, 5w = 5) 0.4%
Col. William Gamble

8th Illinois Cavalry
[430] (0k, 4w = 4) 0.9%
Maj. John Lourie Beveridge

12th Illinois Cavalry (4 Companies)
[192] (Unknown losses)

3rd Indiana Cavalry (6 Companies)
[245] (Unknown losses)
Col. George Henry Chapman
*(Capt. George Washington Shears had
subordinate command of the 12th Illinois)*

8th New York Cavalry
[505] (Unknown losses)
Maj. William H. Benjamin

SECOND BRIGADE
[983] (0k+, 2w+ = 2+) 0.2%+
Col. Thomas Casimer Devin

6th New York Cavalry
[160] (Unknown losses)
Maj. William Elliott Beardsley

9th New York Cavalry
[335] (Unknown losses)
Col. William Sackett

17th Pennsylvania Cavalry
[440] (Unknown losses)
Col. Josiah Holcomb Kellogg

3rd West Virginia Cavalry (2 Companies)
[48] (Unknown losses)
Capt. Seymour Beach Conger

ATTACHED ARTILLERY
[177] (No losses reported) 0.0%

**1st United States Horse Artillery, Battery K
(Six 3-inch Ordnance Rifles)**
[110] (No losses reported) 0.0%
Capt. William Montrose Graham, Jr.

**2nd United States Horse Artillery, Battery A
(Six 3-inch Ordnance Rifles)**
[67] (No losses reported) 0.0%
Lt. John Haskell Calef

THIRD CAVALRY DIVISION
[1,782] (29k, 36w, 40m = 105) 5.9%
Brig. Gen. Hugh Judson Kilpatrick

HEADQUARTERS GUARDS AND ORDERLIES

1st Ohio Cavalry, Company A
[37] (No losses reported) 0.0%
Capt. Noah Jones

1st Ohio Cavalry, Company C
[35] (No losses reported) 0.0%
Capt. Samuel N. Stanford

SECOND BRIGADE
[1,600] (29k, 36w, 40m = 105) 6.6%
Brig. Gen. George Armstrong Custer

1st Michigan Cavalry
[319] (No losses reported) 0.0%
Col. Charles Henry Town

5th Michigan Cavalry
[578] (No losses reported) 0.0%
Maj. Crawley P. Dake

6th Michigan Cavalry
[428] (27k, 35w, 40m = 102) 23.8%
Col. George Gray

7th Michigan Cavalry
[275] (2k, 1w = 3) 1.1%
Col. William D'Alton Mann

ATTACHED ARTILLERY

**2nd United States Horse Artillery,
Battery M (Six 3-inch Ordnance Rifles)**
[110] (No losses reported) 0.0%
Lt. Alexander Cummings McWhorter Pennington, Jr.

CONFEDERATE

ARMY OF NORTHERN VIRGINIA
[4,332 est.] (est. 150k, 4w+, est. 1,500c = 1,650+) 38.1%+

HILL'S CORPS
HETH'S DIVISION
[est. 1,727] (2k+, 4w+, 2w-c+, 69c+ = 77+) 4.5%+
Maj. Gen. Henry Heth

PETTIGREW'S BRIGADE
[510 est.] (Unknown losses)
Brig. Gen. James Johnston Pettigrew (mw)
Maj. John Thomas Jones

11th North Carolina
[120 est.] (Unknown losses)
Capt. Francis Wilder Bird

26th North Carolina
[70 est.] (Unknown losses)
Maj. John Thomas Jones
Capt. Henry Clay Albright

47th North Carolina
[220 est.] (Unknown losses)
Capt. William Crocker Lankford

52nd North Carolina
[100 est.] (Unknown losses)
Capt. Nathaniel A. Foster

BROCKENBROUGH'S BRIGADE
[342 est.] (0k, 57c = 57) 16.7%
John Mercer Brockenbrough

40th Virginia
[110 est.] (Unknown losses)
Capt. Robert Beale Davis

47th Virginia
[70 est.] (Unknown losses)
Lt. Col. John Warner Lyell

55th Virginia
[57 est.] (0k, 57c = 57) 100.0%
Col. William Steptoe Christian (c)
Lt. Col. Evan Rice (c)
Maj. Robert Bruce Fauntleroy

22nd Virginia Battalion
[105 est.] (Unknown losses)
Maj. John Samuel Bowles

ARCHER'S BRIGADE
[275 est.] (Unknown losses)
Lt. Col. Samuel George Shepard

5th Alabama Battalion
[50 est.] (Unknown losses)
Maj. Albert Sebastian Van De Graaff

13th Alabama
[55 est.] (Unknown losses)
Capt. N. J. Taylor

1st Tennessee (Provisional Army)
[50 est.] (Unknown losses)
Capt. Jacob B. Turney

7th Tennessee
[70 est.] (Unknown losses)
Lt. Col. Samuel George Shepard

14th Tennessee
[50 est.] (Unknown losses)
Capt. Bruce L. Phillips

DAVIS' BRIGADE
[est. 600] (2k, 4w, 2w-c, 12c = 20) 3.4%
Brig. Gen. Joseph Robert Davis

2nd Mississippi
[est. 160] (2k, 4w, 2w-c, 12c = 20) 12.5%
Col. John Marshall Stone

11th Mississippi
[est. 120] (Unknown losses)
Maj. Reuben Oscar Reynolds

42nd Mississippi
[est. 190] (Unknown losses)
Capt. Andrew M. Nelson

55th North Carolina
[est. 130] (Unknown losses)
Capt. E. Fletcher Satterfield

PENDER'S DIVISION
[est. 2,605] (Unknown losses)
Brig. Gen. James Henry Lane

PERRIN'S BRIGADE
[810 est.] (Unknown losses)
Col. Abner Perrin

1st South Carolina (Provisional Army)
[130 est.] (Unknown losses)
Maj. Comillus Wycliffe McCreary

1st South Carolina Rifles
[250 est.] (Unknown losses)
Capt. William M. Hadden

12th South Carolina
[150 est.] (Unknown losses)
Col. John Lucas Miller

13th South Carolina
[160 est.] (Unknown losses)
Lt. Col. Benjamin Thomas Brockman

14th South Carolina
[120 est.] (Unknown losses)
Capt. James Boatwright

LANE'S BRIGADE
[570] (Unknown losses)
Brig. Gen. James Henry Lane

7th North Carolina
[80 est.] (Unknown losses)
Capt. James Gilmer Harris

18th North Carolina
[150 est.] (Unknown losses)
Col. John Decatur Barry

28th North Carolina
[60 est.] (Unknown losses)
Lt. Col. William Henry Asbury Speer

33rd North Carolina
[160 est.] (Unknown losses)
Lt. W. C. Horton

37th North Carolina
[120 est.] (Unknown losses)
Col. William Morgan Barbour

THOMAS' BRIGADE
[710] (Unknown losses)
Brig. Gen. Edward Lloyd Thomas

14th Georgia
[180 est.] (Unknown losses)
Col. Robert Warren Folsom

35th Georgia
[160 est.] (Unknown losses)
Col. Bolling Hall Holt

45th Georgia
[190 est.] (Unknown losses)
Col. Thomas Jefferson Simmons

49th Georgia
[180 est.] (Unknown losses)
Col. Samuel Thomas Player

SCALES' BRIGADE
[515 est.] (Unknown losses)
Col. William Lee Joshua Lowrance

13th North Carolina
[30 est.] (Unknown losses)
Lt. Col. Henry A. Rogers

16th North Carolina
[220 est.] (Unknown losses)
Capt. Abel S. Cloud

22nd North Carolina
[60 est.] (Unknown losses)
Col. James Conner

34th North Carolina
[150 est.] (Unknown losses)
Lt. Burwell T. Cotton

38th North Carolina
[55 est.] (Unknown losses)
Lt. John M. Robinson

Kikpatrick's uncoordinated attacks at Falling Waters frustrated fellow division commander John Buford. Had the two Federal cavalry divisions worked in unison, the bridgehead may have collapsed and more Rebels would have been bagged. Once the area and the prisoners were secured, Buford could do little else except watch as an unnamed Confederate on the far side of the Potomac River cut the ropes holding the pontoon bridge in place. Once loose, the bridge uselessly swung downriver. The Gettysburg Campaign was over.

Word that Lee's critically wounded Army of Northern Virginia had crossed the Potomac before Meade was able to bring it to battle gravely disappointed President Abraham Lincoln. "We had them within our grasp," he lamented to one of his secretaries. "We only had to stretch forth our hands and they were ours." Although his rendition of the conditions at the front was not fully accurate, it amply conveyed the deep frustration the president and others were experiencing at Lee's escape.

During the days that followed, the Federal army crossed the Potomac and advanced along the eastern base of the Blue Ridge in pursuit of the Confederates. On July 16, Brig. Gen. David M. Gregg's Federal cavalry division, which had done little fighting thus far during the retreat, engaged two Confederate cavalry brigades over the fords along the river at Shepherdstown, West Virginia. On July 23, a sizable engagement broke out at Manassas Gap between the Federal 3rd Corps and two Confederate divisions, but the uncoordinated Federal attack was abandoned by nightfall. By the end of July, the Federal and Confederate armies were once again facing one another from opposite sides of the Rappahannock River in nearly the same positions they held in May just before the start of the Gettysburg Campaign.

By this time, though, there were many thousands fewer manning their respective fronts. In addition to the more than 23,000 casualties suffered during the three days of fighting at Gettysburg, the Army of the Potomac lost more than 2,000 men (most of them cavalry) during the retreat from the battlefield. The retreat also stripped away about 5,000 more men from the Confederate ranks. Total losses for both armies that June and July in killed, wounded, captured and missing total nearly 60,000.

EPILOGUE

THE CAMPAIGN AND BATTLE OF GETTYSBURG, PA.

JUNE 3 – JULY 14, 1863

The Battle of Gettysburg (July 1-3, 1863) extracted an enormous toll on the Federal and Confederate armies. Generally speaking, both sides lost about one-quarter of their men during just those three days. Many regiments on both sides suffered losses in excess of fifty percent. Robert E. Lee's Army of Northern Virginia, however, was smaller than George G. Meade's Army of the Potomac by more than 20,000. As a result, the losses suffered by the rebuffed Southern army — whose officer corps was also more heavily devastated than Meade's — were much more punishing and much harder to replace.

The purpose of this book has been to detail, as best as the existing records allow, the engagements and acCompanying casualties suffered throughout the campaign from June 9 through July 14. As noted earlier, it is important to keep in mind that many of the smaller engagements claimed hundreds more casualties than the records indicate. As a result, it is all but impossible to provide the specific number of losses with certainty. Careful examination of available records and compilations of available data allow us to make reasonable estimates, however.

The strengths and losses of various commands during the three-day Battle of Gettysburg have been relatively well-documented, and speak for themselves. What has not been closely examined, however, are the losses suffered by the cavalry of both sides throughout the campaign. Doing so reveals some startling numbers.

Many factors other than casualties affected unit strength (in other words, those present for duty on any particular day) of cavalry commands. One important factor that determined this number centered on the issue of mounts. The Federal government provided every cavalryman with a horse; the Confederate government did not. A Southern trooper could be compensated if

his horse was killed in battle, but he had to procure a replacement mount himself. He was usually given a furlough for a short time to return home to do so. Many troopers were detailed to serve other duties away from the regiment as couriers, scouts, ambulance personnel, staff work, and so forth. Recruits joined units during the campaign, and sickness and disease always kept a certain number of men out of the ranks on any given day. The result was that many of these men are not reflected on monthly muster rolls. As should now be obvious, the number of men present for duty on both sides (infantry included) was in a constant state of flux. With all this in mind, let's examine cavalry command numbers. The obvious starting point is the June 9 Battle of Brandy Station and the concluding date is July 14, when Lee's army finished crossing the Potomac River.

Major General J.E.B. Stuart's Confederate cavalry division (the brigades of William E. Jones, W. H. F. Lee, Wade Hampton, Fitzhugh Lee, and Beverly Robertson) totaled slightly more than 9,700 present for duty on June 9. By the end of the battle at Funkstown on July 10 (which was similar in size and scope to Brandy Station), the last engagement by Stuart's cavalry, those same brigades numbered about 5,900 troopers. This represents a reduction of 3,800 men, or more than 39% of Stuart's June 9 strength. While we do not know how many men had lost their mounts, etc. and thus did not show up on the official rolls, this reduced number represents shocking losses for cavalry. (It is interesting and instructive to compare Stuart's loss against infantry commands that fought during the three days of fighting at Gettysburg.)

On the Federal side, Brig. Gen. John Buford's First Division of cavalry was the only one engaged nearly constantly from the beginning of the campaign to its end, from Brandy Station on June 9 through the fighting at Falling Waters on July 14. One regiment, the 12th Illinois Cavalry, was added to Buford's division after June 9. Adding that regiment's strength to those comprising the balance of his division provides 4,580 effectives on June 9. By the time the July 14 battle at Falling Waters was over, Buford's division fielded about 3,575 sabers, or 1,005 fewer troopers. This represents a reduction of nearly 22%.

Brigadier General David M. Gregg's Second Division experienced several changes in its composition during the campaign and did little fighting during the retreat from July 4-14. After the June 9 Brandy Station battle, most of this division's fighting was in the Shenandoah Valley during mid-June while Lee's army was moving north. Gregg's command lost only a handful of men on East Cavalry Field on July 3. At the beginning of the campaign at Brandy Station, Gregg's division suffered approximately 15% losses (331 casualties). The division suffered another 700 losses during the cavalry fights later that June around Aldie, Middleburg, and Upperville. With the addition of the slight losses suffered during the retreat, Gregg's losses throughout the campaign were in excess of 1,000.

The Third Division under Brig. Gen. Judson Kilpatrick was not created until late June. Its first battle as a division was against Stuart's troopers at Hanover, Pennsylvania, on June 30 and it fought steadily through Falling Waters on July 14, earning as evidenced in period documents the famous nickname "Kill-Cavalry" for its impetuous commander. Did he deserve that sobriquet? Judson Kilpatrick received his general's star on June 13. On the morning of the combat at Hanover (June 30), muster rolls for Kilpatrick's regiments give a combined total of just more than 4,000 men. When the final mounted charge by elements of his division ended at Falling Waters on July 14,

Kilpatrick had 3,100 men left in the saddle. The reduction of about 900 troopers in fourteen days represents losses from all causes of nearly 23%, or slightly higher than Buford's estimated losses for the entire five weeks of the campaign. Of the three Federal cavalry divisions, Kilpatrick's (by a slim margin) lost the most men during the campaign, and it lost them in less than half the time.

A number of artillery units (including horse artillery) suffered considerable losses during the campaign. Prominent among them was Capt. John Bigelow's 9th Massachusetts battery, which fought well until it was overwhelmed at Gettysburg on July 2 at the Trostle Farm on southern Cemetery Ridge. Bigelow's command lost 30% from all causes (including Bigelow himself, who was badly wounded) and most of its horses. Southern artillery also suffered heavily during the fighting. The 71 men who made up Lt. Stephen C. Gilbert's Brooks Artillery of South Carolina, for example, part of Longstreet's Artillery Reserve, were heavily engaged on July 2 and July 3 and suffered more than 50% casualties. Many artillery units of both sides suffered losses in excess of 20% during the campaign. For artillery units in particular, these are grievous losses and demonstrate just how close, integral, and exposed many artillery units were in the overall fighting of the campaign.

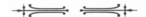

RESOURCES

RECOMMENDED READING

*I*n addition to archival material and web pages, there are untold thousands of books and articles about the campaign and battle of Gettysburg. Most of these sources deal with the main battle of July 1-3, 1863. What follows is a comprehensive list of books (both primary and secondary) about the several dozen actions of the campaign that took place before and after the main July 1-3 battle. These sources, which discuss in varying detail the participants and casualties of these lesser-known engagements, were heavily consulted for this work. The secondary works on this list offer an impressive list of obscure primary sources, and are footnoted as such. We urge readers to peruse these works for additional information.

Most of these combats resulted in wounded or dead men. Each of them in its own way affected the campaign in ways large and small. All of them deserve to be remembered.

- W.P. Conrad and Ted Alexander, *When War Passed This Way*. Shippensburg, PA: White Mane Publishing, 1987 (Rev.).

- Dan Beattie, *Brandy Station 1863: First Step Towards Gettysburg*. New York, NY: Osprey Publishing Ltd., 2008.

- William H. Beach, *The First New York (Lincoln) Cavalry*. New York, NY: The Lincoln Cavalry Association, 1902.

- Charles S. Grunder and Brandon H. Beck, *The Second Battle of Winchester*. Lynchburg, VA: H. E. Howard, Inc., 1989.

- Charles S. Grunder and Brandon H. Beck, *The Three Battles of Winchester: A History and Guided Tour*. Berryville, VA: The Civil War Foundation, Inc., 1997.

■ Kent Masterson Brown, *Retreat From Gettysburg: Lee, Logistics and the Pennsylvania Campaign*. Chapel Hill, NC: The University of North Carolina Press, 2005.

■ Carol Bundy, *The Nature of Sacrifice: A Biography of Charles Russell Lowell, Jr. 1835-64*. New York, NY: Farrar, Strause and Giroux, 2005.

■ Fairfax Downey, *Clash of Cavalry: The Battle of Brandy Station*. New York, NY: David McKay Company, Inc., 1959.

■ Bradley Gottfried, *The Maps of Gettysburg: The Gettysburg Campaign, June 3 - July 13, 1863*. El Dorado Hills, CA: Savas Beatie LLC, 2010.

■ Frederick Shriver Klein, ed. *Just South of Gettysburg: Carroll County, Maryland in the Civil War*. Westminster, MD: Historical Society of Carroll County, 1963.

■ Edward G. Longacre, *The Cavalry at Gettysburg: A Tactical Study of Mounted Operations during the Civil War's Pivotal Campaign, 9 June – 14 July, 1863*. Rutherford, NJ: Fairleigh Dickinson University Press, 1986.

■ Larry B. Maier, *Gateway to Gettysburg: The Second Battle of Winchester*. Shippensburg, PA: Burd Street Press, 2002.

■ Joseph W. McKinney, *Brandy Station, Virginia, June 9, 1863: The Largest Cavalry Battle of the Civil War*. Jefferson, NC: McFarland & Company, Inc., 2006.

■ Stevan F. Meserve, *The Civil War in Loudoun County, Virginia: A History of Hard Times*. Charleston, SC: The History Press, 2008.

■ Hugh C. Keen and Horace Mewborn, *43rd Battalion Virginia Cavalry, Mosby's Command*. Lynchburg, VA: H. E. Howard, Inc., 1993.

■ Scott L. Mingus, Sr., *Flames Beyond Gettysburg: The Confederate Expedition to the Susquehanna River, June 1863*. El Dorado Hills, CA: Savas Beatie LLC, 2011.

■ Frank M. Myers, *The Comanches: A History of White's Battalion, Virginia Cavalry*. Baltimore, MD: Kelly, Piet & Co., 1871.

■ C. Armour Newcomer, *Cole's Cavalry, or Three Years in the Saddle in the Shenandoah Valley*. Baltimore, MD: Cushing & Co., 1895.

■ Eric J. Wittenberg, J. David Petruzzi, and Michael F. Nugent, *One Continuous Fight: The Retreat and Pursuit of Lee's Army of Northern Virginia, July 4-14, 1863*. El Dorado Hills, CA: Savas Beatie LLC, 2008.

■ Wilbur Sturtevant Nye, *Here Come the Rebels!* Baton Rouge, LA: Louisiana State University Press, 1965.

■ Robert F. O'Neill, *The Cavalry Battles of Aldie, Middleburg and Upperville: Small But Important Riots, June 10-27, 1863*. Lychburg, VA: H. E. Howard, Inc., 1993.

■ Eric J. Wittenberg and J. David Petruzzi, *Plenty of Blame To Go Around: Jeb Stuart's Controversial Ride to Gettysburg*. El Dorado Hills, CA: Savas Beatie LLC, 2006.

■ Thomas E. Pope, *The Weary Boys: Colonel J. Warren Keifer and the 110th Ohio Volunteer Infantry*. Kent, OH.: The Kent State University Press, 2002.

■ George A. Rummel III, *Cavalry on the Roads to Gettysburg: Kilpatrick at Hanover and Hunterstown*. Shippensburg, PA: White Mane Books, 2000.

■ John W. Schildt, *Roads to Gettysburg (Revised edition)*. Parsons, WV: McClain Printing Company, 2003.

■ George Sheldon, *Fire on the River: The Defense of the World's Longest Covered Bridge and How it Changed the Battle of Gettysburg*. Lancaster, PA: Quaker Hills Press Inc., 2006.

■ Thomas West Smith, *The Story of a Cavalry Regiment: "Scott's 900" Eleventh New York Cavalry*. Veteran Association of the Regiment, 1897.

■ Taylor M. Chamberlin and John M. Souders, *Between Reb and Yank: A Civil War History of Northern Loudoun County, Virginia*. Jefferson, NC: McFarland & Company, Inc., 2011.

■ J. David Petruzzi and Steven Stanley, *The Complete Gettysburg Guide*. El Dorado Hills, CA: Savas Beatie LLC, 2009.

■ Daniel Carroll Toomey, *The Civil War in Maryland*. Baltimore, MD: Toomey Press, 1983.

■ Eric J. Wittenberg, *The Battle of Brandy Station: North America's Largest Cavalry Battle*. Charleston, SC: The History Press, 2010.

■ Eric J. Wittenberg, *Protecting the Flank at Gettysburg: The Battles for Brinkerhoff's Ridge and East Cavalry Field, July 2-3, 1863*. El Dorado Hills, CA: Savas Beatie LLC, 2012.